St. Louis Community College

Forest Park
Florissant Valley
Meramec

Instructional Resources
St. Louis, Missouri

Writing Horror
and the Body

Writing Horror and the Body

The Fiction of Stephen King, Clive Barker, and Anne Rice

LINDA BADLEY

Contributions to the Study of Popular Culture, Number 51

GREENWOOD PRESS
Westport, Connecticut • London

Library of Congress Cataloging-in-Publication Data

Badley, Linda.
    Writing horror and the body : the fiction of Stephen King, Clive
Barker, and Anne Rice / Linda Badley.
       p.   cm.—(Contributions to the study of popular culture,
ISSN 0198-9871 ; no. 51)
    Includes bibliographical references (p.) and index.
    ISBN 0-313-29716-9 (alk. paper)
    1. Horror tales, American—History and criticism. 2. King,
Stephen, 1947– —Criticism and interpretation. 3. Barker, Clive,
1952– —Criticism and interpretation. 4. Rice, Anne, 1941– —
Criticism and interpretation. 5. Horror tales, English—History
and criticism. 6. Body, Human, in literature. I. Title.
II. Series.
PS374.H67B33   1996
813′.0873809054—dc20   95–38665

British Library Cataloguing in Publication Data is available.

Library of Congress Catalog Card Number: 95–38665
ISBN: 0-313-29716-9
ISSN: 0198-9871

First published in 1996

Greenwood Press, 88 Post Road West, Westport, CT 06881
An imprint of Greenwood Publishing Group, Inc.

Printed in the United States of America

The paper used in this book complies with the
Permanent Paper Standards issued by the National
Information Standards Organization (Z39.48–1984).

10 9 8 7 6 5 4 3 2

Contents

Acknowledgments

I thank the many institutions and individuals who have supported this project. My editors at Greenwood Press, Peter Coveney, Nina Pearlstein, and Jean Lynch have been wonderfully understanding and have provided invaluable feedback in their editing of the manuscript. Middle Tennessee State University provided me with research time through a grant in 1988 and a non-instructional assignment in 1990. I am indebted to my colleagues and students for their support and inspiration.

My Gothic and Horror students deserve special credit for introducing me to contemporary horror fiction, for providing a lively forum for these ideas, and for their impressions and responses over the years. The Feminist Reading and Theory Groups lent energy, ideas, and discussion. Ayne Cantrell read and commented on an early draft. Claudia Spivey House, Shana Eley, and Shelley Wilhite provided research assistance and reading at various stages. The Popular Culture Association in the South and the International Association for the Fantastic in the Arts provided critical forums for parts of chapters 2 and 4. Thanks go to Barrett and Bill for excursions to the drive-in movies in the 1970s, to Dennis for introducing me to popular culture in the 1980s, and to Bob for an introduction to the computer that took root.

Last, I thank my husband and colleague Bill Badley for his insights and ideas, attentions and kindnesses, and continuing support.

Introduction

This book is about contemporary horror fiction as it has shaped and been shaped by three best-selling authors: Stephen King, Clive Barker, and Anne Rice. All three grew up in an increasingly visual and electronic culture out of which they somehow created millions of readers. Still, rather than "author," each might better be defined as a figure or phenomenon whose impact goes far beyond any genre or medium. Each is a scriptwriter, and King and Barker are almost as heavily involved in the film industry as in the production of fiction. Each has a huge cult following, King and Rice in particular.

This book is also something of a "sequel," a continuation of the business of my previous book, *Film, Horror, and the Body Fantastic*. Like most sequels, this one has its own subject and integrity but is informed by the prior text's premises. Both projects, which I originally planned as a single volume, germinated in a special topics course proposal in 1982. Gothic and Horror, as the course was called, was a flagrant appeal to what had all the symptoms of a fad.

My real inspiration at the time was not fiction but horror movies, a long-term guilty pleasure, and a taste for camp. Otherwise I knew little of what I was getting into. I had heard of Stephen King's popularity with students, although I had not read any of his books. I planned to use his novel *The Shining* (1977) as bait and to transfer the passion thus generated back into the "real" texts: the subliterary classics of the nineteenth century, and some standard modern classics—Flannery O'Connor, Shirley Jackson, Franz Kafka, perhaps Joyce Carol Oates. The strategy worked. Mary

Shelley and Stephen King converted students into enthusiastic readers. In the meantime, I became something of a fan.

My students led me to *Danse Macabre* (1981), King's freewheeling study of modern horror not as a genre so much as a personal and cultural experience whose elements—fiction, film, television, comics, and the 1950s—were inseparable. I became interested in horror's encroachment on the popular mainstream, into the Book of the Month Club, Hollywood and avant garde film, and rock culture. What had been a marginal phenomenon—beginning in cult films such as *Night of the Living Dead* (1968), *The Texas Chain Saw Massacre* (1974), and *The Rocky Horror Picture Show* (1975)—had possessed the 1980s. Horror, like the other popular genres, was absorbed into postmodernism. It infected the media with its iconographies. For its themes and metaphors it absorbed sources from advertising to biochemistry to philosophy, becoming more than one of the popular genres or even a genre. Its mythology had spread throughout mass culture, causing us all to think and speak about ourselves and our feelings in peculiar ways.

By the mid-1980s, people were noticing that the horror genre had changed: from the norm-affirming genre Stephen King had pronounced "as Republican as a banker in a three-piece suit" (qtd. in "An Evening" 9) to a carnival of the perverse. My awakening occurred in 1984, when I picked up Clive Barker's *Books of Blood, Volume I* in the local Kroger. Some time later, a student introduced me to Anne Rice's *Interview with the Vampire* as a cult classic from some years back. In Barker and Rice, as in films like *The Evil Dead*, *The Hunger*, *Blade Runner*, and *Dawn of the Dead*, the monsters had become victims and anti-heroes whose difference provoked empathy and fascination. Or they presented us with undeniable images of ourselves. The genre had become symptomatic and diagnostic. A new wave of "deep" or "anti-" horror engulfed the mass market and seemed bent on subverting traditional values, certainty, and identity.

Something like it encroached on academic space, especially the humanities, which became informed by a Gothic, pathological perspective that sanctioned subversion and the perverse. Literary criticism, if the titles were any indication, was a hellish prospect: Hassan's *The Dismemberment of Orpheus* (1971), Foucault's *Discipline and Punish* (1979), Carter's *The Sadeian Woman* (1979), Showalter's *Sexual Anarchy* (1990), Scarry's *The Body in Pain* (1985), Cixous's "The Laugh of the Medusa" (1976), Sontag's *Illness as Metaphor* (1979). Buzzwords like *deconstruction*, *schizophrenia*, *oppression*, *Other*, and even *body* began to sound as Gothic as they were politically correct.

Preparing Gothic and Horror alongside courses in contemporary critical theory, Victorian literature, and contemporary women writers, I could not help but wonder, for instance, how the "madwoman in the attic" of Gilbert and Gubar's title of 1979 related to what was deemed feminism's antithesis: the rape-revenge fantasy (*I Spit on Your Grave*) and the gender bending transformations available to special effects. And so I began to see horror as one of several discourses of the body that use the fantastic—the iconography of the monstrous—to articulate the anxieties of the 1980s and to re-project the self.

In today's culture, a person's self-concept has been increasingly constituted in images of the body. In the ongoing crisis of identity in which the gendered, binary subject of Eurocentric bourgeois patriarchy (in particular, the Freudian psychoanalytical model of the self) is undergoing deconstruction, horror has joined with other discourses of the body to provide a language for imagining the self in transformation, re-gendered, ungendered, and regenerated, or even as an absence or a lack. Like my book *Film, Horror, and the Body Fantastic*, this book is concerned with the cultural origins, technology, and impact of this fantastic "body language"—with the myths and media through which horror has articulated and modified the embodied self.

In *Sensational Designs* (1985), Jane Tompkins examined some American popular classics whose sensationalism, sentimentality, or even popularity has kept people from taking them seriously; for example, Charles Brockden Brown's Gothic *Wieland* and Harriet Beecher Stowe's "sentimental" *Uncle Tom's Cabin*. Tompkins proposed that we find a means for accounting for the value of such texts not on the basis of some temporary aesthetic trend, but for doing "a certain kind of cultural work within a specific historical situation." Popular fiction, she argued, offers society mechanisms for "thinking about itself," for "defining aspects of itself shared between authors and readers, for dramatizing its conflicts, and recommending solutions" (200). This view of texts as doing work, as "expressing and shaping the social context that produced them" (Tompkins 200), I find especially applicable to popular horror fiction today.

Cultural work, as I use the term, is neither positive nor negative: it is, like Stephen King's place in modern culture according to David Atwood, Senior Writer of The Book of the Month Club, "indisputable" (3). My definition of the term *horror* is inclusive, moving between rather than within generic boundaries and media, allowing for elements in a variety of texts and types: Anne Rice's Gothic romances and sadomasochistic pornography, Angela Carter's revamped fairy tales, Octavia Butler's

"Bloodchild" (science fiction), the medical thriller (Robin Cook's *Coma*), serial killer/procedural (Thomas Harris's *The Silence of the Lambs*), graphic novel (Alan Moore's *The Watchman*), pathological nonfiction (Richard Preston's *The Hot Zone*), as well as the novels of King and Barker. I consider the diffusion and implantation of images and mythologies throughout levels of culture essential to the issue.[1]

Chapter 1

Flesh Made Word

SPECIAL EFFECTS

On October 6, 1986, *Time* magazine "covered" Stephen King. The occasion was the publication of *It*, which King had proclaimed his magnum opus and last horror novel. On the cover was a large cartoonish drawing of the "typical" King reader, hair standing on end, eyes transfixed with suspense on "A Novel by STEPHEN KING." The caption, from *It*, was superimposed on the reader's forehead, invoking a connection between effect and cause: "As It saw Eddie looking, Its green-black lips wrinkled back from huge fangs." The reader's face and eyes glowed with light reflected from the open pages. The author appeared in a tiny dust jacket photo in the darkened bottom left-hand corner—sign of the death of the author in the birth of the reader, or perhaps a view of the author as special effect. The cover saluted King's power (similar to *Time*'s power) to embody and affect, to bring the common reader to scalp-tingling, glowing life.

The *Time* cover said that King exploited fear in a way that charged the medium of print and transmitted directly to the body, hence to the visually and electronically literate. Posing as a mass media shaman, he textualized aural, visual, and kinetic sensations, evoked icons from film and television, and narrated in a voice that readers experienced viscerally. If prose fiction was defunct, the Stephen King phenomenon was a long night of the living dead (now entering its third decade). In 1982, Paul Gray had called it, with some justification, "postliterate prose."

Horror returns audiences to preliterate, somatic modes of knowing, and movies, television, and rock concerts most completely recreate the experience of the den or campfire. Sitting in the darkened theater, we re-encounter our earliest dreams. The visual and electronic media have been most directly responsible for the contemporary horror phenomenon. King's fiction, a product of the horror film classics of the 1930s and 1950s, brought a cinematic perspective to the naturalistic novel. As King became an institution and was imitated, the images that inspired him gave renewed life to underground comics, which reinspired fantastic fiction and film.

Modern horror fiction is as parasitic and omnivorous as horror film, incorporating movies and television, theater and the visual arts, with equal gusto. In 1983, Clive Barker, Liverpool illustrator and playwright, inspired by fringe theater, adult fantasy art, and schlocky movies, started writing the short stories that became the *Books of Blood* (1984–86). By 1987 he was directing a film called *Hellraiser* (1988), which became an international hit. Barker's "Son of Celluloid" (1986) is a cancer that absorbs the psychic energy projected by audiences onto the screen, and through its lethal impersonations of classic film stars and genres, evolves into flesh-eating cinema. The story has been collected in the shared world anthology *Silver Scream* (1988), edited by David Schow and with an introduction by *Texas Chain Saw Massacre* director Tobe Hooper. This hybrid form of "splatter-prose" brought the tale of terror into the postliterate era, where inscribing and "writing from the body" was taken to new and knowingly dangerous extremes.[1]

Anne Rice confesses that *Interview with the Vampire* (1976) was inspired not by Gothic fiction—she never finished Stoker's *Dracula*—but by black and white movies (Ramsland, *Prism* 248). In 1985 her eighteenth-century vampire Lestat was restored in a new medium, as a heavy metal rock singer empowered by MTV and a vast subcultural network. Rock music appropriated horror motifs in the late 1970s, beginning with Alice Cooper, Kiss, and Ozzie Osborne; punk and shock rock fused in 1980s Gothic and gave birth to clubs with names like Helter Skelter and Theatre of Blood and groups like Megadeath, Iron Maiden, The Dead Kennedys, Anthrax, and Bauhaus.

As the Gothic was taken up in clothes and lifestyles, the Splatterpunks (derived from the term *cyberpunk* by David Schow in 1986) drew their hard-boiled attitude, driving prose rhythms, and violent situations from heavy metal, cyberfiction, and horror movies. Their infusion of horror film "splatter," epitomized in George Romero's zombie films, into prose fiction, had the purpose of revelation in the flesh, "meat meeting mind, with the soul as screaming omniscient witness" (Skipp and Spector, Introd.,

Book 10). For those who might deplore "no-limits" violence, John Skipp and Craig Spector asserted that there were "also moments of intense, perverse and profoundly disturbing *rehumanization*" (Introd., *Book* 9). In "literary" fiction and film respectively, Bret Easton Ellis's *American Psycho* (1991) and Oliver Stone's metafilm *Natural Born Killers* (1993) are equivalent to or descended from splatterpunk.

Like the punk rebellion against pop rock, as Ken Tucker suggests, the splatterpunks were a stimulus—both in their revolt against Stephen King's pop dread, and in their connection with or influence on writers like Clive Barker, Dan Simmons, Kathe Koja, Joe Lansdale, and Bret Easton Ellis. Spaltter in general, though, is a logical development of the eighteenth-century Gothic revival. Modern horror is often thought to be a degraded form of *terror*, the supposedly refined, "sublime" emotion treasured by the eighteenth-century. Accordingly, *horror* is the product of our mass media–brutalized age. A shift from linear and literate consciousness to postliterate culture, from imaginary terrors to graphic realism, through the proliferation of special effects, is undeniable. But *TV Guide*'s 1990 prediction of horror's return to its "roots" in "psychological terror and subtlety with more impact than an ax to the head" (Lieberman 3) was erroneous, says Walter Kendrick. "There are no such roots, in television or anywhere else" (264).

Dark fantasy has always been a literature of extra-textual effects, their purpose to stimulate strong feeling. The first Gothic novel, Horace Walpole's *The Castle of Otranto* (1764), was the secondary product of Walpole's imitation-Gothic castle, the first of the modern "haunted houses" whose ghosts are elaborate effects. That and the fact that horror is "the only genre named for its effect on the reader," as Gary Wolf has pointed out (qtd. in Hartwell, "Introd." 10), should tell us something.

Horror, whether fiction or film, enacts the formula inscribed in Edgar Allan Poe's "The Philosophy of Composition" in which the text was a machine or apparatus that elicited a specific audience response. Indeed, 1980s horror did not "degenerate" into special effects; it returned to its theatrical roots—in the freak show, the phantasmagoria, the wax museum, the Théâtre du Grand Guignol of Paris, the Theater of Cruelty. The climax of Poe's best loved stories is the reanimated corpse or revolting revelation: the old man's heart beating beneath the floor; the Lady Madeline, bloody and emaciated after clawing her way out of the tomb; M. Valdemar's protracted putrescence, the Red Death. For Poe the "most poetical topic in the whole world" was the death of a beautiful woman ("Philosophy of Composition" 55). The same inspiration was behind the modern slasher film.

The eighteenth-century Gothic was a reactivation of feeling through the senses, a cycle repeated at the nineteenth century *fin de siècle*, and New Gothic revival performs a similar role for our waning century. Patrick Süskind's international best seller *Perfume* (1987), whose monstrous protagonist has an enhanced (and insatiable) sense of smell, turned French symbolist poetry and Huysmons's *Au Rebours* into olfactory fiction for the present. Rice, whose vampire protagonist Louis epitomized late Victorian self-division and decadence, describes horror as "Confusion of the senses, confusion of the mind to overwhelming physical responses" (qtd. in Wiater, "Anne Rice" 43). Speaking of the style of Stephen King, Rice stresses that "Horror and sensuality have always been linked" (qtd. in Wiater, "Anne Rice" 43), and it is no accident that, under two pseudonyms, she had an alter ego as a pornographer. Rice crosses Gothic horror with erotic romance to create the vampire's perspective of heightened consciousness. As to the view that he generates mindless "postliterate" prose, King has said that horror fiction is "necessary . . . not only for people who read to think, but to those who read to feel," a "moral" proposition in a "mad century" that "races toward its conclusion . . . ever more ominous and absurd" (Introd., *Arbor House Treasury* 11). Thus, accounting for King's appeal in Jungian terms, Harlan Ellison felt obliged to construct an elaborate metaphor that has King performing a cultural spinal tap; he "drills into the flow of cerebro-spinal fluid . . . [to] archetypal images from the pre-conscious . . . that presage crises . . . even as they become realities" (77).

Horror is the most physiological genre except for pornography, a fact the fanzines made a running joke—*Fangoria* flaunted a monthly cover foldout poster that proclaimed itself gore's equivalent of *Playboy*. In *Hard Core* (1989), Linda Williams classifies horror film with genres (including weepies, comedies, musicals, and pornography) that emphasizes body spectacle and movement and move bodies of viewers or readers to similar responses (x). As pornography's purpose is to arouse desire, horror's is to exorcise fear. The pleasure of horror's text, Philip Brophy suggests, is "getting the shit scared out of you" (5). Horror delivers a *frisson* that originates as a somatic response. The term *horror* comes from *horrére*, which refers to the "bristling of the hair on the nape of the neck" (Twitchell 10).

UNSAFE SEX

Most critics account for horror in psychosexual terms, as containing a subtext about repressed sexuality, and with good reason. Psychoanalysis was a product of the same nineteenth-century sensibility that produced the Gothic literary classics. Freud's essay on "The 'Uncanny'" (1919), a case study based on E.T.A. Hoffman's "The Sandman," provided a model for psychoanalytic criticism.

Psychoanalytic criticism, Gothic and pathological in its origins, tells us that horror functions as displaced and therefore "safe" pornography. Like pornography, slasher films like *Friday the Thirteenth* employ phallic weapons to "open the fleshy secrets of normally hidden things" (Williams 191). Thus horror appeals to pre-adolescent boys, as James Twitchell maintains in *Dreadful Pleasures* (1985) and *Preposterous Violence* (1989). He argues that horror films provide an adolescent rite of passage, as fairy tales are to children. They are cautionary tales that demonstrate the dangers of unconventional sex, implanting taboos while providing safe outlets for repressed sexual energy and anxiety.

Disregarding for a moment the fact that the majority of readers of horror *fiction* are women in their thirties and forties (Hartwell, "Introd." 5), or the fact that adult themes dominate mainstream and revisionist horror fiction and film (from *Interview with the Vampire* to Cronenberg's *Dead Ringers* to King's *Dolores Claiborne*), what do we make of the trend in which the latent psychosexual contents have been made manifest (*The Rocky Horror Picture Show*, *It*), where subtext becomes overt text? Or where, as in King's *Gerald's Game*, Freudianisms are converted into a pop feminist myth—a myth that disparages phallocentrism, psychoanalysis proper, and Freud? In Barker and Rice, conventional sex is not sublimated but replaced with overt sadomasochism and polymorphic sensuality, and in the films of Cronenberg, Lynch, and Jordan, Eros is coupled with Thanatos in ways that Freud's phallocentric "family romance" does not account for.

In an age that appears ever more post-Freudian, Twitchell's argument is reductive. The horror genre as the product of repressed sexuality, as traditionally defined, is defunct. The thought that we are sexual beings, which reputedly horrified the Victorians, no longer horrifies or even signifies. What does signify since the sexual "revolution" is *Sexual Anarchy*, as Elaine Showalter called it in 1990, sexual anxiety, or, as is perhaps more appropriate in 1995, unsafe sex: the welter of constantly scrambled codes and alternatives and threats and prohibitions and dangers that today's sexually politicized world produces. These were the causes of *I Shudder at Your Touch*, the title of Michelle Slung's best-selling 1991 anthology of "22 Tales of Sex and Horror," its sequel, *Shudder Again* (1993), and kin (for instance, *Hot*, *Hotter*, and *Hottest*

Blood). Contemporary horror is driven by a much broader public anxiety about gender, mortality, and control than Freud could have anticipated.

Freud has become a popular religion, and horror provides many of its symbols (the beast within, the doppelgänger, the "psycho") and rituals (the dream work, totemization of the bad father). Within psychotherapy, false memory syndrome and multiple personality disorder are post-Freudian developments that support, enlarge, yet ultimately undermine Freud's scientific authority. In the humanities, the decentered, deconstructed subject—from Lacan to the French feminists, Baudrillard, Deleuze and Guattari, and imagined in the metaphor of Orpheus's dismemberment— had directly challenged the Freudian ego. The zombie was one graphic version of this metaphor. In another, Barker's short story "The Body Politic" (1986), Charlie George loses his hands to a revolt of members from "the body" as a phallocentric concept: "maybe the grandpappy of his sacred profession, Freud, had been wrong," Charlie's analyst Dr. Jeudwinde wonders. "The paradoxical facts of human behavior didn't seem to fit into those neat classical compartments he'd allotted them to" (Barker, *Inhuman Condition* 86). Contemporary horror has more to do with the loss of what Foucault called Freud's "repressive hypothesis," and the suppression of something else.

THANATOS

"All our fears add up to one great fear," Stephen King wrote in the introduction to *Night Shift* (xvi), "of the body under the sheet. It's our body." It was King who, "Retrofitting the horror novel for the age of MTV, cannily targeted the bad thing, the central obscenity, the dark under all our beds, as *death*" (Gibson xvi). Ernest Becker (*The Denial of Death*, 1973) and Elizabeth Kübler-Ross (*On Death and Dying*, 1965) were among the first to state that death was the modern taboo and final frontier. Freud only belatedly, in *Beyond the Pleasure Principle*, discovered that he had offered no psychology of death. While death for "most people" remains "a hidden secret, as eroticized as it is feared" (xv), says Sherwin P. Nuland in his best-seller *How We Die* (1994), the official belief is that "you don't have to die, that medicine should be able to snatch you from the edge of the grave" (qtd. in May F4). "Whole generations [have grown] up believing that immortality was the general rule," quips Barbara Ehrenreich, "except for those who bothered to smoke" ("Ultimate" 681).

Gothic and horror began to thrive in the eighteenth century as death was gradually removed from public and private experience. As technology harnessed life or Foucauldian "bio-power," Thanatos became nonproductive. The recoil from death is an aspect of two hundred years of Western "progress"—in the sense of "tidying up" that includes effective hygiene, waste disposal, and the banning of odors (Kendrick xv). Thanatos had to enter through the back door. Hollywood glamorized death as violence, contributing to the denial of death as dying, experienced as a part of life, an inevitable natural process (Arlen 280). Death also emerged within iconographies whose manifest subject was birth. In the 1960s and 1970s, birth was demonic or deadly in films like *Rosemary's Baby* (1968), *It's Alive* (1974), *2001*'s disembodied fetus-in-space, and in *Night of the Living Dead* (1968), which gave birth to the zombie.

Walter Kendrick points out that the modern fear of death is different from the older fear of the dead as hostile spirits. Such fear, based in belief and ritual, could be assuaged. But modern horror's iconography concerns a lack of spirits, whether one thinks of nonbeing or the corpse, material death. The real horror is "deadness," or death's aftermath in decomposition, absence, grief (xv). Thus, as Romero and King brought death out of the closet in the 1970s, Thanatos found new rituals. As, in the 1980s, the politically correct term for "health" became "wellness," Thanatos returned with a vengeance. The television news, succeeded by reality-based entertainment, became a wake—interviews with dying victims of disease, close-ups of distressed relatives, televised executions and fatal motor accidents, reenactments of violent crimes. The horror "boom," led by Stephen King, increasingly performed the funeral ritual of "viewing the body." As a character in King's *The Mist* explained in 1980, when the machines, technologies, and religious systems fail, "people have got to have something. Even a zombie lurching through the night can seem pretty cheerful compared to the existential comedy/horror of the ozone layer dissolving" (136). The zombies and their ilk had become our dying and reviving gods.

THE BODY FANTASTIC

The general fear of death, like that of sex, was not the real issue either. Clive Barker confesses his greatest fear has always been "the condition of being flesh and blood. Of minds to madness and flesh to wounding" (qtd. in Booe). In David Cronenberg's films the body had a "mind of its own," said Richard Corliss: it was "a haunted house whose rumblings trigger lust, misery and excruciating pain in the poor tenant. This property is condemned" ("Terminal Case"). The modern horror film, as Philip Brophy put the issue, played "on the fear of one's own body, of how one controls and relates to it" (8).

"Your Body: Friend, Foe, or Total Stranger?" queried the cover headline for the May–June 1992 *Utne Reader.* This confusion about the self as it relates to the body is at the center of many of our present uncertainties. As Pete Boss pointed out in *Screen* magazine in 1986, modern medicine had "recast the unknown" within its parameters (19). On the one hand, the body seemed increasingly within the realm of human manipulation and control, through transplantation, genetic, and reproductive technologies, cryonics, plastic surgery, transsexual surgery, artificial intelligence, and the electronic sensorium. On the other hand, these technologies rendered the body as a sign of the self meaningless, making it a resource or commodity.

Biotechnology, medical imaging, computer and virtual reality technology, and advertising colonize and configure the body, and the definitions of life and death, age, gender, and species are consequently modified, so that the boundaries of the self as a body are incessantly redrawn. As Michel Foucault pointed out in *The Birth of the Clinic*, the new eighteenth-century science of pathological anatomy and the medical "gaze" opened up a new interior space for the body, giving it a fantastic life of its own. But, as the body became increasingly fantastic, it became more than ever the sign of the self, the icon representing the self's existence and unity. Far from being demystified, the body has become the bastion of identity and mystery once reserved for the soul. By the 1980s, the body was not merely a receptacle for the self. The feminist self-help bible published by the Boston Women's Health Collective in 1973, 1984, and 1992, *Our Bodies, Ourselves*, made the point admirably.

In the Circles of Fear and Desire: A Study of Gothic Fantasy (1985), Patrick Day argues that Gothic fiction preceded Freud in creating a concept of an inner life, presenting in fiction what Freud would later reconstruct as a science. In providing forms of dream narrative, Gothic fiction taught readers to interpret their dreams, preparing them for the "dream work." Gothic fantasy not only preceded but partly constructed the popular understanding of psychoanalysis, and was important in facilitating the shift from the religious concept of self as a soul to the secular model of the psyche. Freud exchanged the favor and in turn demonstrated the significance of fantasy.

Today, as the ego is challenged and altered, a comparable shift has occurred from the Freudian psyche to a post-Freudian body, the product of a materialist, postliterate, electronic, image-based culture. Horror coincided with this shift, registering its impact, giving an iconography and language to the emerging model. It is tempting to situate the horror phenomenon within the terms of Foucault's analysis of the discourses of bio-power. Recent horror articulates postmodern dread in the metaphor of a centralized surveillance and power network that appropriates, dissects, and utilizes the body—from *Coma* to *The X-Files*. Cronenberg's concept of the "Video World made Flesh" in *Videodrome* (1983) derives from Foucault's Panopticon (*Discipline and Punish*) and Jean Baudrillard's vision of the subject as schizophrenic and medium, as a sort of human screen. Beyond this vision of the self invaded and inscribed by power, horror betrays an almost mystical fascination with flesh as innerspace, microcosm or medium in which consciousness is transformed: the body as subject. This is the body the French feminists have valorized. The same issues that tear the body asunder, rendering it problematic or profane, also lend the flesh in transformation its own power and turn inner space into a polysemy of subjectivities and languages. If the body is no longer a temple, it is a spirit, and it speaks in wounds.

FEMALE GOTHIC

The body is also, of course, gendered female through woman's designation as the sex, the flesh (versus Word), the wound that never heals. The body is particularly female in horror. Take, for example, slasher films, which in 1989 Clive Barker, as reigning goremeister-host of a USA network special on *The Women of Horror* called "the last refuge of the chauvinist, who can do terrible things to women on the screen." The Gothic novel is equally a "myth of male power," says Showalter (*Sister's* 130), one that Leslie Fiedler has explained as a protest against domestic life. In *Powers of Horror*, French feminist Julia Kristeva adapts Freud, Lacan, and Sartre to a somatic frame of reference even more to the point. She finds horror a fundamental reflex of revulsion against the archaic mother (imagined as an all-powerful, encroaching bodily presence) that initiates separation and ego formation. The term *abject* refers to a liminal state that challenges the boundaries of the self. For the male subject, horror entertainment is an exorcism of the power of the mother, concludes Clare Hanson: by "repassing through abjection," he arrives at a feeling of control. As romance is considered a "woman's genre," horror is male and, more specifically, misogynistic (152).

The monstrous feminine was the true subject of Ira Levin's *Rosemary's Baby* and William Peter Blatty's *The Exorcist*, best sellers (and eventually blockbuster films) that provoked Stephen King to write *Carrie*. Many feminists view *Carrie* as misogynistic. But Carol Clover suggests that we take King's 1981 statement about his intentions, quoted below, at face value:

> *Carrie* is largely about how women find their own channels of power, and what men fear about women and women's sexuality. . . . [W]riting the book in 1973 and only out of college three years, I was fully aware of what Women's Liberation implied for me and others of my sex. The book is, in its more adult implications, an uneasy masculine shrinking from a future of female equality. . . . [Carrie is] Woman, feeling her powers for the first time and, like Samson, pulling down the temple on everyone in sight at the end of the book. (*Danse Macabre* 171–72)

"But where exactly is the horror here?" Clover asks. If, as Claire Hanson argues, woman is the monster, who is the victim? Who is the hero? Like Samson, Clover tells us, Carrie is "all three in turn" (4), and we identify with each. It was feminism that ultimately enabled *Carrie*: it gave "a new language to [Carrie's] victimization and a new force to the anger that subsidizes her own act of horrific revenge" (Clover 4). Diagnosing gender trouble, *Carrie* was a fractured "Cinderella" and compared with feminist revisions of fairy tales, that returned to the older, grimmer oral versions to depict the horrors of patriarchy. In fact, *Carrie* shared characteristics with what Ellen Moers first called "Female Gothic" in 1976 to refer to women writers' adaptations of the Gothic to feminist purposes.[2]

The Gothic has always addressed women's traditional concerns "as well as portraying vividly the place of women and their treatment in society," David Hartwell points out (Introd., *Foundations* 5). Female Gothic fiction switched the codes of male Gothic, using them against themselves to expose oppression and articulate female experience, embodied experience in particular. Thus the Female Gothic is a feminist "anti-"Gothic. Writers ranging now from Mary Shelley and Charlotte Perkins Gilman through Margaret Atwood and Toni Morrison have "stolen" the powers of horror, reclaiming them for women (Jackson 103–4). Elaine Showalter traces the Female Gothic back "through Freud's Studies on Hysteria, 'Dora,' and 'Das Unheimliche,' as well as through Lacan and Kristeva" as part of the effort to "bring the body, the semiotic, the imaginary, or the pre-Oedipal [M]Other Tongue into language" (*Sister's Choice* 129). In *The Madwoman in the Attic*, Gilbert and Gubar "write brilliantly about the anxiety of authorship that women still feel," comments Nina Auerbach. "Their title, and the Gothic thrill that courses through their book, associates this anxiety with pathology" and "the assertion of power" ("Engorging" 158).

In writing "from the body," female Gothic writers shared methods and purposes with some of the graphic horror fictions and films of the last two decades. Both exposed, parodied, or circumvented representations of the body. In some sense both attempted to speak for and through the "abject" flesh. Women have long been drawn to fantasy's subversion of the real (by proposing alternatives) and open, dialogical structures (Jackson 68, 25). In the last fifteen years, women including Tanith Lee, Clarissa Pinkola Estes, Lisa Tuttle, Emma Tennant, Octavia Butler, Johanna Russ, Suzy McKee Charnas, and Anne Rice have moved within the margins of gender and genre, high and low culture, challenging canonicity, and making new myths.

The unwritten female body must somehow be voiced in the language that excludes it, the symbolic, says Kristeva (*Powers*). Alice Jardine proposes the term *gynesis* to refer to this process through which a new language emerges, a project of embracing what was hitherto alien, monstrous, or unclean (73). Gynesis is not confined to women's writing. It can take perverse and misogynistic iconographies. Participating to various degrees of consciousness in this process are male Gothic writers such as Patrick Süskind, Edward Bryant, Dan Simmons, Whitley Strieber, Clive Barker, and Stephen King. The feminine, the body, and Thanatos have been coming into cultural consciousness for some time, in what have only seemed like independent movements. In horror's embodied language, their interdependence is revealed.

WRITING AND THE BODY FANTASTIC

In *Orality and Literacy: The Technologizing of the Word* (1982) Walter Ong argues that in information-age culture, consciousness is increasingly projected into the material world and mass media images. The subject's "inner" reality coincides with the simulacrum, includes and even becomes fantasized bodies. Consciousness is changing. Where Freud hoped to reclaim the unconscious for the ego, postmodern/postliterate consciousness is usurped by information technology, and distinctions between self and world, body and mind, media culture and human reality, live and recorded, collapse.

This model of the self is multifarious and interactive—a post-Jungian and Bakhtinian one, perhaps—appeals directly to X-generation readers brought up on fantasy, role playing, and computer games. The "alt.books.gothic" newsgroup on the Internet, some 656 strong at this writing, consists of people for whom reading and role playing, books and life, are integrated into a totality deemed "Gothic." King's relationship to ideas, especially psychologies, is similar. If he had to choose, he would "be a Jungian rather than a Freudian," he says, however acknowledging Freud's usefulness for "advanc[ing] the importance of dreams. . . . As a

Freudian [and rather like Jung himself], I'm a real opportunist. I'm more apt to use the theories to advance my ideas" (Magistrale, *Second* 4). King (and Barker and Rice as well) turn Freud's talking cure inside out, as Jung did, telling stories about the inner life in archetypal projections and postmodern forms (tales that generate more tales, as in "The Breathing Method"), projecting sites of inner anguish into cultural rites of passage, and, for better or worse, lifestyles.

As the old psychology was translated into the image-based economy of the 1980s and the multimedia of the 1990s, science-fiction, action, horror movies, and Stephen King novels became our epics. King changed the Gothic novel into a "postliterate" prose, a language for an age of secondary (technologically mediated) orality. He writes in formulas like the old bards, appeals to the somatic memory, and uses typography iconographically, subverting print and textuality while incorporating multimedia and hypertexual effects into the book. Posing as a mass media shaman, King textualizes aural, visual, and kinetic sensations, alludes to icons from film, television, and advertising, and narrates in a voice that readers "experience" rather than read. He literalizes the notion of the text as a body and the body as text. As a result, he has become the world's best-selling author. Similarly Barker and Rice have derived their methods and myths from the movies, theater, and the graphic arts. In Barker's *Books of Blood* (1984–86), an equation between body and text, flesh and word is a marginal space—a reality that is neither text nor flesh but both—for stories of transformation and inscription.

Perhaps because of its brutal simplicity, horror film is intrinsically self-conscious, as Brophy explains: it "knows that you've seen it before; . . . that you know what is about to happen; and it knows that you know it knows you know," but also that the cheapest trick still provokes a nerve-jangling response (5). Horror in the 1980s intensified this in-joke with nostalgia—for *Fright Night* reruns, Ed Wood films, *The Twilight Zone*, and horror comics. King and George Romero collaborated to recreate E.C. Comics, with their bloody revenge motifs and twisted endings, in the film anthology *Creepshow* (1982). This anthology defined the early pop horror style, one that did not deny its clichés but realized and lived them out (Brophy 12).

However, modern horror's tendency to self-cannibalism now often ends in subversive *anti-horror* (Douglas Winter) or *metahorror* (Dennis Etchison) in which the medium is exposed as the true monster. Joe Lansdale's "The Night They Missed the Horror Show" plays real-life horrors against the brutalized protagonists' plan to watch drive-in movies. In a blatant contradiction to horror's postliteracy, anti-horror is above all literate: it puts (illiterate) body language to the torturous task of reading its own text. Anti-horror uses conventions subversively, playing against and going beyond them while engaging readers, as in the Stephen King of the metafictions *Misery* and *The Dark Half*. Clive Barker opens each volume of his *Books of Blood* with the following sick joke? epigraph? poem?: "Everybody is a book of blood,/Wherever we're opened, we're red." Initial shock may be followed by disgust and alienation, and eventually, if one reads further, thoughts about the relationship between the pathologically "inscribed" body, the horror genre, and the text.

Barker's "postmodern splatter-prose" is diagnostic, says William Gibson, especially where sex and gender are concerned—a vehicle for "a disturbingly genuine insight into the nature of human sexual dependence." And Anne Rice's frankly erotic reading of Stoker "finally brings the S&M aspect of the vampire text into overt focus" (xvi). Like the films of Cronenberg and Lynch, these fictions present psychosexual issues in a metaphorics of existence as a body, and depict Eros and Thanatos in a sado-masochistic dialogue. Yet in some respects, Barker's sexual politics concur better with ecofeminist science fiction than any sort of horror. Like Barker, Rice has used horror "as an exploratory probe, a conscious technique owing more to modern science fiction than to the pre-Freudian nightmares of Stoker or Lovecraft" (Gibson xvi). Thus Barker has often chosen to write "in drag," as it were, from the embodied experience of a woman, and Rice's "anxiety of authorship" is such that she has identified most passionately with homosexual characters. Meanwhile, her *Vampire Chronicles* move in the direction of romance, toward construction of an androgynous-perverse utopia. Both writers, together with the recent Stephen King—of *Gerald's Game* (1992), *Dolores Claiborne* (1993), and *Rose Madder* (1995), all written from a mature woman's point of view—use body language self-consciously to rethink and reconfigure gender.

Chapter 2 of this book concerns the cultural work of the early Stephen King (1974–1986) by addressing his revitalization of the storyteller's role in "postliterate" culture. King brought the mystique of ancient oral narrators to a popular mythology substantiated by mass media technology. Propelling horror into the mainstream, King provided a psychology of fear and death, founded in the experience of the body, for an age of terrified unbelief. Chapter 3 concerns the later King's (1983–1995) confrontations with the body in writing horror—the body as the corpse (the sight/site of mortality), as the writer's medium, or textuality, and as the monstrous feminine. King's shift into metafiction caused him to rethink relations between embodiment and language, and between the "powers of horror" and gender. In *Books of Blood*, King's designated successor Clive Barker continued and reversed King's emphasis. He brought speculative intelligence, a theatrical literacy, and a cinematic splatter prose to horror's sexual subtext and in the process revitalized the tale of terror. Chapter 4 treats Barker's creation of literate horror fiction from "postliterate" sources and transference of a similar literacy into his films, bringing the genre critical acclaim and opening it to experiment. Like Barker, Anne Rice writes anti-horror that inverts the erotic subtext of the Gothic novel into overt text, the monsters into protagonists, and a reconstituted, enhanced Flesh, an expression of the feminine, into Word: the postmodern body become myth. Her vampires recover their roots in the fertility rituals of the old erotic gods. Chapter 5 examines the Vampire Chronicles as they serve four different audiences: Rice herself (and other lapsed Catholics), sadomasochists, gays, and women.

Chapter 2

The Sin Eater: Orality, Postliteracy, and the Early Stephen King

STEPHEN KING AND THE ORAL TRADITION

Stephen King may have found his calling in a college poetry class in which his teacher (Burten Hatlen) introduced him to Eldridge Cleaver's concept of black "soul." "Is there such a thing as white soul? Is there suburban soul?" Hatlen asked the class. "Something in all of that reached out to me," King says, "because I liked McDonald's and the Dairy Queen [and things like that]. . . . You'd see people bopping in there, and it seemed . . . they *did* have white soul."[1] He has since made it his lucrative business, through the less than subtle powers of horror, to articulate the "soul" of American consumer culture. In the process, King has accomplished what Jane Tompkins calls "cultural work" (200).

When he posed the question about "white soul," Hatlen was thinking of something like cultural consciousness or *nomos*, defined by Eric Havelock as "the custom-laws, the folkways, the habits of a people" (Havelock 24). *White soul* is a contradiction in terms. It refers to mass culture as opposed to racial or ethnic identity. Its roots are in the corporate body, not the spirit of a people. But, if such a thing as a *white*—dominant culture, WASP, mass produced, Disney World, consumer culture, materialist—soul exists, King surely possesses it. As he realized when he called himself a "brand-name author" ("On Becoming") and described his fiction as the literary equivalent of "a Big Mac and a large fries from McDonald's" ("Afterword," *Different Seasons* 504), this confusion of material abundance, *frisson*, and nostalgia with transcendence *is* the soul of American culture. King embraces that confusion and contradiction in his horror fiction, which often reads as a scathing attack on the materialist culture of which it is a preeminent example.

King's fast-food version of the "plain style" smells of commercialism, but that fact makes him the middle-American storyteller without peer, the Homer of "white soul." In less than flattering terms in 1982, *Time* critic Paul Gray pronounced him "Master of Postliterate Prose." He meant that King wrote "prefabricated" or mass mediated prose, fiction that "short-circuits thought," sending readers mentally to the movies and television rather than stimulating imagination. King was truly scary, Gray argued, because he appealed not to readers but to people for whom reality was "at its most intense when it c[ould] be expressed as an animated drawing."

In a 1983 *Playboy* interview, King had a rebuttal ready: "I am writing about a generation . . . grown up under the influence of the icons of American popular culture, from Hollywood to McDonald's, and it would be ridiculous to pretend that such people sit around contemplating Proust all day." He tied off the comment with Henry James's observation "that a good ghost story must be connected at a hundred different points with the common objects of life" (Norden 54). King was hardly unaware of what he was doing. When he was an English major, "good" literature was considered "difficult," psychological, experimental and self-conscious. Burten Hatlen's classes, in contrast to most, suggested that academic, folk, and popular cultures were bridgeable (Winter, *Art* 22). King's role models were the unfashionable American naturalists, who plodded on about the material and social aspects of things and whose style he described as ranging "from the horrible to the nonexistent" ("Afterword," *Different Seasons* 504). He emulated them as part of his rebuttal to the Modernists, their postmodern descendants, and other "avatars of high culture" (King, qtd. in Norden 53). Postmodernists of the 1960s such as Pynchon, Barthelme, Fowles, and Barth incorporated popular culture into their fiction but were notably literary in going about it. King wanted the opposite qualities: a strong storyline, typifying characters, Rabelaisian excess and repletion, a transparent style, and a strongly physical reading experience.

Gray was correct in relating King's appeal to "postliteracy" and thus with visual literacy, technological and cultural change. James Twitchell has found it the "inevitable result of advances in publishing, increasing literacy, shifting demographics, advertising culture, and electronic media" (*Preposterous* 103). In a 1982 foreword "On Becoming a Brand Name," King suggested his own best analog in Charles Dickens, "the first brand-name writer" (42). Dickens reconstructed the novel for the emerging nineteenth-century middle class by drawing on the popular mediums and formulas of the day—the crime sheet, the music hall ballad, pantomime, burlesque, melodrama, *marchen*, the political cartoon, and the serial installment. The great Russian director Sergei Eisenstein called Dickens the first "cinematic" author for engaging the fantasies of a half-literate mass audience. His novels "appealed to the same good and sentimental elements" as film, caused them to "shudder before vice," and like film could "mill the extraordinary, the unusual, the fantastic, from . . . everyday reality" (206). In the 1982 foreword, King slyly commented on how Americans "used to line the docks when the ship bearing the next installment of *Little Dorrit* or *Oliver Twist* was due" (42). Dickens's popularity was viewed not as a sign of a decline in literacy but rather the reverse, as the sign of a new kind of literacy. King's should be viewed similarly for our time.[2]

The King "phenomenon" represents another phase in our present and ongoing "technologizing of the word," as Walter Ong calls it in *Orality and Literacy* (1982). Ong and Eric Havelock (*The Muse Learns to Write*, 1986) argue that contemporary mass culture is increasingly a culture of "secondary orality": although based in writing, it functions, for most practical purposes, through the electronic sensorium. In several respects, postliterate culture is more like the oral culture that produced the Homeric epics than the chirographic and Gutenberg ages that immediately preceded it. King's career is an important response to this shift.

Gray notes that while academic writers like Barth and Vonnegut parodied and ironized mass culture, King took it "dead seriously." In fact, he assumed the mantle of its high priest or bard. He appealed to electronically literate children (and their parents and even grandparents) who were "more familiar" (as King was one of the first to point out) with "Ronald McDonald, the Burger King, and the Easter Bunny than . . . with, let's say, Jesus or Peter or Paul or any of those people" (King, "An Evening" 11). Absorbing the images, sounds, and textures of consumer culture seamlessly into his style, his texts managed to do what nothing else could do quite so well: they made readers forget they were reading. In "short-circuiting thought," King also bypassed the alienated or "dissociated sensibility" that is the inheritance of print culture. Himself a product of an increasingly technologized culture, and lacking the father, both literal and figurative, that literate culture presumed, King partly found and partly created a new literacy and a new literalism, one that reflected the changing consciousness of our time.

As opposed to chirographic culture, which was analytical, historical, self-reflective, and speculative, postmodern culture tends, like oral cultures, to be intuitive, spatially organized, intensely participatory and simultaneous, communal (a global village), and conservative. In pre-literate cultures, the sounded word was power and action: to name was to create, to animate; with literacy the printed word was fact; in postliterate culture, a composite of image and sound bite will move or soothe the world. We have moved from language as representation to language as iconographic speech act.

For Paul Gray, King's popularity is a symptom of crisis; for Walter Ong and Eric Havelock it is probably an example of successful adaptation. In this chapter, I view King as the global village's answer to the oral storyteller—in fictions that have been compared to campfire stories, fairy tales, epics, and ballads. King has himself asserted as much in 1983 when he claimed, "My kind of storytelling" belongs in the "long and time-honored tradition dating back to the ancient Greek bards and the medieval minnesingers" (Norden 55). In personal style and tone he affects the manner of the storyteller, who was an entertainer, philosopher, historian and chronicler, schoolmaster, doctor, and priest in one. King brought that oral bard's mystique to the global village. In the process, his dark fantasy reveals to postliterate culture its far from lily-white soul.

Five characteristics of oral literature are relevant to the King phenomenon: (1) story as situation or scene (visualized by King's uncannily cinematic "Third Eye"), (2) formulaic and repetitive structures, (3) homeostatic as opposed to historical perspective (King's nostalgia tripping), (4) an aural-acoustical dimension, and (5) agonistic and empathic modes.[3] Together, these constitute a newly embodied language and are the real basis of King's appeal.

The Third Eye

According to Walter Ong, in preliterate and oral cultures language is "a mode of action rather than a countersign of thought." The Hebrew *dabar*, which means *word*, means also *event*. In Trinitarian theology, God the Father "speaks" the Second person, his son; he does not inscribe him (Ong 75). People in oral cultures view words as powered and magically potent (Ong 32). Words envision and enact, possessing speaker and listener and becoming a field of action.

Our electronic hearths possess an equivalent authority and power. We absorb film, television, and computer texts much as oral peoples responded to sounded words, immediately and viscerally. Electronic texts have shamanic power to effect virtual "events" as King knows well, and his books are often called "cinematic." "The books are visual," King explains. "I see them almost as movies in my head" (Kilgore 108). He envisioned each chapter of *The Shining* as a scene in a different place until "near the very end, where . . . [as] Hallorann is coming across the country on his snowmobile . . . you can almost see the camera travel along beside him" (Stewart 127). "The Raft" (1985), a story in which four teenagers are stranded in the middle of a Maine lake, is a one-scene encapsulation of the splatter film, complete with a four-page, slo-mo rendering of the monster's ingestion of one deserving jock, foot first, through the cracks of the raft. King "saw" *Cujo* as a single scene rendered in ABC's "Movie of the Week" formula: "everything just flowed from that situation, the big dog and the Pinto" (qtd. in Winter, *Stephen King* 96–97). King's fiction, which is almost too easily transferred to film, makes the reader's body a projector, the story a scene, the text a screen.[4]

Preliterate cultures had no categories for abstracting knowledge, as concepts; these remained "embedded within the human lifeworld," the world of action (69). In "Imagery and the Third Eye," an article in *The Writer*, King advises aspiring authors to focus on "story," situation, and scene. For King, books "happen": "first a situation will occur, then an opening scene. . . . Then I can write the book. The characters don't matter" (Schaffer 115). The essential thing is "story," that "simple caveman invention ('I was walking through the forest when the tiger leaped down on me') that held [an] audience spellbound around a fire. . . . But . . . story springs from image: that vividness of place and time and *texture*" (King, "Imagery" 11). "Story" is not a linear plot but an existential situation or locus. Drawing on the post-Jungian psychology of James Hillman and others, Edwin Casebeer explains King's characters in comparable terms: "A writer such as King does not create personas. Instead, his psyche becomes a locus available for personas to emerge and interact with one another. . . . The resulting text is a nexus upon which King and his readers converge for psychic dialogue" (128). Character is "coextensive with the archetypal. We are visited (or possessed) by identity" (Casebeer 129).

It does not hurt King's image that he characterizes himself as a medium, a writer who draws on primary instincts and deeply embedded memories— and with a direct (Jungian) line to our national crisis center. Or that he says he writes out his nightmares, disdaining notes and outlines (Winter, *Stephen King* 202, n. 38). Or that he writes to stay sane. ("I'm in therapy every day. People pay $135 an hour to sit on a couch. I'm talking about the same fears and inadequacies in my writing" [King, qtd. in "The Novelist Sounds Off," 80].) In a 1980 *Rolling Stone* interview, King described the "actual physical act" of writing as being "like autohypnosis, a series of mental passes you go through before you start" (Peck 101).

Thus, in *The Dark Half* (1989), professor-author Thad Beaumont performs a ritual (smoking, drinking, picking up a pencil), enters a trance, and becomes the best selling writer of gruesome pulp thrillers.

Beaumont also has a special visionary faculty to which he attributes animistic power, a "third eye." King described his own third eye in 1980 as "the eye of imagination and memory" (King, "Imagery" 13). This "inner" eye has evocative power much like that of the spoken word. The third eye does not record events—it projects them, with the reader completing the act: "Imagery does not occur on the writer's page; it occurs in the reader's mind" (King, "Imagery" 12). The first sentence of "The Mist" "starts the reader's internal projector humming," writes reviewer Susan Bolotin. The mist itself descends upon a supermarket as the environment for an infinite number of species—from two-foot-long pinkish bugs, to "flying albinos things" with leathery wings, to huge tentacles attached to things that must be recalled from our own private catalog of Grade B creature features. The supermarket windows provide a screen for this phantasmagoria show.

The mist (linked to the Arrowhead Project across the lake) has the combined attributes of the old 1950s technohorror films, which ought to turn it into harmless parody. But the familiarity, like that of fairy tales (which "regress us instantaneously" [qtd. in Magistrale, Second 4]), disarms readers and lends the story a scary immediacy. Readers are positioned with the characters, who are looking at a window that turns out to be a screen. What you see (the mist) is all there is: "We watched the fog overlay her and make her insubstantial, not a human being anymore but a pen-and-ink sketch . . . on the world's whitest paper, and no one said anything" (410). A Lovecraftian obscurity envelopes everything: "she could not see the underside of it . . . only two Cyclopean legs going up and up into the mist like living towers until they were lost to sight" (490).

King's characters, as Gray says, are always watching movies in their heads. A character in "The Raft" tells the monster to "go to California and find a Roger Corman movie to audition for" (305). King gives postmodern substance to the validated nightmare cliché. Applying naturalistic methods to an environment produced by popular culture, King creates the sense of a shared nightmare. It is no dream; it is a consensual or culturally produced virtual reality.

The "guiding impulse" of horror stories, says Terrence Rafferty in a review of George Romero's film adaptation of King's *The Dark Half*, is an ancient "literal-mindedness." Ideas of evil "take on the bodies of large beasts with powerful jaws; memories . . . become ghosts; and unwholesome impulses and animal instincts tend to pop into being as doubles"

("Bad Blood" 106). As the preliterate mind objectified internal states, projecting fears and desires in archetypal monsters, gods, and heroes, King projects internal conflicts directly on to the big screens of his early texts, from *Carrie* to *The Dark Tower.* Carrie projects her righteous rage telekinetically into conflagration; Arnie Cunningham in *Christine* takes revenge by means of a 1958 Plymouth Fury; incipient domestic violence explodes in *Cujo*, the Trenton family dog gone rabid. *It* (1986) entraps each of the six protagonists in a series of hallucinations, projections of his or her greatest fear in forms directly from horror special effects. Ultimately *It* was a roll call of "all the monsters one last time[.] Bring them all on—*Dracula, Frankenstein, Jaws, The Werewolf, The Crawling Eye, Rodan, It Came from Outer Space*, and call it *It*," as King explained the book to *Time*. The monster was a Tulpa, a creature projected by the mind (Kanfer 83).

An effects wizard (like Spielberg or, again, Dickens), King can bring machines to an appearance of primordial life or give them the powers of gods in the old animistic world. The story "Trucks" (1973) projects fears of dehumanization and extinction brought on by the fuel shortage of the early 1970s. Like the dinosaurs in Spielberg's *Jurassic Park* (1993), the trucks just suddenly *are*: omnipresent in a universal "stench of petroleum" (141), headlights popping on "in unison, bathing the lot in an eerie, depthless glare." The trucks have the "squared-off shoulders of prehistoric giants" (130). The human race takes a time trip back to the caves, to "[D]rawing pictures in charcoal. This is the moon god. This is the tree. This is a Mack semi overwhelming a hunter." No, even further back than that, to a race of production line zombies "in Detroit and Dearborn and Youngstown, and Mackinac" (*Night Shift* 142). *Christine* (1983), whose monster is a 1958 Plymouth Fury, a literal metaphor for the deadly American romance with the automobile, possesses her teenage driver Arnie Cunningham. Behind the wheel, he transforms in effects sequences adapted from *The Howling* (1980) and *An American Werewolf in London* (1981): his face "twisted and sunken" until "only the nose is thrust forward," he changes into an "ancient carrion eater" (322).

In King, things do not "fall apart": they come alive, run amok, implode, and explode. As Twitchell notes, pyrotechnic destruction is central to *Carrie* (1974), *'Salem's Lot* (1975), *The Shining* (1977), *The Stand* (1978), *The Dead Zone* (1979), *Firestarter* (1980), and *Christine* (1983), thereby displaying his special ability to "anatomize explosive violence from the inside out" (117), slowing it down "as do films shot in slow motion" (116). Reviews of King's novels typically alternate between praise (for the author's direct treatment of serious themes) and excoriation for "gratuitous grisliness" (Doniger), for the machine that gets going and won't, for two hundred or so pages, stop. But repetition is the point. King's novels return to a very old form that relied on externalization, ritual reenactment, redundancy through accumulative and rhythmic structures, and agonistic struggle.

Fairy Tales, Formulas, and Children

The concept of "oral literature" is an anachronism, a contradiction in terms, Ong reminds us. The spoken word was subject to instant decay, so that oral literature had imposed on it a mnemonic burden. Parry described the Homeric epics as consisting of "devastatingly predictable formulas and equally standardized themes or functions." To *rhapsodize* (from the Greek *Rhapsoidein*) meant to "stitch songs together" (Ong 132). Oral organization was formulaic, accumulative (episodic rather than "plotted"), and redundant, taking shape as the existential context (current events, setting, and audience) demanded. The oral storyteller drew from a repertoire of proverbs and other set expressions, or scenes grouped loosely in catalogs or aggregates.

Because the oral specialist performed speech acts, repeating formulas on demand to fulfill a contract with an audience, he or she was less the inspired genius than an assembly line worker or court clerk. Originality was unthinkable; reliability mandatory. King's readers have contracted to be frightened in exchange for catharsis and the illusion of control, which contract King fulfills every few months after turning out his daily quota of 1,500 words. King seems to enjoy characterizing himself as a hack, a whore, a "brand name" author who produces a commodity. He is the only writer to have had five books simultaneously on the *New York Times* bestseller lists, which he has headed for twenty years.[5] "The Breathing Method" (*Skeleton Crew*, 1985), in which a group of men gather periodically to recite tales of the uncanny, is one of King's metaphors for the author's role. Above the fireplace in the library are the words of the toast raised as each tale is begun: "It is the Tale, not he who tells it" (Norden 55). Tales preexist and preclude tellers, who are "authors" only as they subsist within the marketplace. Their work is a matter of conserving culture.

King exploits the power of archetypes. He tells ancient stories, filtering them through modern Gothic and fantasy conventions. His fictions, opening in suburban or small-town America—Castle Rock, Maine, or Libertyville, Pennsylvania—have the familiarity of the house next door and the 7-Eleven. The characters have the trusted two-dimensionality of kitsch;

they originate in clichés such as the high school "nerd" or the wise child. From such premises, readers move through a densely rendered atmosphere resonant with a popular mythology: advertising, MTV, and comic books as well as traditional sources. When he "plug[s] directly into mass-produced images," using language the way a baseball fan "behind the home-team dugout uses placards, to remind those present of what they have already seen" (Gray), he is repeating formulas as the oral performer did. King's redundancy is purposeful, as in preliterate cultures, in which an event existed in the event of remembering. Ong suggests an analogy with the preschool child who requests the same stories over and over: for both ancient and modern pre-literate listeners, the tale exists only in the oral-aural continuum, and gains resonance and meaning through repetition.

Ben C. Indick had the right idea, in his essay on King's *The Eyes of the Dragon* (1987), when he imagined "the wide eyes and open mouths" of children listening to "tales told around fires" and later to Homeric histories and still later to the "lays of the minstrels" and the "vivid pictorial dramas . . . we call the mystery, Miracle and . . . Morality plays" (189). King writes from all of these oral traditions—campfire stories, epics, romances, and allegories—often at the same time.

King writes from within a consumer culture that is as transitory as oral culture, but also far more self-conscious of its ephemerality, and whose distinguishing trait is uncertainty. Media technology makes hype possible; it also ensures that the star or trend that is here today will be gone tomorrow. We are subjected to constant shock: "More information washes over us than washed over any other generation in history—except for the generation we're raising. . . . This flow of information—it makes you very nervous about everything," King says (qtd. in Spitz 183). Horror responds to this anxiety by intensifying it, by "mak[ing] us children": "That's the primary function of the horror story—to knock away all of . . . the bullshit we cover ourselves with, to take us over taboo lines" (Peck 93). "We" are like the primitives huddled in the darkness—the chaos of signals that we call the information age—waiting for a clear and indisputable sign.

"None of us adults remember childhood," says King, whose hyperrealism attempts to recapture its intensity: "Colors are brighter. The sky looks bigger. . . . Kids live in a constant state of shock. The input is so fresh and so strong. . . . They look at an escalator, and they really think that if they don't take a big step, they'll get sucked in" (qtd. in Peck 95). In King's version of the Romantic tradition, "losers," the infirm or "challenged," minorities, and children are privileged with insights and powers—the alcoholic poet Jim Gardener, mentally disabled Tom Cullen, deaf-mute Nick Andros, stutterer Bill Denbrough, underdogs Carrie White and Arnie

Cunningham, African-Americans Dick Halloran and Sister Abagail, "special" children Danny Torrence and Ellie Creed. The survivors in *The Stand*, who are divested of social conventions, recover the "state of nature." The child is the father of the man. By way of Bruno Bettelheim, King views horror stories as "nothing more than fairy tales for grown ups. And one way to get a grown up is to open up that conduit to the child he was." Because they tap memories that return with uncanny power, fairy tales are "the scariest stories that we have," King told Tony Magistrale in 1989 (*Second* 4).

James Twitchell argues that King's appeal, like that of action film and video games, is almost exclusively to adolescent males.[6] But King holds the record for the most Book of the Month Club (BOMC) Main Selections (fourteen), provoking BOMC to create The Stephen King Library, which offers the 27 King novels in "treasurable" hard cover editions ("The Complete Stephen King"), and suggesting that Twitchell is way off the mark. Like Robert Bly or Clarissa Pinkola Estes, King's cultural work involves evoking the "inner child" in his multi-generational audience. Fairy tales were never really "for" children anyway. The folktales they have come down from were told by elders as the guardians of tradition to a community audience. In the nineteenth century, when Dickens's novels were circulated around the Victorian household of family and servants, and often read aloud, or when the author himself performed public readings from his Christmas Books, the traditions of the oral community as extended family continued. Stephen King novels are similarly a family affair, passed from parent to child (or vice versa).

As Bettelheim explains, many fairy tales begin with the death of a parent or ancestor, or an aging parent's decision to let the heir take over after proving him- or herself worthy (8). The protagonist, an initiate, must meet with loss or change, and encounters fundamental existential dilemmas that, as Jung pointed out, occur several times over a life. As a modern novelist in a self-conscious culture, King sums up national and cultural experience as well.

King's early books resemble Dickens's or the Brontës' in their domestication and modern "fracturing" of fairy tale and Gothic formulas and in fulfilling Bettelheim's theory of the cathartic and educative function of fairy tales. *Carrie* is a dark modernization of "Cinderella," with a bad mother, cruel siblings (peers), a prince (Tommy Ross), a godmother (Sue Snell), a ball, and a theme in which a persecuted victim recovers her female power. *Christine* is a fairy tale for postliterate males—*Carrie* for boys as the revenge of the nerds. The novel memorializes the youth and car culture of the 1950s in this version of "Cinderella" in which the high school nerd changes into a hood, acquires a beautiful girlfriend (the princess), and destroys the bullies who formerly humiliated him—all through the agency of a magical car, a 1958 Plymouth Fury, "One of the long ones with the big fins." Arnie's transformation is a body makeover, like the car's. *Pet Sematary* is based on W. W. Jacobs' "The Monkey's Paw" and the formula of the fatal wish come true. *'Salem's Lot* is *Dracula* come to *Our Town*. Often King's characters and places have mythical or typifying names: Carrie White, John Smith, Louis Creed (whose cat is named Church), Libertyville (Pennsylvania), Castle Rock, Jerusalem's Lot (corrupted, into 'Salem's Lot).

Fairy tales state existential dilemmas "briefly and pointedly" in stereotypes and formulas in which "evil is as omnipresent as virtue" (Bettelheim 8), but the figures in many of the tales are unequivocal, "not ambivalent as we all are in reality." Polarization (projection of internal conflict on "positive" and "negative" objects) allows the child to learn to deal with emotional and moral distinctions. Amoral tales with ambiguous characters (like "Puss 'n' Boots") reassure the child that success can be achieved (Bettelheim 9–10). Thus, the boy in *'Salem's Lot* is "a bigger-than-life archetypal eleven-year-old boy. And a lot of the kid characters in the books are strong and good" (qtd. in Kilgore 104). Barlow, the King vampire in *'Salem's Lot*, is Dracula raised to the nth power. In *The Dark Half*, the storyteller himself is polarized into the Good author (the clumsy and moderately successful literary novelist Thad Beaumont) and the Bad author (George Stark, his pseudonym and inspired pulp writer). The campy *Creepshow* includes types such as the henpecked professor-husband and the insufferable bitch wife, or the Gothic, all-consuming patriarch who terrorizes his daughters with the line, repeated as a ghastly-farcical refrain, "I want my cake!" Ambiguous characters such as Carrie are protagonist-victim-monsters with whom we identify as the story metes out justice from her perspective. (King's early novels usually provided a semblance of the fairy tale consolation. Thus the exceptions, the family-centered *Cujo* and *Pet Sematary*, were especially shocking for ending with the death of a child.)

"Round" characters were the product of literacy and memory, of consciousness that could turn in upon itself. King's characters are not introspective in the usual sense. They are postliterate schizophrenics whose inner space is laid graphically before us, in the blood-filled elevators of the Overlook Hotel or in cinematographically realized flashbacks or in flames. King gets us inside the skins of his protagonists by giving them his own preternaturally sharp third eye. Whether we really empathize with

Arnie Cunningham or not, we cannot doubt the intensity of his physical sensations. Similarly the clairvoyant Danny Torrence

> shrieked. But the sound never escaped his lips; turning inward and inward, it fell down in his darkness like a stone in a well. He took a single blundering step backward, hearing his heels clack on the white hexagonal tiles, and at the same moment his urine broke, spilling effortlessly out of him.
>
> The woman was sitting up.
>
> . . . . Her dead palms made squittering noises on the porcelain. Her breasts swayed like ancient cracked punching bags. There was the minute sound of breaking ice shards. She was not breathing. (*The Shining* 218)

King's characters may be "flat," but the worlds they move in are "hyper-realized" in primary colors.

Roland, the "gunslinger" and knight errant of the postapocalyptic *The Dark Tower* is "like something out of a fairy tale or myth, the last of his breed in a world that was writing the last page of its book" (King, *Dark Tower: Gunslinger* 42). According to Douglas Winter, he is "a simulacrum of the classic elements of heroic mythology": a quester wandering through a wasteland of broken-down machines, gasoline pumps, highways, and railroads (66). King's epic fantasy *The Stand*, often compared to J.R.R. Tolkein's *Lord of the Rings*, is perhaps the most beloved King book. It is also a postapocalyptic Western: small groups of survivors of a superflu struggle across the American continent, attempting to rebuild civilization. The adversary is the "Walkin' Dude" named Randall Flagg who draws loners and outlaws to Las Vegas; he is opposed by tribal Mother Abagail Freemantle, who is also the childlike seer. As in the Greek epics or the Hebrew Bible, *The Stand*'s stereotypes are absolute figures around which to organize information. *The Stand* (like the oral epic) is copious, redundant, organized by aggregates (associated clusters that provide structures for storing information), amplification, and set formulas—epithets, proverbs, songs, speeches, messages, rituals, and omens—rather than tight plotting. Fran Goldsmith's diary (like Mike Hanlon's diary in *It*) stands for what is left of literacy and history. As in the oral epic, history is contextualized, embedded within the human life world of polarized action and struggle.

Needful Things (1991) has "a huge cast," King says, calling it a "throwback" to *'Salem's Lot* and *The Stand*, "where I threw in 50 or 60 characters and then said, 'Shit!' and threw in about 30 more" (qtd. in

Ashton-Haiste 30). A disaster or crisis is often the focal point for assembling a vast number of characters. *Carrie*, King's first novel, and *'Salem's Lot*, his second, destroyed whole towns and in the process took an inventory of culture.

King is known for setting up a "complete, mundane, comfortable world with name-brand products and familiar language" (Thomases and Tebbel 207), a world like our own whose repletion of surfaces is a disavowal of its real ephemerality. That King's "worlds are echo chambers of popular culture" (Twitchell *Preposterous* 104) is consistent with his role as "oral" historian and compares with Homer's use of copia—the catalogues of men and artifacts. In a 1981 interview, King describes the reader as "a guy in space" who, lacking historical context, needs to be brought down to a semblance of earth, anchored to a hyperreal or created "environment that the reader can identify with totally" (qtd. in Thomases and Tebbel 207).

As in preliterate culture, the information flow is the only "real thing." Some things are "certain," King explains, in that they "run through society. Anywhere . . . somewhere there's going to be a Coke sign. People identify with Coke" (qtd. in Thomases and Tebbel 207) to the extent that for many it is not merely a soft drink but, as Stuart Ewen suggests, a badge of identity. In our eternally remade culture, Coke (or its like) replaces the cross, the flag, or the ancestor.

Adapting the methods of the American Naturalists to contemporary popular culture, King makes his characters and settings "dense" with demographic signs. Like Disney World or Norman Rockwell's paintings, his texts combine naturalistic detail with the comforting two-dimensionality of TV sitcoms and kitsch. In a culture of advertising, brand images can attain a semblance of permanence through their omnipresence and become our archetypes. Coke *is* the "real" thing.

Homeostasis and Nostalgia

Oral literature "invested a great deal of energy in saying over and over what has been learned arduously over the ages." Oral culture is by nature conservative (Ong 41–42). But Ong, Havelock, Millman Parry, and Claude Lévi-Strauss have stressed that (in contrast to literate societies) preliterate societies were homeostatic, living "very much in a present which keeps itself in equilibrium," explains Ong, by "sloughing off memories" that have lost relevance (46). There was no sense of linear chronology as we know it. The oral narrator began an epic *in medias res*, meaning not (as commonly thought) at a particular midpoint in a chronological narrative, but at whatever scene or formula was called for. Performances were not repeated verbatim. The bard's memory consisted of "a float of themes and formulas" out of which stories were constructed (Ong 6). Oral traditions reflected present cultural values (Ong 48). Oral history was inconceivable. Postmodern history is similarly nonexistent.

In 1971 William Irwin Thompson wrote that Americans' idea of history is "a shattered landscape in which the individual moves through a world of discontinuities" (12), and where a person no longer has a "history" as a single, linear identity developing from birth to death and "is free to change lives and wives as often as he has the energy" (18). In the 1980s and 1990s, this serial view of the self became commonplace. Replacing linear history was a cyclical pattern of retrogression, nostalgia, and renewal. Postmodern psychology shifts the emphasis from the ego to a more fluid idea of the self in time and place. "Today is the first day of the rest of your life," we were told in the 1980s. Self-help books such as *Passages* proclaimed that we go through (indeed are) a series of different stages or crises—childhood, adolescence, young adulthood, mid-life, old age— whose constant is the passage itself, or the process of psychic death and rebirth. Popular culture is obsessed with rites of passage, which objectify flux and commemorate change. Each "passage" makes us adolescents in that we confront primary terrors, regress, take stock, discard, and begin again. King's novels concern, and provide rites for, these passages.

In the postmodern scene, history is homeostatic, relative rather than objective and linear. This perspective became obvious in the 1980s in movies that celebrated or examined nostalgia in generational cycles. *Back to the Future*, *Peggy Sue Got Married*, and *Blue Velvet* conflated time, blurring the boundaries of the generation "gap"; parents became adolescents again and vice versa, or the audience was invited to be a part of both generations at the same time (*Blue Velvet*). The conflation was uncannily pleasurable and sinister. Since the 1950s, American culture has looked back roughly two decades or a single generational span—with the 1950s retroactivated in the 1970s, the 1960s beginning in the 1980s, and the 1970s in the 1990s.

The early and middle novels of Stephen King are informed with this pattern. King is Rousseauistic, depicting good children, corrupt parents, and evil institutions (Magistrale, *Landscape* 95–97), and a world in which cyclical renewal is necessary. A pattern, as Joseph Reino also notes (2-3), is the lost father who is replaced by a writer-figure and a stopgap culture created out of the "pop" remnants of American culture (*'Salem's Lot*'s Ben Mears, the Losers' Club, whose group therapy and regression serve the same purpose). Like postfuturist science fiction films of the 1980s, King's landscapes are haunted with the debris of the accumulated, corrupt past, and the future is ever in doubt. In *The Stand*, most of the world's people have been destroyed by plague, but not their corpses, abandoned cars, or ٍne world's weapons. "Everything is lying around waiting to be picked up again," remarks one character. Trashcan Man, pyromaniac and walking arsenal, is also a technological wizard. The Walkin' Dude is the sociopath haunted by and haunting with political memories waiting to come around again; he recalls attending school with Charles Starkweather, meeting Lee Harvey Oswald in 1962, riding with the Ku Klux Klan, cop-killing with black men in New York City, and whispering plans to Donald DeFreeze about Patty Hearst (Winter, *Stephen King* 59–60). Flagg (the Walkin' Dude) draws his fellows across the desert to Las Vegas. King's chosen few are American Adams whose solution is to begin again, creating small alternative communities. Hence Fran Goldsmith and Stu Redmond leave the world's last community in Colorado and return to Maine—to start over.

King's world is one of permanent "historical amnesia," as Fredric Jameson calls it. Conservative nostalgia substitutes for a temporal perspective and effects a sense of continuity and permanence through spatialized time, as Stuart Ewen points out, or history as style (111–34). Vivian Sobchack notes a similar trend in "postfuturist" science fiction from *Blade Runner* (1982) to *Back to the Future* (1985): "excess scenography" inflated the value of space, of *mise-en-scène*, while temporal distinctions were "conflated" and "homogenized" (274). As in the Gothic, the setting very nearly *was* the film. Or, rather, science fiction dissolved into Gothic.

"Retro" culture, its product, maintains cycles of continuity against the threat of constant dislocation. King retrofitted the horror monsters of 1950s reruns of the already nostalgic 1930s film classics. In a culture that maintained itself through nostalgia, the hoarier the cliché, the better. In King's novels, according to Paul Gray, life becomes "stock footage" and "ancient history the Flintstones." What Gray doesn't say is that for many it is the Flintstones or nothing at all.

But King is also "postmodern," says Robert Kieley, in depicting a nation "exposed over and over to itself, as an enormous mirror, part trite situation comedy, part science fiction, part cop show." As national rites of passage, King's books focus on our era of diminished expectations. They especially fit the 1980s, when America saw itself less in the image of Lincoln than as Ronald Reagan, a "dazed behemoth with padded shoulders" (Kiely).

This sensibility is obvious in *Christine* (1983), which, like *Back to the Future*, was a compendium of the 1970s as 1950s retro culture. The novel was a scaffold to which King attached copia from folklore, pop culture, and from the mobile youth culture that had come down from the 1950s by way of advertising, rock songs, television film, and national pastimes. *Christine* is flooded with the fragments and rhythms of fifty-some rock songs from the 1950s through the 1970s—with the 1970s songs (by Bruce Springsteen, the Beach Boys, and Elvis Costello) standing as jaded versions of their prototypes. The spiritual source of this mythos is Christine's haunted radio, her "soul," which is stuck on a Golden Oldies station, thus determining the plot, with "Teen Angel," "In My Room," and "Dead Man's Curve" proving most fatal. Vintage rock also structures the novel into three sections (with rock lyrics heading each of the 51 chapters) and arranged in Leslie Fiedler's terms, in *Love and Death in the American Novel*, as "Teenage Car Songs," "Teenage Love Songs," and "Teenage Death Songs," the first two categories collapsing into the last. *Christine* is a recapitulatory rock musical in which *deja vu* substitutes for history.

The Gothic is by nature nostalgic and a critique of nostalgia: its essentials are regression, haunted space designed to recapture (primal) psychic energy, and in the recovery of feeling, a sense of rebirth or transcendence. *Christine* is nostalgia about the horrors of nostalgia, a "dark parable about the death of the American romance with the automobile," enacting its "last gasp" (Winter, *Stephen King* 125) or final backfire. Thus the 1958 Plymouth Fury is a time machine, a spatial metaphor for trips taken in and out of time.

Christine is also a fine example of how reading Stephen King conserves through ritual. King recalls the moment that inspired him to write *The Stand*, of hearing a preacher "dilating upon the text 'Once in every generation the plague will fall among them.'" He liked the phrase (it "sound[ed] like a Biblical quotation but [was] not") so much that he typed it out and tacked it over his typewriter (*Danse Macabre* 371). In 1990, with much fanfare, the "original" version of *The Stand* appeared, enlarged by some 350 pages and several new characters. The ritual of rereading thus becomes the Second Experience. The Second Experience, moreover, hits baby boomers at midlife and becomes part of its ritual of wiping out, taking stock, and starting over. Both generations seem to find the second or third time around richer, more Biblical in its plenitude. In May 1994 *The Stand* was back on the paperback best-seller list. The occasion was the ABC television miniseries, updated for the age of AIDS it seemed to predict, and premiering on Mother's Day.

King's tales of terror are rituals of the most fundamental sort, of redemption, regression, abjection, and return. For at least two generations they have been a collective act in which cultural memory was reinstated, a culture's looking back to get its bearings. As King's recitations, these tales of monsters, machines, brand images, and old TV icons, viewed nostalgically or elegaically, go on offering provisional structures for a dissolving and re-forming culture.

The "Grain of the Voice": King's Oral/Aural Narrative

The 1986 magazine *Time* cover story provided a list of King's patented "tics and tropes." Below are six (out of nine):

> *The Disgusting Colloquialism*: "She drew in a great, hitching breath and hocked up a remarkably large looey onto the top of his head." *The Brand-Name Maneuver*: "Here sits a man with Bass Weejuns on his feet and Calvin Klein underwear to cover his ass." *The Comic-Strip Effect*: "Whack-WHACK-Whack-WHACK—And suddenly it was in his hands, a great living thing that pumped and pulsed against his palms, pushing them back and forth. (NONONONONONONO)." *The Burlesque Locution*: " 'Goodafternyoon, deah leady,' Richie said in his best Baron Butthole voice. 'I amn ain diah hneed of three ticky tickies to youah deah old American flicktoons.' " *The Fancy Juxta-position*: epigraphs from Virgil and *Mean Streets*. (Kanfer 74)

What these examples have in common, and an aspect of the comic book style, is an acoustical dimension: printed words must be sounded out and heard by a bodily ear, their oral-aural dimension retrieved.

King is not the "first to turn his fiction over to the echo chamber of mass culture," Gray remarks, mentioning postmodernists Barthelme, Pynchon, and John Barth. King's novels are the other side of what John Barth called a "literature of exhaustion" that confronted the crisis of literacy with *Lost in the Funhouse: Fiction for Print, Tape, Live Voice* (1968). The "author" of Barth's "Life-Story," confined to print, blurts out in direct address to "The reader! You, dogged, uninsultable, print-oriented bastard, it's you I'm addressing, who else, from inside this monstrous fiction," and asks "How is it that you don't go to a movie, . . . play tennis with a friend, make amorous advances ?" (127). However particularized and challenged "you" feel after reading this passage, Barth's author concludes that his reader is himself. King prefers an even more direct assault on his readers' senses. Rather than turn the barrier of print itself into self-conscious art (as Barth does), and drawing on the comic-book, he gives his fiction a sound track. He bludgeons typography until it performs. In "The Body" (1982), the narrator is crossing a railroad bridge when a train materializes:

The freight's electric horn suddenly spanked the air into a hundred pieces with one long loud blast, making everything you ever saw in a movie or a comic book or one of your own daydreams fly apart, letting you know what both the heroes and cowards really heard when death flew at them: WHHHHHHHONNNNNNNK! WHHHHHHHHONNNNNNNK (*Different* 358).

King sees to it that his books "not only read well, but listen well" (Kilgore 116). "It's the total experience of a book to read it aloud," opines King. "It's a much more intimate experience to listen to a novel. . . . The page has a shape . . . a form of its own. . . . But when you listen . . . you can fall totally into [the story]" (qtd. in Beahm 128). It is hardly surprising that King is a fan of talking books (the King children earned their allowances by taping books for him to listen to while driving) and has recorded many of his own. While many authors are poor readers (and don't know it), King is the exception. "Usually if someone gets through one paragraph I'm dancing in the aisles," says Jim Barrigan, director of Penguin-Highbridge Audio. King "opens up his Jolt cola, takes a swig, and off he goes. . . . He's an editor's dream because he can go through three or four pages of the book without one mistake" (Green 43).

King shifts typography into iconography, representing sound as sound. In "The Raft," for example: " 'Help,' Rachel screamed. 'Help it hurts please help it hurts IT HURTS IT HURRRRTS————' " (288). What more can you say? King reclaims the discounted or discredited language of the body, especially the body in pain.

The first lines of *Misery* (1987), therefore, can be comprehended only when read phonetically: they must be pronounced and heard:

> umber whunnn
> yerrrnnn umber whunn
> fayunn
> These sounds: even in the haze. (3)

Author Paul Sheldon is awakening from an automobile accident and a long drugged sleep. The passage communicates Sheldon's swim back into consciousness, his registration of the sounds of the words, "Your number one fan," spoken by Annie Wilkes, a former nurse obsessed with Sheldon's romance novels. The phonetic spellings force us to read the text aloud or "as if" aloud. We are plunged into Sheldon's existential situation, his failure to comprehend words as words, his embodiment. We enter active oral-aural consciousness. For audiences already "there," such typography replenishes the one-dimensional, enclosed medium of the printed page.

During the crisis of orality in Greek culture, in the fifth century B.C., when writing was new and lacked the authority of speech, many written texts similarly called attention to themselves, "speaking" of their limitations and also of strange new powers. Havelock translates a scene from Euripides' *Hippolytus* (428 B.C.) in which a murder victim's husband discovers on her corpse a note naming her killer. "The tablet shouts, it cries aloud," he exclaims, overcome less with grief than with surprise at the novelty of text: "Look, look at what I have seen in written letters (*en graphais*)—a song speaking aloud!" (lines 877–80, qtd. in Havelock 22).

In the eighteenth century Lawrence Sterne showed a comparable self-consciousness about the printed text. King forces his text into a postliterate aural-accoustic dimension, allowing the reader to get the sense of "being there." And although Sterne and King play with the text as if it were a toy, both seek to evoke a sense of the evocative power of the spoken word in oral culture.

All sound is dynamic, but especially oral utterance, which originates inside living organisms and thus has magical power. The spoken word is always an event, a moment in time, lacking the "thinglike repose" of the printed text (Ong 32). To represent the oral African-American community, Toni Morrison seeks a "visceral or emotional response as well as an intellectual response . . . with the audience" and opens the text to the participation of the reader and a chorus (Morrison, "Rootedness" 330). Morrison may be the best example of the oral novelist that we have. King's "pop," white, mass-produced version of "soul" (and however much it pretends to a homogeneity of American culture that does not exist) affects similar qualities, in particular the visceral sense of a voice—or, rather, voices. King's short stories are often first-person narratives. "Mrs. Todd's Shortcut," narrated by crusty Homer Buckland, is one of several in dialect. The novel *Dolores Claiborne* (1993) is narrated by a garrulous sixty-five-year-old woman as a single taped confession. One of King's most widely recognized "tics" is the use of italics to enhance typography, lending the text acoustical power (however paradoxically through a kind of iconographic signification). Italics shift the typography, enabling readers to hear the more-than-literal word, returning them to the uncanny voice of the unconscious.

Italics most commonly stylize proverbial expressions and messages, flashbacks, fantasies, clairvoyant utterances, intuitions, and/or auditory hallucinations. With the help of italics, the Creed family cat Church, recently returned from the dead in *Pet Sematary*, "speaks" to his master:

"I'm here to tell you that you come out the other side with your purr-box broken and a taste for the hunt. . . . I'm part of what your heart will grow now. . . . Tend your garden well" (192). Earlier in the novel a hit and run victim speaks from the collective voice of the Micmac burial ground:

> The dying man was making a gurgling sound in his throat. He tried to speak. Louis heard syllables—phonetics, at least—but the words themselves were slurred and unclear. . . .
>
> "Caaa," the young man said. "*Gaaaaaaa*—-". . . . Then Louis thought he might have had an auditory hallucination. *He made some more of those phonetic sounds and my subconscious . . . cross-patched the sounds into my own experience*. . . . A swooning, mad terror struck him and his flesh began to . . . move up and down his arms and along his belly in waves. . . .
>
> "The soil of a man's heart is stonier, Louis," the dying man said. "A man grows what he can . . . and tends it." (74)

Later, picked up by Jud Crandall, *"The soil of a man's heart is stonier"* recurs as a refrain throughout the novel—its fatal, faintly Biblical *sound* reverberating beyond the page. Italics signify an opening in the text, a gap in fabric of reality through which the collective unconscious speaks. In "The Reach," italics similarly represent a community voice, whether represented by an individual—for instance, Stella Flanders, who has never left Goat Island—or the spirits who come to meet her when, ninety-five years old and dying of cancer, she decides to cross to the mainland:

> She heard voices, but was not sure they actually spoke:
>
> > *Take my hand, Stella—*
> > *(do you)*
> > *Take my hand, Bill—*
> > *(oh do you do you)*
> > *Annabelle . . . Freddy . . . Russell . . .*
> > *John . . . Ettie . . . Frank . . . take my*
> > *hand, take my hand . . . my hand . . . (do*
> > *you love).* ("The Reach," 565)

The typography indicates a transcendence of ordinary textuality in contrapuntalism. "Do the Dead Sing?" asks the voice. The answer is another question, "Do you love?" It is answered in what she perceives to be a ghostly chorus, a self-transcending affirmative.

Italics often lead into internal rhyme and elaborate, ballad-like patterns of incremental repetition—a question, a phrase, a quotation, a proverb—as in Stella's "I stay here because the mainland is too far to reach" (553), and "The Reach was wider in those days" (*Skeleton* 560). The reach is water, time, memory, community, and finally life. The question "Do you love?" thematically and tonally links contrasting stories in *Skeleton Crew*: in "The Reach," in "Nona" (where it is a terrifying self-indictment), and in "The Raft," where it is a fragment of a song. In the beginning of the story the question is associated with summer love and, by the end, with loss and failure and death. The skillfully balanced contrasts in the stories go on indefinitely and give a sense of King's considerable aural range.

King recalls the first record he ever owned, a 48 with "Hound Dog" and "Don't Be Cruel." Finding rock was like finding something "very, very powerful, like a drug, like a rush. It made you bigger than you were.... Then watching *American Bandstand* and seeing . . . really ugly [people]. . . . They look[ed] like me! But the music made them big, too" (Schaffer 115). Rock music is a big part of the King mystique. "Every day at 9 A.M., . . . [he] climbs into a T-shirt and jeans, swallows a vitamin pill, drinks a glass of Maine tap water and turns on some hard rock on WZON" and writes until 5 P.M. (Kanfer 83). In many oral cultures, narratives were (and still are) chanted to music, especially drums and stringed instruments, which stabilizes or varies the text. In *Christine*, King's patterning, incremental repetition, and (as the horror mounts) a pulsing, driving rhythm provide a "musical" accompaniment to the action. This has an obvious appeal to people who channel surf or listen to music or watch television while reading. Like writing, reading is no longer a single-minded, solitary activity. King's novels make sense within the intermediary contexts that the present generation of readers encounter. As they prepare children and adolescents for adulthood, they also initiate them into the global village.

Many characters discover their identities as writers first through telling stories to friends (Gordie Lachance in "The Body" and Bill Denbrough in *It*). The writer's role is a response to a community, and King's speaking narrators often act as the community storyteller performing on demand. In "The Body," the narrator Gordie transcends embodiment and finds his calling by telling stories to his friends, and the oral situation represents a special pre-adolescent space in which "real" community or presence existed. In *It*, Bill Denbrough, introspective stutterer-cum-successful professional writer, must perform as the Losers' spokesman. Wisdom may derive from the "inner child" but it can reveal itself only in the power of utterance. Denbrough is "called" to lead the group in the Ritual of Chud, which is a kind of shouting match. We are reminded to read phonetically:

Dropping his voice a full register, making it not his own (making it, in fact, his father's voice, although Bill would go to his grave not knowing this . . .), drawing in a great breath, he cried: "HE THRUSTS HIS FISTS AGAINST THE POSTS AND STILL INSISTS HE SEES THE GHOSTS NOW LET ME GO!" (*It* 1056)

In this demonstration, the dialogic voice of the community (the father and the symbol of the ancestor as foundation, the Turtle) wins out against the monophonic voice of It (Magistrale, *Second* 115–19). Conversely, writers who lack an audience, who are blocked or secretive, go berserk (Jack Torrence, Thad Beaumont as Richard Stark).

Vision separates, abstracts: sound is a unifying sense. We listen with the whole body, surrounded by sound, becoming the sound. Creating an acoustical dimension in which the book seems to speak, King's enhancements "read" somatically, opening up typographic space to a sense of context. My students explain that when they read King's fiction they forget themselves. They forget where they are. They forget they are "in a room." They forget they are reading.

Oral Agonistic and Empathic Modes: The Death of the Author

Readers lose themselves in King's novels because Kingstyle seems to be no style. King takes a hack's pride in having no affectations or aesthetic purposes (outside of liking to scare people) and his own inner compulsion. He writes because he can't not write. His comment on the style of the American Naturalists as "horrible or nonexistent" is telling: it is the lack of style that he chooses as trademark. Peter Straub was immediately taken with King's "unprecendentedly direct" style: "It was not at all a literary style, but rather the reverse. It made a virtue of colloquialism and transparency. . . . [I]t moved like the mind itself . . . like a lightning rod to the inner lives of his characters" ("Meeting Stevie" 10). "Vox pop" Richard Corliss more recently termed it (38). The absence of a style gives King a voice, and thus an illusion of presence, of a body. In an essay from *Image/Music/Text*, Roland Barthes uses the phrase "the grain of the voice" to describe what one hears "deep down in the cavities" of the body of a singer (181). Beyond the song, the singer, and the style, and lacking identity or personality, the "grain" is the "body in the voice as it sings" (188) that testifies to authenticity. Through his disavowal of "literary" style, King acquires (at least the impression of) such a "grain" or "body." His books have "rhythm" and "weight," says Michael McDowell, and thus "work for most readers in a way that they perceive as visceral" (95). King reaches down to what Sartre valorized in Camus (and Roland Barthes considered impossible): "writing degree zero." Or, as Charles L. Grant describes the King phenomenon: "It's a voice there in the work, King sitting on the back porch with a beer in his hand. . . . 'So let me tell you a story that'll scare the shit out of you'—even if it's five hundred pages long, you listen" (30). The author as guy next door.

As Ong tells us, the verbomotor lifestyle of primary orality tends to unite people in groups: it "fosters personality structures that are more communal and externalized, and less introspective than . . . among literates" (Ong 69). King's noises presume the immediate presence of a "listener," project an instant audience, and lend him a credibility that goes with the territory. Says Nina Auerbach, "we believe him" whether he is quoting *Moby Dick* or saying " 'EEEEEOOOOOOARRRHMMMMM!' or 'Hurts! It *hurrrrr*—.' " ("Not With a Bang"). The aural-acoustical dimension of King's rhetoric extends far beyond the text in an ongoing dialogue with readers and critics (and himself), creating an arena (or, rather, multi-media center) for the writer's public personality. King multiplies himself in prefaces, forewords, introductions, afterwords, and notes that are dog-eared, revered, and intoned by fans. He writes and speaks with the authority or (what is even better) the untutored "common sense" and anti-intellectual humor of the "average man" on nearly everything. His approach to writing the text of a volume on gargoyles, a coffee table book and collaboration with the photographer f-stop Fitzgerald, is a case in point. In it King swears he knew nothing about the subject, researched nothing, and wrote as he promised to, from his "nerve endings" ("It wasn't laziness; . . . the more empiric knowledge I gleaned on the subject of gargoyles, the worse I would write about them" [*Nightmares* 7–8]).

Frequently King turns anti-intellectualism into oral "literature," in the sense that writing takes on the properties of oral agonistic. In the foreword to Underwood and Miller's *Fear Itself*, he counters the "brand name" accusation with the self-appellation, the "Green Giant of . . . the 'modern horror story' " ("On Becoming" 15). Thus raising the insult to a hyperbolic flattery, he finishes the round with a literary allusion: "Perhaps the first brand-name writer was Charles Dickens" ("On Becoming" 42). His strategy descends from the oral form called "flyting" or reciprocal name calling, with King inverting the vilification on himself. (He gained early expertise when he wrote a college newspaper column called "King's Garbage Truck.")

King's stylistic trademark, if he has a single one, is "excess," says Michael Morrison. He "revels in crude behavior on the page." A "literary bull in the china shop," he "not only breaks glassware to get your attention, he defecates on the floor" (Morrison 263). King's scatological expressionism compares with the oral storyteller's liberal use of the agonistic, the language of gore, grimaces, grunts, and groans. Hence King confesses in the "Notes" to *Skeleton Crew*, "I got to thinking about cannibalism one day . . . and my muse once more evacuated its magic bowels on my head. I know how gross that sounds, but it's the best metaphor I know of, inelegant or not, and believe me when I tell you I'd give the little Fornit Ex-Lax if he wanted it. Anyway, I started to wonder if a person could eat *himself*" (571). This note explains the inspiration for "Survivor Type," the tale of a doctor marooned on an island who subsists on parts of his own body. King's metaphors, even when describing his own style, are somatic: they seek to "reinvest" literary clichés with body language.

Much of King's content, as in nineteenth-century *belles lettres*, dramatizes and acts out the implied author's relations with his readers. Proverbs and riddles are used in oral culture "not simply to store knowledge but to engage others in verbal and intellectual combat," and one riddle sets the stage for another appositional or contrasting one (Ong 44). In his "Afterword" to *Different Seasons* King answers the objection that he lacks "literary elegance" by claiming to give instead "good weight," which he translates thusly: "if you can't run like a thoroughbred you can pull your brains out. A voice rises from the balcony: 'What brains, King. Ha! Ha, very funny, fella, you can leave now!'" (504). Joseph Reino expresses consternation with this sort of behavior, which he calls "image-mutilation" and regards as compulsive (Preface [ix]). Regardless of taste or compulsion, it is one of King's tropes. Paradoxically it validates readers' experience of the texts, enhancing their sense of the voice and the person. Ultimately it recontextualizes the writer and the reader in a site that recalls the oral community.

Oral literature was agonistic not only in its manner of presentation but in its content, its celebration of physical excess and its ardent descriptions of violence. Blood flows freely in the oral tradition. Citing psychologist J. C. Carothers, Ong points out that as literates tend to interiorize schizophrenia, people in oral cultures more often act it out: rather than psychic withdrawal, they show "external confusion, leading . . . to violent action, including self mutilation and violence to others." Special terms designate this behavior: "the old-time Scandinavian warrior going 'berserk'" or the Southeast Asian "running 'amok'" (Ong 69). The detailed depiction and ritualization of violence was a logical extension of this perspective. Ong notes how Books VIII and X of *The Iliad* "rival" the most sensational of today's television shows and movies (Ong 44). The grisliness of the oral versions of the "classical" fairy tales is by now well known. *Carrie*'s reversal of *Cinderella*'s happy ending, for instance, recovers the gruesome revenge elements of the tale's folk originals (the stepsisters' heels are sliced off and a dove pecks out their eyes). *Carrie* is Cinderella in the body language of menstrual blood and raging hormones. King's adolescent joy in grimaces and groans, the *Mad* magazine humor, and the staple of "grue" hardly need mentioning. Writing exorcises demons that would otherwise erupt, as the blocked Jack Torrence of *The Shining* (1977) demonstrates. King's writer-protagonists are invariably prone to grotesque oral or scatological performances or extreme violence, suggesting Kristevan relationships between writing and horror, the body and the text. *Misery* (1987) portrays writing and reading as a grotesque physical battle of the sexes (with needles, axes, and typewriters)—to the death. Or King's writers produce literalized metaphors in which their characters come to violent physical life (*The Dark Half*, "Secret Window, Secret Garden"). Red, the narrator of "Rita Hayworth and the Shawshank Redemption" (1982) reveals to the reader that he has concealed the one-hundred-page manuscript about the quasi-legendary prison career of Andy Dufresne in his rectum (enlarged by gang-banging encounters with the prison "sisters"). In "The Revenge of Lard Ass Hogan" (in "The Body," *Different Seasons*) a fat boy gets even with his tormentors by vomiting all over his fellow contestants at a blueberry pie-eating contest and starts a gut-wrenching chain reaction in the audience.

In *Danse Macabre*, King explains his appeals to the gag instinct as a last resort: "I recognize terror as the finest emotion, and so I will try to terrorize the reader. But if I find I cannot terrify him/her, I will try to horrify; and if I find I cannot horrify, I'll go for the gross-out. I'm not proud" (37). The engagement with an audience undermines King's corporate image, authorial stance, and textual closure and so enhances the King phenomenon. The dialogic text means that King is "in love with his readers, as someone in his income bracket might well be," writes Susan Bolotin. This cozy relationship spills over into the now countless books of Stephen King commentary, Stephen King calendars, Stephen King quiz books (Spignesi 1990 and 1992) and games, *Castle Rock: The Stephen King Newsletter* (Jan. 1985–Dec. 1989), *The Stephen King Companion* (Beahm), *In the Darkest Night: A Student's Guide to Stephen King, Teacher's Manual: The Novels of Stephen King* (Zagorski), and *The Shape Under the Sheet: The Complete Stephen King Encyclopedia* (Spignesi).

This phenomenon in turn spills over into the news magazines that follow him under the headings of Business or Show Business as often as the book section.[7] "Do you know me?" he asked rhetorically, looking at you through your TV screen. This American Express commercial assumed that King's face is a familiar image, a fact that makes him unique among authors. As King has asked, "What does it mean when somebody who is a novelist is invited to appear on 'Hollywood Squares'?"

King is the author not as Logos but as *image*. Whereas this makes a movie star unreachable, it makes an author approachable. When we read "him" we hear his voice and see his face. He is so much a part of the popular culture that flows through his books that he has become just like you and me. It is not merely that his books "echo" popular culture and advertising; it is that Stephen King is ubiquitous. Although he now writes occasionally for *The New York Times Book Review* or *Life*, we are more likely to see him on television or (in paperback) at the local discount or grocery store. His relatively newfound critical acceptance has done anything but set him at a distance; now that he is an American institution, you are "invited" to "Enter into a special relationship with Stephen King"—so says the cover letter for The Stephen King Library (Weinberg). The advertising brochure intones: "Once in a generation, a special writer attains both best-selling popularity and great critical acclaim. . . . The Stephen King Library is being launched in recognition of the achievement of this '20th century Edgar Allan Poe.'" King's celebrity status doesn't taint the Northeastern homespun, family-man-and-Bangor-citizen. King's public role is so frag-mented, apparently, as to resemble the "average" American's life. It doesn't hurt that for one hundred dollars, a fan could join him in 1986 around a Maine campfire and listen to him tell stories (*Stephen King's World of Horror*).

King sometimes seems to prefer performing his fictions—whether in the form of *Stephen King's World of Horror*, a television drama series (*The Golden Years*), directing movies (disastrously, in *Maximum Overdrive*, 1986), screen writing (successfully in *Sleepwalkers*, 1992, and *The Stand*, 1994)—more than writing them, and recalls Charles Dickens's near de-fection to the theatre. As Ong points out, in eliminating the narrator's voice, print "mechanically as well as psychologically locked words into space" and created a firm sense of closure and distance. The Victorian novel, especially in Dickens, was an exception and displayed signs of "lingering feeling for the old oral narrator's world" (Ong 149). The address to the "Dear Reader" indicated the author's sense of audience and context, and monthly installments encouraged unprecedented reader engagement with the characters and the author.[8] Dickens's addiction to dramatic readings from his novels is even more revealing. His favorite scene—Sykes's murder of Nancy from *Oliver Twist*—was also his most theatrical in the Grand Guignol style. Eisenstein quotes Stefan Zweig's description of the "three- quarters of a mile" long lines of people who waited for tickets to a Dickens reading in New York (207). Contemporaries report that Dickens's genius as a performer was as great as his writing talent. His fiction "partook of the theatrical," says Philip Collins, and in giving readings from that fiction he was demonstrating "his long-standing debt, as a writer, to [this calling]" (xviii). Likewise King, a mass-media guru for the global village, uses whatever means to make the page an arena of spectacle and struggle.

As King's performances are novels, his novels are theatrical performances. Sometimes it seems as if he would rather demonstrate or teach the books than simply write them. The brand-name dropping, thought to be a sign of King's anti-intellectualism, is part of a heuristic gloss that runs throughout and beyond the fiction. Don Herron is correct in describing it as "much like what you'd expect from a professor," providing "themes, recurring *motifs*, cross-references" (133). In this respect, it contrasts with academic postmodernists who delight in burying their themes in arcane codes and allusions that are in the end self-referential. King does the opposite: he writes a horror fan's version of *Dracula* ('*Salem's Lot*). He explains literary allusions in terms of the mass media, producing a cross between Classic Comics and Cliff's Notes, or between T. S. Eliot's notes on *The Waste Land* and the CD-ROM multimedia edition of *Grollier's Encyclopedia*. As part of King's analysis of the American way of death, Louis Creed of *Pet Sematary* finds himself thinking "'A fine and private place . . . but none, I think, do there embrace.' Who? Andrew Marvell. And why did the human mind store up such amazing middens of useless junk anyway?" (*Pet* 285). The answer is on page 286 of the novel, where Jung's collective unconscious is explained. By the end of the novel, after burying his son's corpse in an Indian burial ground that resurrects its contents with naturalistic simplicity, Louis feels "less than human now, one of George Romero's stupid, lurching movie zombies" or an escapee from "T. S. Eliot's poem about the hollow men. *I should have been a pair of ragged claws, scuttling through Little god Swamp. . . .* Headpiece full of straw. . . . That's me" (*Pet* 372).

King is serious in referring to his fiction's "good weight." As speech acts, having the force of utterance from within the body, words do have substance, context, power, impact, *frisson*. Truly moral fiction must make you feel (King, Introd., *Arbor House Treasury* 11). And a good tale, Poe has asserted, is one that produces an emotional or visceral effect. King's appeal is "visceral" also in the specific sense that he is perceived as speaking-listening-feeling presence. Here is Book of the Month Club editor-in-chief Brigitte Weeks advertising *Needful Things*, the Fall 1991 Main Selection:

> the reason we care about [King's] novels is that we care about his people. . . . We feel the pain in Polly's twisted hands. . . . Most of all . . . we sense that Stephen King cares about us, his readers. Once again, he says it best: "I love the people who read my stuff. . . . I love them because they listen." (10)

Weeks's "Stephen King" is a smarmy, all-American empath. He creates contexts within which his feelings—especially his feeling for pain—are extended to readers, who are not readers so much as listeners, and who in listening are "healed." This King, moreover, needs us. His image as a man who goes through a "Freudian exorcism" every time he writes is appropriate to our time, for our priest must be "one of us."

A plurality of voice, body, boy next door, public figure, teacher, entertainer, and family man, King has become everything but that alienating figure, The Author. Decentering and deconstructing the authorial role, he is the community storyteller. "[W]riters, actors, and actresses are the only recognized mediums of our society," King, quoting Thad Beaumont (from *The Dark Half*) told Tony Magistrale (*Second Decade* 11). Hence Stephen King: empath, medium, shaman, healer. As his zombies and vampires became our dying and reviving gods, representing and absolving us of our own cannibalism, King had become our high priest by the end of the 1980s. In a 1983 *Playboy* interview, he suggested that his role derived from that of the

> old Welsh sin eater, the wandering bard who would be called to the house when somebody was on his deathbed. The family would feed him their best food and drink, because while he was eating, he was also consuming all the sins of the dying person, so at the moment of death, his soul would fly to heaven untarnished, washed clean. (King, qtd. in Norden 54)

In "absorbing and defusing all your fears and anxieties and insecurities," the Sin Eaters are "taking them upon ourselves":

> We're sitting in the darkness beyond the flickering warmth of your fire, cackling into our caldrons and spinning our spider webs of

words, . . . sucking the sickness from your minds and spewing it into the night. (King, qtd. in Norden 54–55)

The "spider webs of words" are the medicine man's poultices, an absorbing, healing medium for the cultural body. But that body is, after all, fantastic. And because he "sells" lies, consolations, and absolutions, and will die with a full stomach—as he readily admits—King is "headed straight for hell" (Norden 54–55).

Indeed, horror as King had defined it by the end of the first decade of his career, was like most such rites of passage and absolution, was anti-intellectual, conservative, and self-recuperating—"as Republican as a banker in a three-piece suit." It was an oral tradition in several senses. Or as King said in 1983, it had an "effect of reconfirming values, or reconfirming self-image and our good feelings about ourselves" (King, qtd. in "An Evening" 9). In King's second decade, things would become less simple.

Chapter 3

Stephen King Viewing the Body

In the early 1970s, when everyone else thought horror was fueled by sex, King targeted the thing Freud had most notably neglected, "the central obscenity, the dark under all our beds, as death" (Gibson, "Foreword" xvi). Two incidents in King's childhood may have provided a basis for his obsession.

When he was two years old his father, Donald King, disappeared—permanently. In the fall of 1959 or 1960, Stephen found a box of his father's old 1940s paperbacks in his aunt's attic together with a sampler of stories from *Weird Tales* magazine, a collection of H. P. Lovecraft stories, and some rejection slips from men's magazines—evidence of Donald King's attempts to write horror and science fiction (*Danse Macabre* 99–102). In recounting his discovery in *Danse Macabre*, King lingers over the "shiny overcoating" on those (Avon) paperbacks, a "cross between isinglass and Saran Wrap" (101), suggesting these objects' talismanic power over him. As in fairy tales and Dickens's novels, King's protagonists are orphans searching for their true parents—and ultimately (as adults) for community. His fiction is a search for the father who walked off and left a box of weird tales in his place, who left his son haunted with stories about absences and hauntings that must be told or lived.

In the second trauma, four-year-old Stephen evidently saw a friend run over by a passing train. Years later, the author wrote in *Danse Macabre*, "my mother told me they had picked up the pieces in a wicker basket" (90). He claims to have no memory of the incident. As a horror writer, he has been picking up pieces of the body ever since.

King has written over and over about this combination: the missing father and the confrontation with the body that "calls" a boy to become (if not a man) a horror writer. It is the kernel that informs King's metafictions and the "King myth" that informs popular culture. The first of these was "The Body," a novella drafted in 1973 or 1974 (Winter, *Stephen King* 207) and published in *Different Seasons* (1982) under the section heading, "Fall from Innocence."

THE BODY IN "THE BODY"

After the death of his football-hero brother, twelve-year-old Gordon Lachance is alienated from his father and finds companionship with three friends. "The Body" follows the gang's journey to find the corpse of a boy who has been killed by a train. This story is equally a Kristevan allegory of the body, a descent into embodiment, the underworld of chthonian nature, followed by an ascent to textuality. The corpse "seen without God and outside science," Julia Kristeva explains, "is the height of abjection. . . . It is something rejected from which one is not separated" ("Approaching" 127). His act of viewing the body marks Gordon's reclaiming of the "powers" of horror:

> For a moment it seemed all right, a more natural deathscene than any ever constructed for a viewing-room audience by a mortician. Then you saw the bruise . . . and the way the corpse was beginning to bloat. . . . You remembered that gassy smell . . . like farts in a closed room. He was a boy our age, he was dead, and I rejected the idea that anything about it could be natural; I pushed it away with horror. ("The Body" 417)

In his revulsion, Gordie pronounces the scene unnatural, detaches himself from the body, and enters the symbolic order of culture and language. In a Stephen Kingish pun Gordie remarks on how the "kid was disconnected from his Keds"—has been literally knocked out of his shoes—"beyond all hope of reconciliation" (405). As the scene's interpreter and the gang's storyteller, Gordie takes on the role of the medicine man (Biddle 96) or sin eater.

In "The Body," the corpse is the last of numerous references—scatological, sexual, and oral—to loss of bodily control. Two embedded stories, representing Gordie's development into Gordon Lachance, the best-selling horror writer, are also allegories of the body. "Stud City," the twenty-year-old Gordon's first published story, betrays its author's immaturity in more than the title. It is "an extremely sexual story written by an extremely inexperienced young man" who had "been to bed with two girls and . . . ejaculated prematurely all over one of them." "Stud City" 's attitude toward women, Lachance admits "verges on actual ugliness—two of the women . . . are sluts, and the third is a simple receptacle" ("The Body" 322). Virginia, Chico's stepmother, represents the sexual aspect of the chthonian mother Gordon defeats in the act of writing. (The more mature Gordon peeps out of two sentences in "Stud City": "Love may be as divine as the poets say, but sex is Bozo the clown bouncing around on a spring. How could a woman look at an erect penis without going off into mad gales of laughter?" ["The Body" 312]).

"The Revenge of Lard Ass Hogan," the story young Gordie tells Vern, Chris, and Teddy, is another Kristevan scenario. As Chris says, it "ain't a horror" but horror's carnivalesque ("Gross but funny" ["The Body" 362]) mask/masque. When in the film adaptation (*Stand By Me*) Lard Ass spouted purple puke "like the combined fountains of Rome," the on-screen hilarity and the theater audience as well reached, according to *National Review*'s John Simon, "gargantuan dimensions. The scene seems to go on forever and gives a wholly new [embodied] meaning to the phrase 'purple passage'" (Simon 60)—as purple *rite* of passage and as communication medium. Lard Ass's passage to maturity means descending into the chthonian underworld ("his whole head disappeared into the pie-plate" [370]) and emerging triumphantly as the hero as artist: (blueberries "flew" from the pie-dish, "staining the tablecloth around him like a Jackson Pollock painting" [371]). His revenge begins in an abjection ritual in which daring to lose control—willfully, publicly, and infectiously—gains him power and perverse respect. Lard Ass is King's comic paradigm of the writer as agonist, who transcends embodiment through the body.

On another front, "The Revenge of Lard Ass Hogan" is *Carrie* in drag. Lard Ass is ridiculed because his obesity makes him soft or abject like a woman, but like the (French feminist) hysteric, he becomes a sorceress. As a metafiction, we should see Lard Ass's triumph as comparable to writing like a woman, from the body, entering the symbolic order through its back door.

The embedded stories are juvenilia King published originally in college magazines (Winter, *Stephen King* 107). As Leonard Heldreth notes, the two stories are in different typefaces (72), suggesting a mastery of several voices. These variations, like King's other typographical enhancements, signal dialogic or polyphonic narrative. It is writing as speech act, postliterate prose. "The Body" only appears to be one of King's more literary stories, a Portrait of the Artist as a Horror Writer. Through a Proustian regression, however, he returns to the oral community of friends and dialogic forms. In King's metafiction storytelling is a "talking cure" but in a literal, social, and Jungian sense. "The Revenge of Lard Ass Hogan" never has a final form, retaining its vitality in oral performance. It is requested (by best friend Chris) and interrupted by audience participation: "There ain't no *Gretna* in Maine" (Vern); "Shut up and let him tell the story" (Chris); "*Whole* pies?" (Teddy) [362–64]).

Paradoxically, the *act* of writing is "done in secret," like masturbation, twelve-year-old Gordie notes. Writing on the one hand is a private ritual, a regression and return through which one gains self-integration and control, as Leonard Heldreth stresses, and on the other a bonding activity or dialogue that makes the thought of mortality less lonely (74). Isolated by writing, the twenty-year-old Gordon recalls listening to his brother's bedtime stories, and is comforted by that recollection. Fourteen years later, the successful novelist knows that people write stories to "*understand the past and get ready for some future mortality; that's why all the verbs in stories have -ed endings. . . . The only two useful artforms are religion and stories*" (395). Gordon's headnote to "The Body" also emphasizes the need for "*an understanding ear*" (289).

KING'S WASTE LAND

King did not confront the body or the subject of death so directly again until *Pet Sematary* (1983), the graphic and disturbing anatomy of the medical perspective he began in 1979. Most of the earlier novels had been adult fairy tales or supernatural epics that buried the real spectre in the subtext. *'Salem's Lot* (1975) attributed the disappearance of an entire town to vampirism, displacing fear of death as fear of the undead. In *The Stand* (1978), in which a superflu destroyed most of the world's population, King took horror to another level of power, acting out a fantasy of invulnerability through destroying and rebuilding the world. "I felt a bit like Alexander or . . . Johnny Rotten," he wrote in *Danse Macabre*. "No more Ronald McDonald! No more *Gong Show* or *Soap* on TV—just soothing snow! No more terrorists! No more bullshit! . . . I got a chance to scrub the whole human race, and *it was fun!*" (373).

It was far from the earlier admission that "the body" was "a boy our age, he was dead, and I rejected the idea that anything about it could be natural" (417). Through the supernatural coping mechanisms of genre horror, King had "always shied away from . . . the aftermath of death," as he admitted to Douglas Winter in 1984. "The funeral parlors, the burial, the grief . . . the guilt." *Pet Sematary* was about "a real cemetery" (*Stephen King* 132).

As an encounter with mortality, *Pet Sematary* initiated a period of reflection and return and self-analysis. Writing the novel was disturbing, "like looking through a window of something that could be." Determined "to go through with it, to find out everything, to see what would happen," King found the book "ceased being a novel" and became a Sisyphean task (qtd. in Winter, *Stephen King* 131). In 1979, he finished the first draft and put it in a drawer. Two years later he pulled it out and looked at it again. "I thought it was a nasty book" (Winter, *Stephen King* 131).[1]

Pet Sematary was Stephen King's version of *The Waste Land*; it was a cultural diagnosis that indicted his own "white soul." Protagonist and King-surrogate Louis Creed, a doctor at the University of Maine at Orono, has little philosophical or psychological preparation for death. A rational materialist (a lapsed Methodist married to a non-practicing Jew), he has no formal creed (other than the Hippocratic Oath). When under stress he returns to a fantasy of driving an ambulance in Disney World as the head of Walt's "resurrection crew."

A children's pet cemetery provides an initiation ritual for Louis, his wife Rachel, and his children Ellie (six) and Gage (two). An elderly neighbor and father figure Jud Crandall takes the family there for their "first eyeball to eyeball with death," necessary in "[T]hese days" when "no one wants to . . . think about it" (*Pet* 60). Later, Louis realizes that Ellie knows more about "Ronald McDonald and Spiderman and the Burger King" than "the whole *spiritus mundi*" (*Pet* 198). The world of religion, myth, and ritual is signified in conspicuous absences or reversals. Time is indicated through references to seasons and holidays, with each commemorated more incoherently as the year goes on, and with Louis's son Gage's death and grotesque resurrection occurring sometime around Passover or Easter.[2] *Pet Sematary* goes over the themes of late modernism, and has similar cultural work to do. King anatomizes mass culture as an evasion of death and life, as simulacrum.

Louis stumbles through his son's funeral in a haze of grief and alcohol, dimly conscious of buying a coffin with his Mastercard, of a fist fight with his father-in-law in the funeral home as grief is displaced in hypermasculine violence (culminating as the two men knock the coffin from the trestle and a small hand spills out), of the "violently green" Astroturf at the graveside, and of a pizza and a painting of a clown at Howard Johnson's. The banality of this death is overwhelming. Louis's coping mechanisms are offered by a youth-oriented mass culture—by rock music (The Ramones), *The Wizard of Oz*, Disney World (his idea, apparently, of heaven), and American naturalism—forces that merge to compose a powerful denial.

Pet Sematary critiques the modern medical perspective, as Foucault does in *The Birth of the Clinic* (1975), as something that mystifies and dehumanizes death at the same time—cloaking it in esoteric language and confining it to sterile sanctuaries. The simulacrum and the hospital collaborate in *The American Way of Death*, as Jessica Mitford put that issue in 1963, and *Pet Sematary* is its post mortem, 1980s style. On the one hand, it is Disney World, ritual as miniaturization and evasion. On the other, it is materialistic and violently alienating.

The pet cemetery is arranged in Druidic rings that allude to Stonehenge (connoting human sacrifice and cannibalism as well as mystery) to suggest the real primitivism behind modern medical "miracles" (King, qtd. in Winter, *Art* 134). It is the outer circle of a Micmac Indian burial ground that sends the dead back in a state of soulless half life, resurrecting with brutal literalness. A succession of accidents, heart attacks, strokes, and deaths—Jud's wife Norma, Louis's two-year-old son Gage, Jud, and Rachel—and resurrections follow.

The turning point is the death of Gage. Louis is a heavy father as a baby boomer with a Peter Pan complex. Obviously at issue is Louis's bioethical creed, his belief in saving the only life he knows, the material. But this desire is based in a patriarchal lust for immortality through the son, expressed first in an agony of sorrow and rage, then ghoulishly, as he disinters his son's corpse and makes the estranging discovery that it is like "looking at a badly made doll" (*Pet* 342). Performing his task, Louis degenerates into a "resurrectionist" from a Victorian shilling shocker or "a subhuman character in some cheap comic-book story" (*Pet* 333). The reanimated Gage appears to have been "terribly hurt and then put back together again by crude, uncaring hands" (*Pet* 388).

The Wendigo, which presides over the supernatural elements in the novel, is a Native American spirit associated with cold, isolation, dislocation, and cannibalism. King appropriates it, associating it with American materialist values and the bioethical dilemmas of the 1980s. The Micmac burial ground where it resides offers a frozen, naturalistic prospect, a high plateau where the stars make him feel "infinitesimal, without meaning" (*Pet* 134), a barren ground where piles of broken stones (as in "The Hollow Men") are the only markers. But the hollowness of Louis's bioethics is truly shown in his habit, when under stress, of taking mental trips to Orlando, Florida, where he, Church, and Gage drive a white van as Disney World's "resurrection crew." In these waking dreams, Louis's real creed is revealed: its focus is on Oz the Gweat and Tewwible and Walt Disney, that "*gentle faker from Nebraska*" (*Pet* 376)—two wizards of science fantasy.

Louis's disintegrating state of mind, which reflects that state of modern culture, is replicated in intensifying textual incoherence and fragmentation. He is increasingly haunted by cartoon visions of Mickey Mouse, Goofy, Gage, and Church, which mix surreally with fragments from Marvell and Eliot and the *Wizard of Oz*. Louis's wizardry is reflected also in the narrative perspective and structure, which flashes back in Part 2 from the funeral to his sun-drenched fantasy of a heroically long, flying tackle in which he snatches Gage from death's wheels. Louis's resurrection schemes reflect a culture-wide Frankenstein and Peter Pan complex, realized in the postmodern monster he has begotten. Wielding his father's scalpel and cannibalizing his mother, Gage is the measure of a generation.

The baby boomers, King explained in *Time* in 1986, "were obsessive" about childhood. "We went on playing for a long time, almost feverishly. I write for that buried child in us, but I'm writing for the grown-up too. I want the grown-ups to look at the child long enough to be able to give him up. The child should be buried" ("The Novelist Sounds Off"). In *Pet Sematary*, King had disinterred and anatomized that buried child. In the novels to come he would bury the child again, this time with formal rites.

Drafted in 1979, when King was teaching creative writing and Gothic literature at the University of Maine at Orono, *Pet Sematary* was the hub of a group of stories that marked a culture's mid-life crisis and a similar turning point in King's career. He would subsequently turn to anatomize the material culture he so often claimed to be speaking for. *Pet Sematary* also foreshadowed his later turn from conventional (*'Salem's Lot*) and fanciful (*Christine*) horror and toward existential themes and experimental, self-aware forms—to the regressive, polyphonic structure of *It* (1986, begun in 1979) and to the metafiction of *Misery* (1987) and *The Dark Half* (1989).

If *Pet Sematary* affirms any source of community, culture, and belief, it is the form and ritual of the children's pet sematary. Its concentric circles form a pattern from their collective unconsciousness, a pattern that mimes "the most ancient religious symbol of all," the spiral (*Pet* 286). *It* makes *Pet Sematary*'s merely hinted consolation into its primary focus and structural device. In *It*, a group of children similarly create a provisional community and a mythology as a way of confronting their fears, as represented in It, a metamonster, the serial-murdering, shape-shifting bogey that haunts the sewers of Derry, Maine. In 1958, the seven protagonists, a cross-section of losers, experience the monster differently, for as in George Orwell's *Nineteen Eighty-Four* (1949), It derives its power through its victim's isolation and guilt and thus assumes the shape of his or her worst fear. (To Beverly Marsh *It* appears, in a sequence reminiscent of "Red Riding Hood," as her abusive father in the guise of the child-eating witch from "Hansel and Gretel.")

In an ominous passage early in *Pet Sematary*, Louis dreams of Disney World, where "by the 1890s train station, Mickey Mouse was shaking hands with the children clustered around him, his big white cartoon gloves swallowing their small, trusting hands" (31). To all of *It*'s protagonists, the monster appears in a similar archetypal form, one that suggests a composite of devouring parent and mass-culture demigod, of television commercial and fairy tale, of 1958 and 1985: as Pennywise the Clown, a cross between Bozo and Ronald McDonald and John Wayne Gacy, the serial killer who performed as a clown. As in *Christine*, *Pet Sematary*, and *Thinner*, the monster is material culture itself, the collective devouring parent nurturing its children on "*imitation*[s] of *immortality*" (*It* 1138). Like Christine or Louis's patched-up son, Pennywise is the dead past cannibalizing the future. Thus twenty-seven years after its original reign of terror, It resumes its siege, whereupon the protagonists, now professionally successful (but childless) yuppies, must return to Derry, like the ex-hippies of *The Big Chill* (1983), to confront as adults their childhood fears. Led by surrogate horror writer Bill Denbrough, who now stutters only in his dreams, and Mike Hanlon, librarian and historian, they defeat It (at last revealed as a huge female spider, the pre-Oedipal mother once more) both individually as an allegory of psychoanalysis and collectively as a rite of passage into adulthood and community.

"WORD MADE FLESH, SO TO SPEAK": *THE DARK HALF* AND *MISERY*

It was attacked in reviews as pop psychology and a "badly constructed novel" and the puerility was partly intended. (Its inspiration was a beloved image: the entire cartoon cast of the Bugs Bunny Show coming on at the beginning.) *It* would be, he promised, his last horror novel, a nostalgic calling forth of all the monsters at "clearance-sale time. Everything must go" (King, qtd. in Kanfer 83). The book was one important rite in what would be a lengthy passage, a looking backward and inward, regressing and taking of stock. The last chapter begins with an epigraph from Dickens's *David Copperfield* (1849–1850) and ends with an allusion to William Wordsworth's "Intimations of Immortality," from which King takes his primary theme and narrative device, the look back that enables one to go forward. In the 1970s King's fiction was devoted to building a mythology out of shabby celluloid monsters to fill a cultural void; in the postmodern 1980s, he began a demystification process. *It* was a ritualized unmasking of motley Reagan-era monsters, the exorcism of a generation and a culture. As in *Pet Sematary*, where the monster often appeared as a cross between Oz and Walt Disney, the monster-clown Pennywise came uncomfortably close to resembling most that "gentle faker" from Bangor, Maine. For *It* (the novel) was also an analysis of King's cultural work over the preceding decade.

After *It*'s extensive exploration of childhood, King took up conspicuously adult characters, issues, and roles. In *The Eyes of the Dragon* (1987), he returned to the wellsprings of his fantasy: he wrote a fairy tale for his daughter Naomi, then thirteen. King told much the same story as before but assumed the mantle of the elder and oral narrator. As a fairy tale for adults, *Eyes* summed up and reconfigured many of the oral and mythic elements in King's early work: the presence of a voice, the improvisational tone, the archetypal characters. While he continued to cultivate "voice" or textuality, he sharply restricted character and situation in order to examine writing itself as a mode of knowing and as a speech act. The book introduced King's self-conscious phase, a move away from vast gestures, epic sweep, huge casts, and easy consolations. It picked up where *The Shining*, "The Body," and "Survivor Type" had left off and directly addressed the issues inherent in his peculiar role. Beginning with *Misery* (1987), he would write metafictions that interrogated his own role as horror writer and celebrity. In 1989 he explained that "what I have written about writers and writing in the last five years or so has been a real effort . . . to understand what I am doing, what it means, what it is doing to me, what it is doing for me . . . [to] understand the ramifications of being a so-called famous person" (*Second* 11). *Four Past Midnight*, published in 1990, was a turning point, a "[L]ooking back over the last four years" and seeing "all sorts of cloture [sic]" ("Two Past Midnight" 250).

An earlier, and by far the most dramatic, example of King's deconstruction of "Stephen King" was the creation and subsequent revelation in 1984 of his pseudonym Richard Bachman. He published the five Bachman books over an eight-year period, he has claimed, to limit his official output to two novels a year. Bachman soon grew into an identity with a biography and photographs (he was a chicken farmer with a cancer-ravaged face), dedications, a narrative voice and social vision, and a naturalistic mode in which sociopolitical speculation combined or alternated with psychological suspense. In 1985, when the novels (with one exception, *Thinner*, 1984) were collected in a single volume attributed to King *as* Bachman, the mortified alter ego seemed buried. Bachman's demise raised the question of what "Stephen King" really was, not only for his readers but also for King. Yet, far from disturbing the interest or the trust of his readers, the revelation enhanced his reputation and sold more books.

As evidence of a dark alter ego, Bachman didn't do King any harm. The squeaky clean family man acquired depth, a dark soul, something more than desirable—indeed necessary—in a shaman. Shortly after Bachman's internment and beginning with *Misery* (1987), King began a series of metafictions whose subject was the King phenomenon itself, especially the writer-reader relationship. *The Dark Half*, which came next, in 1989 (after a decent four-year interval following the pseudonym's decease), was the story of Bachman. The novel was a self-interrogation and an allegory of a relationship that is at least three-fold: between the writer, his imagination or "genius" (his "third eye"), and his public image.

Protagonist Thaddeus Beaumont is a professor and moderately successful literary novelist devoted to his family. But he has been living a secret life of twelve years through George Stark, the pseudonym under which he emerged from writer's block as the author of best-selling crime novels. Stark's genius finds its most vital expression in *his* protagonist, the professional crime boss Alexis Machine. Like King, Beaumont is found out and forced to disclose and destroy his pseudonym and ritualizes the event with a graveside service and *papier mâché* headstone. Destroyed as a fiction (or released from sublimation), the pseudonym bursts out of the grave in physical form. The series of murders that follow (of the people responsible for the pseudonym's "demise") is narrated in Stark's graphic prose style, with Stark's control of the text at this point standing for his power over Beaumont's life, literally to take Thad's wife and children (twins, of course) hostage. What Stark wants is to live in writing, outside of which writers and characters do not exist. King draws on a literature of the double and the detective story, including Stevenson's *The Strange Case of Dr. Jekyll and Mr. Hyde* and Sophocles' *Oedipus Rex*, in which protagonist must discover the demons within himself before he can stop the plague.

The alter ego is a physiological as well as psycho-literary phenomenon: Stark is Thad's cannibalized twin. At age eleven Thad had a series of headaches and seizures, and a surgeon removed from his brain the fragments of his sibling. Stark's origins and their physical juxtapositions suggest that they are Apollonian and Dionysian parts of a whole, a dynamic or dialogue that compels the writer. Thus King literalizes his idea of the visionary "third eye." Tony Magistrale found Stark's separate physical existence hard to suspend disbelief in: "One moment we are asked to view Stark as a secret sharer of Beaumont's most private inclinations; the next minute these two men are as different from one another as a suburban professor and an urban street punk" (*Second* 65). But Magistrale is reading the novel as psychological fiction, with a modernist, Freudian model in mind, where King's models are Barth, Jung, and Nintendo games.

As a medium, the author's job is to "create a bifurcation in the reader's mind," King told Magistrale. One half "says this is all make-believe, words on a page; the other half is living that life, becoming more and more real. That is power" (qtd. in *Second* 11). Stark is a demonstration of that reality and that power. He is a caricature of the ancient literal-mindedness inherent in postliterate horror. Thus King renders him as a graphic pun and allows him literally to take over. The epigraphs and allusions in the novel are from and to Stark's books. He murders people connected with Thad's decision to bury Stark, most of whom are connected with the literary business—Thad's agent, editor, fan/informer, and a local man who is bludgeoned with his own prosthetic arm. Stark also murders literature, inscribing its corpse with a straight-edged razor, meaning a triumph of body in the worst sense—of "stark" and mindless violence, gore, seriality, copycat killers—over literacy and textuality. Stark is a cliché realized through a collective fantasy, projected in part by Beaumont, in part by readers, and hence by culture. Thus King blurs boundaries between Stark and *his* character, Alexis Machine, whose actions are the models for Stark's (or is it Beaumont's?) murders. The ambiguity lent by a third term in this allegory of doubles embodies a larger confusion shared by the reader and the writer between an author, his persona, and his character. The confusion extends to the medium in which Stark thrives best, the shared hallucination of mass mediated space.

King "is tactful in teasing out the implications of his parable," says George Stade. No character *says* "that reality inevitably leaks fiction, which then floods reality, that reality and fiction feed on and feed each other" (12). Instead, combining comic book flatness with the naturalism of a graphic novel, King gives textuality visceral "life." Of course, Stark describes it best when explaining himself—as "word made flesh, so to speak." The act of will that forces his exit is revealed in the structure of the book. King flouts expectations by reversing his usual procedure, glutting the first half of the book with Stark/Machine's rampages, reconstituting the character of Beaumont in the last half. Beaumont's story falls away as Stark's razor-sharp action emerges; as Stark loses physical cohesion, Beaumont's contemplative metafiction dominates. He performs a series of automatic writing exercises and self-interrogations, alternating between his typewriter or pen and Stark's pencil. In the showdown, Beaumont controls body and mind to regain textual power while Stark writes to remain embodied. Meanwhile Stark's last book, *Steel Machine,* taking shape in pencil, reveals huge gaps and repetitions of the word "sparrows" and "the sparrows were flying"—sparrows being King's metaphor for psychopomps that bear souls to the land of the dead. The text ends in a "scene from some malign fairy-tale" (423) as Stark is borne away by flocks of sparrows and makes a final imprint as a black hole in the sky.

On the Usenet newsgroup on Stephen King, James MacLeod compared reading the *Gunslinger* books to playing Donkey Kong, a Nintendo game. The Stark half of *The Dark Half* has the berserk momentum of a video game. Stark's character and "logic" come as much from pulp fiction, adult comics, and computer graphics as from psychological or literary sources. He is the action game raging to take over Beaumont's and King's text—or textuality, literacy, and decency altogether.

But as text within text, "Stark" also engages readers in the text's creation, cultivating literacy. Like the metafictional detective stories of Jorge Luis Borges, the computer fiction of Michael Joyce or Stuart Moulthrop, or the old epistolary novel, King's metafictions effect a level of "hypertexual" engagement.[3] Here we have the King of the introductions, notes, and afterwords telling us how and why he does what he does, the experience of "the author" overlapping with his fictions proper. These are merged with the story, however, engaging readers in the production of the text.

Readers are finally encouraged to read the novel as a *roman à clef.* At the outset, in an "Author's Note," King makes sure the Bachman myth informs our experience: "I'm indebted to the late Richard Bachman for his help and inspiration. This novel could not have been written without him."[4] Like Bachman, Stark is the pseudonym declared dead and buried, exorcised as private demon, only to be resurrected as a body irradiated by the "Stephen King Phenomenon." Thus the "real" Bachman gives *The Dark Half* flesh and blood. *The Dark Half* alludes throughout to King: Stark is buried in Homeland Cemetery in Castle Rock, Maine, King's territory. This is the land of the uncanny, that unremembered (all too familiar) territory and, as in *Pet Sematary*, the collective unconscious. The large hole in the turf in front of Stark's fake gravestone remains the central mystery of the novel: it corresponds with the gap or intersection in the text in which meaning is constructed and fictions take independent life.

In the context of the "King myth," *The Dark Half* is a farewell to automatic writing and "action" heroes, comic books, and postliterate prose. At the end of the book Thad says good-bye to the "lovely visions that third eye sometimes presented" (413) and sends off George Stark, a flock of sparrows bearing his decomposing body away. At the same moment, "King," the author who has merged postliterate prose with academic metafiction and "Stark" violence with a moral tale, transcends both Stark and Beaumont. The third eye goes on seeing. The sin eater goes on eating.

The purgation of Stark/Machine, like the revelation of Bachman, is finally cathartic and reassuring for the reader. And in confessing Stark/Bachman, King becomes more saintly in his readers' eyes. Like a number of celebrities (including First Lady Emeritus Betty Ford, televangelist Jimmy Swaggart, and actress-cum-author Elizabeth Taylor), through periodic sinning, public confession, and mass mediated absolution, he becomes "one of us."

King didn't really send off Richard Bachman, of course; he incorporated the alienated, cancer-ridden chicken farmer's perspective into his work. As a pseudonym Bachman had allowed him to be not only pessimistic but more introspective and "literary" and, once introduced as a "part" of King, allowed him to write his series of self-exploratory metafictions: *The Dark Half*, *Misery*, and the novellas "Secret Window, Secret Garden" and "The Sun Dog" (in *Four Past Midnight*, 1990). King has explained that he is often "unaware of what he's really writing until after he is done. It's like drawing pictures in a dark room, and then a sudden illumination shows you what you've been drawing" (Magistrale, *Second* 7). These allowed him to view the relationships of writer, reader, and text in clear relief, focusing more narrowly than before, through two or three characters, on the relationship between writers, readers, and text. *Misery* was conceived as Bachman's book (Beahm 168) but revised and published as King's in 1987. *Misery* was also the first of his novels to get good reviews.

Misery was about "the powerful hold fiction can achieve over the reader" as personified in Annie Wilkes, a psychotic former nurse addicted to romance novels. After he crashes his car during a blizzard on an isolated Colorado road, best-selling romance writer Paul Sheldon is rescued, drugged, and held prisoner by Annie, "Number One Fan" of his heroine Misery Chastain (of whom he has tired and killed off). This "Constant Reader" becomes Sheldon's terrible "Muse," forcing him to write (in an edition especially for her) *Misery's Return* to life. Like the witch from Hansel and Gretel or the Bad Mother, Annie punishes Sheldon's attempts to get free by amputating his foot and thumb with an ax, "exercising editorial authority over his body" (264). And like Scheherazade, the oral storyteller, Sheldon must publish, perform as demanded, or literally perish.

Misery is unusually cerebral and bitter for King. Among other things, the novel is about the experience of being cut to fit fan expectations. It also attacks America's "cannibalistic cult of celebrity": "[Y]ou set the guy up, and then you eat him" (qtd. in Kilgore 109). *Misery* is a sophisticated satire both on and for the postliterate reader. Before his car accident, Sheldon has attempted to enter the ranks of literary novelists, not only by killing off Misery and his romance series, but also by writing *Fast Cars*, a grimly realistic novel that he feels good about. Annie is dismayed at its lack of "nobility" and then enraged when she reads it: "It's filthy," she says. "It's also no good" (39).

Annie punishes Paul by forcing him to burn his manuscript (his only copy) and write *Misery's Return*, which will bring the nineteenth-century romance heroine back to life. Annie and her obsession represent the preliterate world associated with Scheherazade as the storyteller in thrall, compared to sexual slavery. With *Fast Cars*, Sheldon has achieved "male" textuality, enters into the symbolic, which liberates the writer from the historical-physical context, from presence and audience. (Ironically his "other" fast car has driven him into a snow bank and the arms of Annie Wilkes.) Forcing him to burn his text (his manhood), Annie destroys his (writing's) independent life, and plunges him back into ancient darkness, where he is chained once more to his audience, to his body.

Thus the situation is gendered: textuality and literacy are male, and Paul Sheldon's readers are "ninety percent of them women" (25). The set of oppositions generated by the conflict of Paul and Annie, writer and reader, includes the masculine and feminine. Speechless, helpless, unfocused as a baby at the beginning of the novel, Paul recapitulates child development. "Annie is the mother; . . . the monstrous feminine, the castrating female," presented as all-engulfing (Hanson 150). She is Sheldon's terrible Muse, a female counterpart to Scheherazade's misogynistic Shahyar, and more. Annie comes to embody all that Sheldon's heroine Misery's name suggests. She is the misery traditionally attributed to the female as "the sex." Like "an African idol out of *She*," Annie is a "big but not generous" woman without "feminine curves": she gives Paul "a disturbing sense of solidity, as if she might not have any blood vessels or even internal organs" (7). Here her total objectification identifies her also with the mother in the Kristevan scenario of abjection, where the child's entrance into the symbolic is signaled by revulsion from the mother's engulfing body. Thus Annie in her depressive phase, brought on by premenstrual syndrome, softens into more than usual shapelessness, a visual metaphor for the Mother as "the point where meaning collapses":

> This massive . . . strangeness which, if it was familiar to me in an opaque and forgotten life, now importunes me as radically separated and repugnant. Not me. Not that. But not nothing either. A "some-

thing" that I do not recognize as a thing. A whole lot of nonsense which has nothing insignificant and which crushes. At the border of inexistence and hallucination, of a reality which, if I recognize it, annihilates me. (Kristeva, "Approaching" 126)

Annie is the Stephen King "gross-out," suggesting (as Hanson says) that horror is a predominantly male rite of abjection. As she "softens," first bingeing on ice cream, then smearing it on herself, and finally mutilating herself, Sheldon hardens. He literally works out: he recaptures his strength, lifting the typewriter (an ancient Royal) over and over to strengthen his arms. The typewriter and the text symbolize an act of protest against crushing meaninglessness. As in the Kristevan scene, writing emerges out of physical revulsion and an act of separating from the Mother, a struggle Sheldon envisions as a rape ending in the triumph of the symbolic over engulfing flesh. Annie, says Hanson, is a "catalyst" bringing Sheldon out of the darkness of infancy "to the wielding of textual power" (152). The text of *Misery's Return* also rises to the occasion: "Annie was right; the story was turning out to be a good deal more gruesome than the other Misery books. . . . This book, he began to understand, was a Gothic novel, and thus more dependent on plot than on situation. The challenges were constant" (154). Sheldon's definition of the Gothic corresponds with Leslie Fiedler's view of it as masculine protest.

If indeed *Misery* incorporates Bachman's vision, Bachman allowed King to write a politically incorrect novel about gender. Magistrale admits that it is "about the destructive, potentially castrating nature of women." Annie Wilkes is mentally unstable, but she is "one of the few women in King's canon who posseses real power, and she does not know how to handle it responsibly" (*Second* 126).

But *Misery* is also more generally, like "The Body," about writing and the body: the experience of the body, "feminizing" embodiment, and the body as text. King chooses as epigraph to Chapter 2, a proverb from Montaigne, which says that *"Writing does not cause misery, it is born of misery."* It is as Elaine Scarry suggests in *The Body in Pain: The Making and Unmaking of the World*: one writes to articulate embodiment, the condition of existence epitomized in physical pain, and which can be articulated only indirectly through metaphor or fiction. Expressing physical pain "eventually opens into the wider frame of invention" (Scarry 22).

In the beginning Sheldon is embodied, and the reader experiences the text as his physical struggle for articulation against pain. The seemingly meaningless sounds of the first words of the novel ("umber one fayunn") announce Paul's regression into aphasia, his dispossession of the world.

In the early stages, as he is dozing and waking, he thinks in an allegory of pain. It is "something like a horse race. At first King of Pain was far in the lead and I Got the Hungries was some twelve furlongs back. Pretty Thirsty was nearly lost in the dust" (34). At last visually conscious, he is just barely able to identify his legs as shapes: "His left knee—a throbbing focus of pain—no longer seemed to exist at all. There was a calf, and a thigh, and then a sickening bunch in the middle that looked like a salt-dome" (35). Only after the renaming of his parts, recognizing and reconstructing himself, can Sheldon complete the making of *Misery's Return*. As the typewriter throws keys, Sheldon writes in the missing characters, and handwritten text threatens to take over the typescript. Yet the text's regression into manual writing corresponds with Sheldon's increasing unity of being and control, his emergence out of pain. (As the typewriter degenerates as a writing tool, it becomes proportionately vital to his reclaiming of physical power, and it becomes the weapon that kills Annie.) The text of the metafiction *Misery* emerges with the agony that produces *Misery's Return*.

Beyond this allegory of writing out of bodily misery, *Misery* suggests that the Constant Reader *is* the author's text. Indeed, the hallucinatory opening of the novel leaves doubt as to whether the book is other than a dream. And if, as King said, it is about the "powerful hold fiction has on the reader," Annie results from Paul's success in attracting and addicting readers. Misery's last name *Chastain* (suggesting *chain, chastise, chastity*) alludes to Annie's (and the Reader's) repression, which her addiction to romances encourages. In the long run Sheldon needs and serves the terrible Reader/Muse more than he defeats her. Sheldon's writing is like Annie's reading—an addiction, linked with the pain-killing drugs she alternately offers and withholds. The relationship is a terrible co-dependency, a sadomasochistic marathon. Sheldon survives by finding out how "To get her *gotta.*" The *gotta* being the drive or compulsion or sickness that compels a person to go on—that makes you *have* "to find out what happened next" (224). "The *gotta* which had kept them both [writer and reader] alive" (226). The irony underlying this battle of the books is that Sheldon's antagonist, like Scheherazade's, is absolutely necessary to his writer's life. When he plots the novel more rigorously than in his previous books (suggesting a triumph of the linear and "masculine"), he discovers that his constant sadistic reader is also his best reader, the one who stimulates the fear of death that (according to Hélène Cixous) enables the male to "get it up." Indeed, Sheldon concludes that *Misery Returns*, the product of this sadomasochistic ritual we have shared—and not his "literary" novel *Fast Cars*—was his masterpiece.

The body Sheldon defeats, whether Annie's or his own (or the generic) is "the feminine." Yet Sheldon triumphs only by restoring and reinstating Misery—the romance character and the "female" body, the figure who embodies for Sheldon the misery of writing. Therefore, Sheldon writes not only against the feminizing body; he writes "from the [female] body" in the Cixousian sense, and after an agonizingly long labor gives birth (*Misery Returns*). *Misery* is finally about writing as an encounter with the Anima, whether the female Constant Reader, the "female" body, or the woman in oneself (Frazier 95–97). This encounter means, as in the case of Cronenberg's Brundle, Sheldon must "become" a woman. Thus he is able to invest his heroine with some of his own misery (Magistrale, *Second* 129). Annie is the means for Sheldon's recovery of the feminine he has discarded (in *Fast Cars* and the snow bank) and that is essential, it seems, to his writer's life. Writing requires the "female" flesh it attempts to transcend, and King's novel *Misery* is about the procreative struggle of male word and female flesh for ascendancy over the authorized text.

Misery finally compels readers, male and female, to identify with Sheldon's epistolary misery as a physical struggle, an agony, a battle with drugs and pain, and thus, by implication, with King, who rises to the occasion. But readers are also uncomfortably characterized in Annie. Male or female, we cannot help but note that our activity has a counterpart in Annie's addiction to romances. We turn the pages of *Misery's Return* and *Misery* in sync with Annie as she devours the text. We may, like Clare Hanson, be further disconcerted when the novel culminates in Sheldon's triumphant textuality, imagined as "our" rape.

The jacket copy claimed that King "owe[d] his fans a love letter. *Misery* is it." The flap was consistent with the novel in playing on self-referential elements and provoking readers to think about some rather discomforting things. Richard Corliss compares reading the book with watching the film: King's novel "doesn't stop till your expectations and his energies are depleted . . . wrung out, and he wants you to feel he's exhausted too from some Wrestlemania, this fine fuck." The last sentence of *Misery* comes "from an author who has purged his demon by writing about her" ("By the Book" 38). It is dated "Lovell, Maine: September 23rd, 1984 / Bangor, Maine: October 7th, 1986: *Now my tale is told*" (310). Sheldon and King, writer and writer, text and subtext "come" subversively together.

The analogy between the writer's body and the text, and between virility and creative juices, censorship and castration, is hardly new. Overt allusions throughout remind us that the situation is like that in *The Collector* (Paul wonders if John Fowles' first novel is on Annie's shelf.) On page

159, he writes, "Another day lost in the funhouse with Annie," alluding to John Barth's metatext about being in thrall to the Muse. As Barth returned to Scheherazade in his program to revitalize a "literature of exhaustion," Sheldon is revitalized by the Constant Reader, his terrible Muse and Whore. King's text explores, as Hanson says, itself and in the process "the genesis of all King's fiction, . . . the origins of what he calls his 'Gothic' horror" (149). King contrasts male Gothic-horror with what he apparently views as Female Gothic Romance.

Misery, perhaps the most literate of King's novels, is a middle-aged, gender-troubled, Kristevan version of "The Body." It openly competes with academic metafiction but on King's terms and, within those terms, succeeds. It made its mark as a postliterate version of postmodernism, striking normally hostile critics with its vitality that many other such allegories often lack: "good weight" as well as wit, human interest, vitality of prose style, the "gotta." *Misery* is anything but abstract. Readers experience reading and textuality in visceral and aural terms, experiencing the textual equivalent of the oral agonistic. At the end, cinematic terms like *rinse* and *wipe* remind us that Sheldon (and yes, King) is now sitting at a screen, using a word processor. Having regressed and returned, Sheldon transfers his recovered energy over into a civilized—and also clearly postliterate—setting. Most of all, King flaunts his superiority at "writing from the body" in the simplest sense of producing a visceral effect.

But in other ways the metafictions subverted the Stephen King phenomenon. They told how writing is misery, yet to be at a loss for words is to be entrapped within the body. Words aspire to displace bodies, so that the birth of the Author often means the death of the woman (often the wife) in King's stories. And the Author has ultimately little control over his texts. The Reader imprisons the Author, demands, and in effect writes her own romances. Worse, she is a serial killer whose homicidal mania is sublimated in and inspired by the text. The text moves out of the Author's control also as a persona impelled by the phallic power of the pen. Beaumont exorcises Stark, but there is no more evidence that his "literary" novels are good than of the excellence of Sheldon's *Fast Cars*.

King's last metafiction, "Secret Window, Secret Garden" (in *Four Past Midnight*, 1990), undermines the concept of authorship itself. It is Barthes's "The Death of the Author" for postliterate prose. A writer discovers to his horror that he may be a plagiarist, and the uncertainty is the horror, suggesting the postmodern perspective in which all texts are derivative and either consciously intertextual or plagiarized. The open secret in "Secret Window, Secret Garden" is King's recognition that there is no Stephen King.

"Bachman," as the intended author of *Misery* on the other hand, may have expressed genuine horror and a genuinely dark King. *Misery* fits Fiedler's definition of the Gothic as an expression of hypermasculine horror of the feminine, as Hanson argues, and specifically of the feminine as the state of being embodied, without textual Author-ity. *Misery*, moreover, was focused directly on the target. Recent studies of misogyny, homophobia, and fat-phobia in King's novels suggest how squarely his horror is centered in the body's frailty and the horror of the chthonian mother.[5]

Abe Peck of *Rolling Stone* asked King if writing horror was "like Boy Scout camp, sitting around and telling a story," and he replied,

> No, it's a lot more sinister than that. I don't know if we talked about this or not, but at one point somebody said, "What do you think Kubrick wants from *The Shining*?" And I said, "I think he wants to hurt people."
>
> Well, maybe I was just saying what *I* want. My idea is that you should be able to suck somebody in and really hurt them. (Peck 101)

King's misgivings about *Pet Sematary* even after publishing it suggest that it was "Bachman" who wrote that novel: "It's a terrible book—not in terms of the writing but it just spirals down into darkness. It seems to be saying nothing works and nothing is worth it, and I don't really believe that" (Modderno 144–45). The Bachman books have a similarly alienated pessimism. As Tony Magistrale suggests, Bachman supplied King with a Hyde, a necessary voice to "indulge his darkest fantasies and speculations" (*Second* 63) and "explore a side of himself that is far removed from his image" as a devoted father and husband, and participating citizen of Bangor, Maine. "In the end Bachman served as a means of liberating King's art" (*Second* 65–66).

The Dark Half explored more directly the part of King the writer that wanted to "hurt." Stark is as monstrously hypermasculine as Annie is monstrously feminine. Like Arnie Cunningham empowered by Christine, Stark drives a big oil-burning car with a bumper sticker reading "HIGH-TONED SON OF A BITCH" (430). Stark's hypermasculine "drive" (epitomized in Machine) is linked with writing: the slasher/writer embodies a threefold analogy between penis, knife, and pen[cil]. Like a hard-on, Stark-Machine leads Beaumont headlong through the book until, in the showdown at the end, Beaumont learns to sublimate his aggression in politically correct, literary efforts.

The Dark Half apologized for King's violence and misogyny even as it vented it. However devastating its real implications (which are similar to the message of Oliver Stone's now infamous film *Natural Born Killers*, 1994), *The Dark Half* seemed to say the correct thing and was a safe book. Earlier, and more significantly, "Bachman" had allowed *Misery* to be what Magistrale calls an "unsafe book," an attack via Annie Wilkes on a "composite" of "conflicting forces—from the demands of an expectant audience to the disparaging remarks of academic critics and reviewers—that seek to confine the art of Sheldon/King into reductive and therefore safe categories" (*Second* 126). A comment in King's introduction to *The Bachman Books* is in similarly gendered terms: "My 'Stephen King publishers' were like a frigid wifey who only wants to put out once or twice a year, encouraging her endlessly horny hubby to find a call girl. Bachman was where I went when I had to have relief" ("Why I Was Bachman" ix). But more than that, "Bachman" allowed King to cross taboo lines to project and identify sources of tension and alienation.

One difference between King and Bachman, it became evident, was that Bachman saw through the "white soul" that "Stephen King" as global village bard epitomized. The Bachman books are unrelentingly pessimistic and often disturbing. They depict a debased social landscape: the elements of popular culture that are treated with affection in his mainstream books—for instance, the name-brand mythologies—become the waste land we have seen in *Pet Sematary*. The protagonists are alienated, from the beginnings of the novels, and the future, as Magistrale describes it, "is devoid of love, stable relationships, and any real degree of sociopolitical freedom" (*Second* 63). This is telling when three of the five novels are science fiction: *Roadwork*, *The Long Walk*, and *The Running Man*, two of which compare the future to a game show in which the stakes are life and death. *Thinner*'s protagonist Billy Halleck—a complacent, affluent, obese lawyer responsible in a hit-and-run accident—is reduced by a Gypsy's curse to a shadow of his former self and given a dark vision of "white soul." In the primary metaphor he eats compulsively to fill his empty soul, stopping at fast-food outlets along the highway. Yet he shrinks and hollows out to an image consistent with his truer spiritual state. Regarded as "terminal," he loses faith in the social institutions that once supported him. He ends up thinner: ruined and alienated. The reader is left with a view of a world that is, as in George Romero's film *Dawn of the Dead*, "literally feeding on itself" (King, qtd. in Winter, *Stephen King* 205, n. 10). To put the issue mildly, there were no fairy tale consolations for Richard Bachman. *Rage* (1977, 1985) is narrated by an alienated student who shoots his algebra teacher in front of the class. As they sit in stunned silence, he sits down behind the desk. " 'This,' [he says] pleasantly, 'is known as getting it on' " (*Bachman* 33).

In June 1993, a high school student named Gary Scott Pennington performed a similar act a few weeks after doing an oral book report on King's novella *Rage* (Reed 44). Annie Wilkes, George Stark, Alexis Machine, and "Richard Bachman" suggest the extent to which King the Sin Eater is haunted by such events, and these characterizations that literally embody violence—social violence and the horror writer's violence—are obviously exorcisms. Their embodiment is also a cautionary tale about phenomena such as Pennington, or Mark Chapman's infatuation with *Catcher in the Rye* before killing John Lennon, or John Hinkley's fixation on Jodie Foster through her role in *Taxi Driver*, or the "Carrie Killer." In *The Dark Half*'s central metaphor of word made flesh, King referred to the "copy cat" killer and acknowledged the collectively projected realities that texts can become, the possibility that the public fascination with serial killers, for instance, actively breeds them. He exposed the danger inherent in his own sin eating, that in absolving society of its guilt by taking on its projections, in healing them, he feeds the collective disease that makes them sick. The healer thus perpetuates the disease. This acknowledgment partly demystified the real-life serial killer "phenomenon" King had helped create. But King's association of himself (and "Bachman" and Bachman's novels) with the serial killer could not help but lend mythic power to the serial killer "phenomenon" in turn. In the process, the serial killer enhanced "Stephen King."[6]

FLESH MADE WORD, OR THE WOMEN'S ROOM: *GERALD'S GAME* AND *DOLORES CLAIBORNE*

As King commented in 1989, "Bachman killed his children before they were out of infancy. I've noticed that in the work I am doing now, if there are any children they tend to be older . . . and all these things seem to be keeping . . . progress with my own life" (Magistrale, *Second* 4–5). After writing as Bachman for eight years, and asserting the conscious control required of *Danse Macabre* and *Pet Sematary*, King was able to step back and write with more "literate" self-awareness. Yet, in spite or because of this increasing self-consciousness, through the postmodern 1980s and now in the anxious, gender sensitive 1990s, he has continued in his role as America's Sin Eater. In his most recent phase, he has moved from metafictional self-exploration to self-expansion. He has engaged in role playing and gender shifting, testing or moving beyond the limits of the horror genre as he formerly defined it, and taking risks. The screenplay

Sleepwalkers (1991) and novels *Gerald's Game* (1992), *Dolores Claiborne* (1993), *Insomnia* (1994), and *Rose Madder* (1995) take up gendered issues that are more often the territory of Clive Barker and Anne Rice: among them abortion, religious fanaticism, sadism, masochism, domestic violence, and incest. Three of these books are as King has said, part of a belated effort to understand women by writing from women's points of view (See Magistrale, *Second* 5), *from* (rather than merely in horror of) the female body. Testifying to the seriousness of this effort, *Gerald's Game* is dedicated "with love and admiration, to six good women," all originally named Spruce, among them King's wife and novelist, Tabitha Spruce King. *Dolores Claiborne* (1993) is dedicated to Ruth Pillsbury King, his mother.

Gerald's Game is a survivor's story based in a classic Female Gothic situation: the woman trapped in the house and terrorized by her husband. Over a seventeen-year marriage, Jessie Burlingame has been coerced into playing the victim's role in a sado-masochistic bondage and discipline game. At their lakeside cottage on a warm night in October, already naked and handcuffed to their bed, Jessie refuses to play Gerald's game. When he persists, Jessie kicks him in the groin, he goes into shock, collapses, and dies of a heart attack. The novel consists of her sensations, memories, associations, and thoughts during the twenty-eight-hour ordeal, during which she recovers memories of sexual molestation by her father. Connecting Gerald's sex game with her father's, she begins to understand her oppression. Recollecting further, she engages in imaginary dialogues with long-dead friends, who provide alter egos to her habitual role as "Goodwife Burlingame." Jessie recovers a will to live and strength to endure pain—enough to mutilate her wrists and struggle free of her shackles.

Misery blamed a sadistic and all-devouring matriarchy for the protagonist's victimization. *Gerald's Game*, as its title announces, condemns patriarchy. The latter "corrects" the misogyny implicit in *Misery*, transposing its situation and setting into Female Gothic and taking the woman's point of view. Both novels are feats of ingenuity. The setting is the bed, which makes tortured body language not only exploitable but essential. In both, the gendered body is a prison, trap, torture chamber, and medium. As Sheldon is the male author shackled to the demands of an insatiable woman/reader/muse, Jessie's bondage represents the sexual slavery of women. Where Annie turns from the Constant Reader into an archetypal bitch goddess, Gerald is dead meat from the beginning, and becomes a reference point for female rage. In response to Annie's increasing abjection, Sheldon rises to the occasion. Horror also makes Jessie powerful. The sight and sound of a stray dog (a bitch?) devouring her husband's body rouses her instinct for survival. From the opening scene, the male body is abject, positioned as Other. Sheldon is called on to discard, reconstruct, and resurrect himself through writing; Jessie recovers her deep resources. The difference is that Sheldon's antagonist is Annie and Jessie's is her context and herself. And where Sheldon must recover physical and textual power, Jessie must discover hers. She becomes the Cixousian hysteric whose body speaks unconscious truth. Alone with her thoughts, without food or water, and for two nights in complete darkness, she becomes preternaturally attuned to sounds and smells, returns to oral/somatic consciousness, undergoes disintegrative regression, recovers memories of past traumas through somatic cues, smells in particular, and undergoes reintegration. This psychosomatic event triggers her assumption of control over her body, a matter of getting outside of her skin, quite literally, of using her body as a tool even while staying in touch with its perceptions.

Jessie's story alludes to novels of women's awakenings that are now required college reading, from Charlotte Perkins Gilman's "The Yellow Wallpaper" to Kate Chopin's *The Awakening* to Atwood's *Surfacing*. In the 1983 *Playboy* interview, King used the words of "that fine poet Anne Sexton" to describe what writing meant personally for him: "I am able to 'write myself sane'" (Norden 44). Jessie's story is also modeled on the incest survivor's narrative that has become a reductionist psychological cliché, one that, as Wendy Doniger notes, "exploits the contemporary American obsession of those who define themselves a victims and orient the rest of their lives around their victimization. . . . Mr. King relies on the victimization scenario for the whole structure of his novel" (3). Such a text made Stephen King not an imitation feminist so much as a poor one.

Gerald's Game was, among other things, a public rite of self-correction, and self-correction sells as well as anything these days. As a massively popular entertainer, King participates in mass culture's co-option, domestication, and (also) inclusion of once marginal causes and groups. If 1970s feminism had given force to Carrie's rage, it also energized *Misery*'s masculinist backlash and provided a female body language for Jessie's recovery in *Gerald's Game*. King's sudden sensitivity in the 1990s to old gender troubles suggests the extent to which feminism—even French feminism—has become a common language and enabling myth.

But in *Gerald's Game* and subsequent novels, King returned to the roots he put down in his first published novel *Carrie* (1974). Like the stories in Angela Carter's *The Bloody Chamber* and Anne Sexton's *Transformations*, *Carrie* was a fractured fairy tale of Cinderella's revenge, whose violence returned to older oral versions that gave women more power. King has called *Carrie* "a book about women" that expressed "a lot of male fears—about menstruation and about dealing with women who eat you up" (Peck 95). In 1983 King admitted that the charge of stereotyping women characters was "most justifiable," and he extended the criticism to his "handling of black characters":

> Halloraan, the cook in *The Shining*, and Mother Abagail in *The Stand* are cardboard caricatures of superblack heroes, viewed through rose-tinted glasses of white liberal guilt. And when I think I'm free of the charge that most male American writers depict women as either nebbishes or bitch-goddess destroyers, I create . . . Carrie—who starts out as a nebbish victim and then becomes a bitch goddess, destroying an entire town in an explosion of hormonal rage. I recognize the problems but can't yet rectify them. (qtd. in Norden 47)

In an interview with Tony Magistrale in November 1989, King explained that *Carrie* was part of an effort, recently reinstated, to "understand women and try to escape the stereotyping that goes on in so much male fiction" (*Second* 5).

Carrie had provided challenges, not the least being the unfamiliar, intimately female nature of the subject matter. King became ill at ease, and he threw an early draft of the first few pages into the kitchen trash basket: "as I arrived at . . . [the opening scene] I suddenly realized that I (1) had never been a girl, (2) had never had a menstrual cramp or a menstrual period, (3) had absolutely no idea how I'd react to one. . . . I had been in a girl's shower room exactly once" ("On Becoming" 21). Tabitha King found the discarded pages and persuaded him to finish the book. Paradoxically, King and Carrie were in precisely the same alien territory for the first time, that of the sex, the female body. Through the feat of empathy that writing it required, *Carrie* somehow became a powerful diagnostic, treating menstrual taboos and the Judeo-Christian origins of misogyny with uncommon boldness for 1974. Carrie is the victim of her mother, who has been inculcated with Judeo-Christian misogyny. Mrs. White demonizes her daughter's body, flesh of her flesh, and therefore constructed under patriarchy in terms of Sin and Death. Carrie is the Female Gothic heroine imprisoned in the "maternal legacy" of the female body (Showalter, *Sister's Choice* 128) perceived as antagonistic to a sense of self, as the following passage could not demonstrate more clearly:

> "And God made Eve from the rib of Adam," Momma said . . . [thumping] Carrie with the side of her foot and Carrie screamed.

"Get up, woman. Let's . . . pray to Jesus for our woman-weak, wicked . . . souls.

"Momma—". . . .

"And Eve was weak and—say it, woman. Say it!"

"No. Momma, please help me—"

The foot swung. Carrie screamed.

"And Eve was weak and loosed the raven on the world," Momma continued, "and the raven was called Sin and the first Sin was Intercourse. And the Lord visited Eve with a Curse . . . of Blood . . . and Eve found that her belly had grown big with child." (54)

In the end, Carrie has become "a kind of monstrous hero," says Clover— "hero insofar as she has risen against and defeated the forces of monstrosity" and monster in her demonic excess (4).

Dolores Claiborne is equally about a woman who has become a monstrous hero. But Dolores has consistently refused to be a victim. She is not only "the major character" in the story; she "dominates" the book's "landscape" (Magistrale, *Second* 5). And where Carrie's vengeance is the stuff of gossip and legend, Dolores narrates her own story. Terrence Rafferty calls the novel King's "most stubbornly literary" book, "lurching back and forth in time on the waves of the narrator's unruly emotions" ("Under a Cloud" 93). It is a dramatic departure from his ordinarily transparent style and linear plotting (93). Suspected by the police of murdering her wealthy employer Vera Donovan, Dolores explains her role in the death of her husband, Joe St. George, thirty years before. In the process, she accounts for her life, a bleak, narrow existence on Little Tall Island off the coast of Maine. King's strongest and fullest female character, Dolores not only refuses to be a victim; she sees to it that Joe falls down a well shaft—on June 20, 1963, during the total eclipse of the sun—thus ending his molestation of their thirteen-year-old daughter Selena.

Dolores's voice is at first hard to take, and more than one reviewer remarked her scatological garrulity. "I guess you'll have to fix this up some, won't you?" she tells Nancy, the stenographer. "I'm just an old woman with a foul temper and a fouler mouth," Dolores admits, "and that's what happens, more often than not, when you've had a foul life" (5). She opens with a lengthy (twenty-page) series of descriptions of Vera's use of her excretory functions as a form of power and pleasure (the "dirty old bag had her a shit savings account . . . only I was the one who got the withdrawals" [27]) on her "bright" days. The passion and eloquence of Vera's anal retentiveness matches that of Lard Ass Hogan's gargantuan bingeing and purging. However, its purpose is not anything so noble or adolescent as revenge. This book has a different kind of body language. Beyond its effectiveness in an arena of oral agonistic, its purpose may be like that of Angela Carter in *Nights at the Circus* (1984) whose swashbuckling and monstrously heroic narrator employs a bawdy, blustering, belching, farting, body language as part of her refusal to be a lady. Another is to show what it is like to be an old woman, one with "nothin to do but die in an upstairs bedroom on an island far from the people and places she'd known most of her life" (44). Still another is to present a Female Gothic version of the Kristevan scenario, for Dolores views Vera, among many other things, as her mother, huge and shapeless in senility. It reflects, perhaps, King's horror as a child at finding himself alone with his obese, bedridden grandmother's corpse (described in the story "Gramma"), his own horror as an adult watching his mother die of cancer (described in the story "The Woman in the Room"), and his mother Ruth Pillsbury King's experience as caregiver to her aging parents.

Gerald's Game's Jessie Burlingame is ambiguous because her sanity and strength are, after all, in doubt. Her uncertainty is calculated like the point of view in Henry James's *The Turn of the Screw*. Jessie's final trial in *Gerald's Game* is the image, apparition, or hallucination of a spectral male figure in a dark corner. Its existence in the gap of the liminal calls her flashbacks to scenes of molestation into question and hints at schizophrenia. *Dolores Claiborne* is a different kind of survivor's story. Its ambiguity is rooted in sterner stuff. The total eclipse of the sun by the moon, associated with female power and the body (anima, shadow, womb) provides the moment for Dolores to lose her husband down a well, described as a light-devouring black hole. Like Thad Beaumont, Dolores has a dark third eye for her intuitive, dangerous side, which provides another image of eclipse.

Dolores does not lose touch with the natural world or her task, whether it is to tell her story, rid the world of the scurrilous Joe, or clear away the "dust bunnies," the "bunch of ghost-turds" (47) whose gray nastiness haunts and terrifies Vera in her dotage. True to her name, Dolores (Madonna Dolorosa, dolorous, morose, ill-tempered) Claiborne (clay born, cthonic) remains steadfastly in the natural world and simultaneously represents the mother destroyer. Like Vera (whose words, "Sometimes you have to be a high-riding bitch to survive. . . . Sometimes being a bitch is all a woman has to hold onto" [*Dolores* 169] provide the motto of the book and who may have killed her children as well as her husband), Dolores is not *nice*. For that reason—for her resistance to the grieving victim stereotype—we admire her. She is Annie Wilkes liberated from romance novels, absolved and vindicated.

The well-made film adaptation scripted by Tony Gilroy and directed by Taylor Hackford and outstanding for its purposes, improvises what Rafferty sees as a "warm mother-daughter soap opera," drawing on the same pop psychology as *Gerald's Game*: we watch as Mother Dolores forces the churlish, hard drinking Selena to remember her molestation and confront her victimization. King's book is informed by the more interesting idea, that "women's suffering doesn't have to turn them into victims, and that there's something heroic about the hard shells they develop to protect themselves from a hostile environment" (Rafferty, "Under a Cloud" 94). The novel vindicates the "bitches" of the world, the point being that "without your guts, Dolores Claiborne, you're just another stupid old woman," as Vera puts it (300). The novel reveals the mother-daughter estrangement in flashbacks, leading to Dolores's choice of daughter over husband. But the incest survival plot is a minor part of the narrative, and bad memories, especially for Vera, are all too close to the surface. However melodramatic its ingredients (incest, murder, a suspicious car accident, an eclipse), the novel is a subtle revelation of a relationship, an intensely ambivalent one, between "two bitches livin on a little chunk of rock off the Maine coast," as Dolores puts it, "how they passed the years in that big house, two bitches who ended up spendin most of their time bitchin at each other" (299), and who cared more for each other than for anyone else.

King succeeded in writing a woman-centered novel and also in enhancing, indeed multiplying, his persona. How much his feminism should be trusted, I do not know. Before the 1990s, taken as a whole, King's women have been a horror story. Vera Donovan and even Dolores Claiborne can be viewed in a long line of death bearing mothers. The ultimate horror is the inner-child-devouring female spider that is It's final form and whom Bill Denbrough destroyed with the words, "Try this, you bitch! TRY THIS ONE OUT! DO YOU LIKE IT? DO YOU LOVE IT?" (1093).

The It-Spider's antithesis (or antidote) is Beverly Marsh, whom King has described as just "one of the boys" in the Losers' Club until she must "serve" as earth mother and "symbolic conduit between adulthood and childhood. . . . It is a role that women have played again and again in the lives of boys: the symbolic advent of manhood through the act of sex" (qtd. in Magistrale, *Second* 6). As Mary Pharr notes, this "orgy of flesh and spirit" is "eucharistic," each Loser "finding grace and courage and manhood through Bev's body" (31). What does Beverly find? Her role. As Pharr notes, King's women have long been judged by what Kay Mussell calls the "domestic test" for determining worthiness of romance heroines: they were "good" if they exhibited sexual control, modesty, intuitiveness, selflessness, and caring (Mussell 89–90). They were "bad" if they had opposing qualities, particularly if sexually active (Nadine Cross), or powerful (Annie Wilkes). Dolores and Vera are true exceptions.

King's efforts in writing about women have been a long time coming. In his 1995 review of Louisa May Alcott's *A Long Fatal Love Chase* as an example of the "woman stalked/woman in peril" subgenre, he is not above plugging his latest novel, *Rose Madder* (1995). (The latter, he notes, is also the story of an abused wife who leaves and is stalked by her obsessed husband [17].) Whatever the case, King's nod to feminism has been prompted less by the "alternative" Alcott than by the enormously success- ful Clive Barker and Anne Rice, who preceded him in explicitly gendered and gender bending "writing from the body."

Chapter 4

Clive Barker Writing (from) the Body

With *Books of Blood*, an obscure playwright and illustrator named Clive Barker launched the "post-King era of horror fiction," as William Gibson has called it ("Introduction" xv). "You read him with book in one hand and an airsick bag in the other," King joked in 1986, adding "That man is not fooling around" (qtd. in Kanfer 83). Perhaps more importantly, Barker was as intellectual and politically subversive as King was not.

Barker challenged the modern horror genre as King had exemplified and defined it. "A lot of horror is written to reassure people the values they bring to the book are . . . correct," Barker said in 1990, with King in mind, adding, "I'm not writing horror to reassure people" (Booe). King's "white soul" domesticated and mainstreamed horror; Barker privileged the different or marginal. His protagonists were people on the fringes: actors, gays, prostitutes, small-time crooks, women, and often the monsters themselves. King's horror stories were the product of a brilliant stereotypography and overstatement in which clichés are lived out fully. Barker claimed to "deromanticize" and "renew" the genre, "stripping" it of "knee-jerk conventions" (Strauss 92). Beyond that, "I like to think there's a kind of 'celebration of perversity' in *Books of Blood*," he said in 1986, "that's a response, simply, to normality" (Wiater, "Catching" 46).

Douglas Winter's term "anti-horror" points out this subversive element in Barker's work. Anti-horror inverts "the typical horror story . . . on itself," asking the reader to "view the traditional images in a new way" (Nutman, "Douglas E. Winter"). As King had reinvented the horror novel,

Barker revitalized the tale of terror, relocating it in the iconic, the grotesque, and the ironic. For he also made it a vehicle for ideas, forcing a "reactionary" genre to take on taboos and open up to controversial issues: the politics of gender, feminism, male violence against women, homosexuality, AIDS, urban blight, Marxism, violence in the media, pornography, and censorship. Using a title that promised blood to attract hard-core fans to a form they did not usually read, Barker turned "splatter" into an iconography of confrontation and paradox. He enhanced horror's capacity to disturb with techniques adapted from theatre, literature, and visual arts. Like King, Barker realized that horror could reach a mass audience with ideas they might not otherwise entertain. "I'm trying my damnedest," Barker has explained, to address "quite complex and elaborate ideas," and if "you give people a chance, if they want it, they'll get it" (qtd. in Burke 72).

Barker's early literary career as a playwright explains a great deal. He was the center of The Dog Company, a marginal theater group that specialized in mime, improvisation, anti-theatre, and Grand Guignol. Their sketches often depicted the miscegenation of fantasy and reality, of image and word. The plays, most of which Barker wrote and directed, provide glimpses of the later writer. *Poe*, an early one-act mime play, presented the author's dream life in a series of images and vignettes. *Dangerous World* (1981), which (according to the program notes) followed poet/painter William Blake from his deathbed into the "garden of his imagination," presented such delights as "the blood-sipping Ghost of a Flea," "the epic allegorical figure of London," and the marriage of Heaven and Hell (*Dangerous World* program notes). *Colossus* was an improvisational piece about Barker's favorite artist Goya. *Books of Blood* would extend this cross-referencing of visual and literary arts. In *The Secret Life of Cartoons* (1983), an anarchic comic strip rabbit entered the lives of real people.

It was The Dog Company, with its roots in the absurd and various theatres of cruelty, that seems to have inspired much of Barker's anti-horror.[1] He carried over the same perverse anti-theatricality, spectacle, shock, and emotional ambivalence. He mixed comedy, the erotic, the disgusting, and the pathetic, maintaining an exhilarating tension in the modulation from one emotion into the next.

But before he was a playwright or student, Barker was an illustrator, and probably the most obvious characteristic of his early work was his visual imagination. For Barker, writing seems to be another kind of iconography, and he refuses to make distinctions between painters like Goya and Bosch and "visionary" writers like Gabriel Garcia Marquez and

Jorge Luis Borges. Two heroes are William Blake and Jean Cocteau, for whom any genre was subordinate to "inner vision" (Burke 19–20). Barker envisions his concepts, often sketching them first and only later articulating them as words. Visiting his studio in 1989, Stanley Wiater found drawings scattered over the floor, "Midnight sketches, done feverishly," which became "a starting place for something" the next morning ("Clive Barker" 11). Everything he does is by hand to maintain the connection of hand, eye, and word.

As "powerfully visionary" in the larger sense "as he is gruesome" according to Ramsey Campbell (xi), he practices a politics of subversion that originated in the act of reading and writing from the body. A collection of his drawings entitled *Clive Barker, Illustrator* (1990), and ranging from early expressionistic brushwork pieces to elaborate color illustrations for *Books of Blood*, reveals the extent to which his iconography is based in the human figure. Because writing is imaging, Barker feels an almost moral imperative to show precisely what others think should in all decency be covered. He says he owes as much to Mapplethorpe as to Poe:

> The kind of horror fiction I write is primarily interested in tearing away the veil. Confrontation with the image, seen clearly. I'm trying to see what the wound means. And the only way . . . is to look at the wound. (qtd. in Gracey-Whitman and Melia 418)

Monique Wittig has written that the "fascination for writing what was never previously written and the fascination for the unattained body proceed from the same desire" (10). Barker uses the metaphor of the literalized body to express in flesh and blood that which Freud, Lacan, Barthes, Kristeva, and Foucault have merely discoursed of. The *Books of Blood* were a perverse "recitation" of the body as a text—a dissection, an "exploratory probe," as William Gibson says. Each "reading" presumes the metaphor in which the literal body stands for the real and transgresses the law of the symbolic order. In this metaphor, "opening" the body means reading our deepest (pre-Oedipal) selves. Biological images are metaphors for ideas. Flesh becomes word, text becomes wound, part becomes whole, and cliché is embodied, often painfully. The titles alone are multivalenced with word play: paradoxes ("The Life of Death"), puns ("In the Flesh," "The Skins of the Father"), metonymies ("The Body Politic"), oxymorons ("The Confessions of a Pornographer's Shroud"), inversions ("The Inhuman Condition"), allegories ("The Age of Desire"), allusions ("Son of Celluloid"), and ironically twisted clichés ("Human Remains").

READING THE BODY POLITIC

In Barker's ink brush piece entitled *Minds at War* (in Burke 3), two male figures in profile square off belligerently, reenacting some archaic antagonism, as from their heads jut the smoking ruins of ancient cities. "In the Hills, the Cities" (in *Books of Blood*, Volume I) works with a similar visual concept of power and conflict: the people of the Yugoslavian city Popolac join together in a network of straps and harnesses to construct a colossus and march out to perform ritual battle with their twin city Podujevo. The colossus is "the body of the state," explains Vaslav. "It is the shape of our lives" ("In the Hills" 201). As a citizen, he has watched it form, "a living proverb," "a spectacular reality" beyond ideology. It is "the head [literally] in the clouds." From the perspective of two English tourists, however, it is a terrifying negation of the human subject, its legs taking "strides half a mile long," each man, woman, and child "sightless" and (they thought) "deathless, in their lumbering, relentless strength" (197).

Popolac is a revision of the science fiction cliché of society as machine by way of Michel Foucault's vision of power embodied and harnessed through a network of forces and relations, economic, social, and political. The description of Popolac, recalling *Discipline and Punish: The Birth of the Prison* (1975), suggests

> a masterpiece of human engineering: a man made entirely of men. Or, rather, a sexless giant, made of men and women and children. All the citizens of Popolac writhed and strained in the body of this flesh-knitted giant, their muscles stretched to the breaking point, their bones close to snapping. ("In the Hills" 206)

Terror leads to horror with the breakdown of structure: someone "buried in the weak flank" of Podujevo dies of the strain, beginning "a chain of decay in the system. One man loosed his neighbor and that neighbor loosed his, spreading a cancer of chaos through the city" (187–88). When Podujevo falls, creating a river of blood clogged with human corpses, Popolac goes mad with confusion.

"In the Hills, the Cities" is also a study in structural contrasts: between order and chaos, between the collective and the individual, the citizens that are the city and the English tourists who are threatened by its fall. Mick, a shallow clothes designer, and Judd, a political journalist, are a homosexual couple touring Yugoslavia who have discovered that they are temperamentally and politically incompatible. When making love, however, they are a miracle of movement: "They locked together, limb around limb, tongue around tongue, in a knot only orgasm could untie, their backs alternately scorched and scratched as they rolled around exchanging blows and kisses" (177). Like the people in the city they are choreographed into a thing of grotesque beauty. Realizing the meaninglessness of their relationship and his life up to glimpsing this miracle, Mick catches on to the giant's foot as it leaves the ground and is swept up, the earth "gone from beneath him . . . a hitchhiker with a god" (209).

Barker has explained that the colossal image was directly inspired by two paintings by Goya (*The Colossus* and *Saturn Devouring His Children*) and more generally the magic realism of Gabriel Garcia Marquez, which defamiliarize common concepts by literalizing them in marvelous images and events. The grotesque elements of the scene are matched by terror and moments of revulsion by the awe that terror generates; what political position or which set of emotions prevails is left up to the reader. The story is typical only in demonstrating Barker's ambivalence—his qualification of one issue with another one that bears on it, and a complementary technique of reversing emotions midway through a story and putting a spin on the conclusion.

"In the Hills, the Cities" is a metonymy, a literalization of the idea of the state by way of a Foucauldian metaphor of bio-power. "The Body Politic" from *The Inhuman Condition* (1986, originally *Books of Blood, Volume IV*) depicts a paradigm shift in which the stable ego and centered identity, the self enthroned in the head and defined by the parameters and functions of "its" body, is overthrown by a revolt of hands. The right hand, a synecdoche and a Messiah, a temporary protagonist, severs the left from the wrist of Charlie George, a packager whose hands ordinarily work for him all day long. The freed limb, dragging a hatchet, liberates other hands and limbs, leading to a bloody revolution of the body from "the body."

As we have seen, part of the fun in "The Body Politic" comes from witnessing a Dionysian dismemberment of the Freudian ego. Charlie's psychoanalyst Dr. Jeudwinde is discredited early on, when he attempts to interpret Charlie's dreams: "Usually the penis predominated in his patients' dreams, he explained, to which Charlie replied that hands had always seemed more important than private parts. After all, they could change the world, couldn't they?" (65). Dr. Jeudwinde's faith in the Freudian ego breaks down under overwhelming evidence of "Charlie," a body with several minds of its own. He wonders whether attempting to be rational about the human mind is a contradiction in terms (86). "Mind" as the self's center or unity is negated and revealed as a construct of language. As Charlie tries to put his thoughts into words, he finds metaphors insufficient:

The hands were everywhere, hundreds of them, chattering away like a manual parliament as they debated their tactics. All shades and shapes, scampering up and down the swaying branches. Seeing them gathered like this the metaphors collapsed. They were what they were: human hands. That was the horror. (97–98)

Language betrays us in the most common figures of speech, as Barker's sight gags demonstrate: "her nails, her pride and joy, found her eyes, and the miracle of sight became muck on her cheek" (149). Charlie learns that the unity he has considered himself is a figure of speech. After a struggle in which he uses the (attached) Left to lure the Right, he is followed by its mob of revolutionaries up a fire escape. As he jumps to their collective death, the revolution of hands is defeated. But Charlie's martyrdom is ambivalent, ending in his euphoric contemplation of the koan "What is the sound of one hand clapping?" (88).

Barker has in mind several schools of postmodern psychology that view the individual as changeable and multiple rather than stable and singular. "The Body Politic" ends with the meditations of a doubtful identity named Boswell, who has spent his life "going wherever his legs would take him" (89). After colliding with a train, he wakes in intensive care and encounters his amputated legs, tagged for the incinerator but livelier for the separation. "Having made their presence known to him they left him where he lay, content to be free" (102).

And did his eyes envy their liberty, . . . was his tongue eager to be out of his mouth and away, and was every part of him, . . . preparing to forsake them? He was an alliance . . . held together by the most tenuous of truces. . . . [H]ow long before the next uprising? Minutes? Years? He waited, heart in mouth, for the fall of Empire. (102)

The Marxist themes of "The Body Politic" are real enough, as in "In the Hills": the story is set in the drab, aimless oppression of the working classes of the Thatcher era, and the hands seek and find masses of homeless brothers, beginning with the YMCA on Monmouth Street. But the Marxism comes by way of Deleuze and Guattari's schizoanalysis, which opposes psychoanalysis with ego breakdowns and "breakthroughs." Against the "oedipalized territorialities (Family, Church, School, Nation, Party), and especially the territoriality of the individual, Anti-Oedipus seeks to discover the 'deterritorialized' flows of desire" and to escape the established codes, celebrating the dissolution of the self (Seem, Introduction xvii). In "The Body Politic," Barker's stroke of genius is to take the

Freudian Body literally and depict its trauma in graphic terms. Even more to the point is "The Age of Desire," from the same volume, which uses schizoanalysis against phallocentrism. Jerome Tredgold, a test subject at the [David] Hume Institute, succumbs to a "chemically induced state of compulsive sexuality" (Meyer and Van Hise 116). The experiment is part of Dr. Welles's plan to initiate an "Age of Desire": "the Dream of Casanova," of "Sex without end, without compromise or apology." "The World had seen so many Ages: the Age of Enlightenment; of Reformation; of Reason. Now, at last, the Age of Desire. And after this, an end to Ages, perhaps to everything" ("Age" 200). Like the citizens of Popolac and Podujevo, Jerome is the ordinary man "deployed" as bio-power.

At first, his erotically enhanced vision merely shows him that as Deleuze and Guattari explain, "sexuality is everywhere" and that capitalism is an economy of desire (293) dominated by a specular-phallic economy of signs: "on advertising billboards and cinema marquees, . . . the body as merchandise. Where flesh was not being used to market artifacts of steel and stone, those artifacts were taking on its properties. . . . [B]uildings beleaguered him with sexual puns" ("Age" 201). Jerome is eventually consumed by a fire somehow fueled by the "beady eye at his groin" ("Age" 200), the phallic gaze. He becomes

> just a plinth for that singular monument, his prick. Head was nothing; mind was nothing. His arms were simply made to bring love close, his legs to carry the demanding rod any place where it might find satisfaction. He pictured himself as a walking erection, the world gaping on every side. Flesh, brick, steel, he didn't care—he would ravish it all. (206)

Thus the gaze is linked with sexual violence. (The experiment is coyly named Project Blind Boy in honor of Eros and his misplaced arrows.) Jerome visualizes clichés from romantic songs—metaphors of "paradise, of hearts on fire; of birds, bells, journeys, sunsets; of passion as lunacy, as flight, as unimaginable treasure" (186), and his lust culminates in grotesque literalizations of romance. "Give me your heart," he croons to Officer Boyle (191) before tearing out and physically possessing that organ. In this phallic-specular economy, Jerome fetishizes whatever he sees and is compelled to pry open and make visible, to possess and "feminize" whatever is "hidden."

But Jerome's phallocentrism is transcended in an important shift of emphasis. He becomes an embodiment of Deleuze and Guattari's desiring machine, which calls into question the established order of the society that creates it. From a more Foucauldian perspective one might say that an "implantation of perversions" in Jerome confuses his sexuality. Rather than opening, penetrating, and possessing, he begins filling holes—*any* holes—figuratively healing wounds and intermingling with the natural world. The serial rapist becomes polymorphously perverse and at one point has sex with a wall: "The sun had fallen full upon it, and it was warm; the bricks smelled ambrosial. He laid kisses on their gritty faces, his hands exploring every nook and cranny. Murmuring sweet nothings, he . . . found an accommodating niche, and filled it" (194). As his body changes, Jerome regresses to pre-Oedipal empathy with the world and comes "alive to the flux and flow of the world around him"—the paving stones seem to catch fire from him and then burn with their own flames. The world thus fantastically eroticized, his mind is "running with liquid pictures: mingled anatomies, male and female in one indistinguishable congress," a "marriage of his seed with the paving stone" (194–95). In the final scenes, he merges with "all the suffering world" (215), and in an affirmation of life, revolts, like Sisyphus, against all death. He confronts his creator Dr. Welles, who is burning records and killing monkeys, and pleads for their lives.

"The Age of Desire" concludes in one of Barker's perversely "happy" endings. Engineered in every sense of the term by the Hume Institute, the metabolic chaos that Jerome becomes is perversely liberating, and like Frankenstein's creature or Robocop, the monster as victim, Jerome has a radical innocence that destroys his makers. He becomes the revolutionary "desire machine" that wreaks havoc within the System, the machine of coercion. Most of his victims are associated with the Hume Institute or the law, and the majority of them are men. Jerome comes to represent, in addition to compulsory sexuality under late capitalism or a Freudian dream of castration denial, the transcendence of the body through the body. He experiences a terror and ecstasy that transcends conventional pleasure and unitary standards of value.

The story of Jerome transgresses liberal-Marxist political correctness also, however, and manages to please no one completely. It disturbs idea mongers with its sexual violence and it disturbs gore hounds with its radical sexual openness. Barker frequently refers to his breaking the taboo in which horror's sexual subtext must remain hidden to "work" and says that he consciously brings "that subtext into the more prominent position of text" (Strauss 92). He refers to a need to address not only "the issue of sexuality in horror" but also "the issue of many kinds of sexuality in horror."[2] In his fiction, there are sex scenes of every sort, between men, between women, "there are orgies, there are people fucking walls—there is just a sense that we are sexual beings and that . . . horror fiction is about the body—which over and over again it is" (qtd. in Hughes 391). It is therefore not surprising when Barker's comments on fantasy refer to postmodern psychology and social theory. In addition to Deleuze and Guattari, Foucault, and Lacan, his ideas draw heavily on feminist psychoanalysts (such as Cixous and Kristeva) and object relations psychologists (Chodorow) who emphasize the pre-Oedipal relationship with the Mother. Collectively, Barker's comments cohere as a theory of fantasy as a subversive art. Like Rosemary Jackson, Barker thinks that fantasy subverts the norm by presenting alternative realities. The fantastic provides a vicarious regression to unstructured pre-Oedipal experience in which possibilities seem infinite, where the world is "full of tactile and potential sensual experiences, which are at root sexual, but also about pleasure in all its diversities. . . . Then . . . we get educated out of that. . . . We get told we have to be this way or that and preferably this!" (Barker, qtd. in Dair 393). Fantasy constructs scenarios in which "those barriers are broken down again. So many of the monsters . . . are about appetite and the fears of appetite" and the need to "tame" appetite. "And yet it stays with us as a possibility" (Barker, qtd. in Dair 393–94). For Barker horror or abjection, as in Kristeva, is the darker aspect of our recognition of what we desire, the experience of the "bisexual" Mother. By awakening the powers of horror, the fantastic brings us back to an infant's openness to possibility, in which life and death are relative states of metamorphosis, of changing shape at will, talking with the animals. There, like the transforming Jerome, we encounter our fears and desires as potentialities and are open to new experience.

The fantastic therefore becomes "usefully dangerous" in providing images for "socially subversive" ideas, says Barker (Gracey-Whitman and Melia 404). These images enter the dream lives of readers, making them receptive to change:

> Our fears and hopes for our bodies, our ongoing anxiety about the decay that begins at eighteen. Our sense of ourselves as sexually whole; the part of us that remains polymorphously perverse. . . . [P]eople will accept those kinds of images and ideas in a fiction in a way that they . . . [wouldn't in a] psychoanalytic treatise. Or . . . through their analyst. (qtd. in Gracey-Whitman and Melia 406)

Dark fantasy reconnects readers to the body experienced in childhood as a radical openness to experience, and so becomes politically subversive.

In a similar way, Barthes, Kristeva, and Cixous intend to subvert the symbolic order by "writing" from the body.

BOOKS OF BLOOD AND ÉCRITURE FÉMININE

Working in the genre that (outside of pornography) is most readily equated with misogyny, especially in film, Barker walks a fine line. On the one hand, he condemns the mass media's exploitation of women (Dair 394), indicting horror film as "the last refuge of the chauvinist" (*Women of Horror*). At the same time, *Books of Blood* advertised itself as the equivalent of splatter film in prose and courted hard-core horror fans. Barker's "tear[ing] away the veil" is problematic when the very act of looking at the body as an object, according to some feminist theory, means dehumanizing the subject.

French feminist Monique Wittig ran into a similar problem in *Le corps lesbien*, which subverts language as part of her effort to reclaim the female body for women. Her preface foregrounds the issue. There she stresses that she is violating not the female body but the symbolic order's construction of it as an object of male desire. It is the logos that she disrupts, voicing the unvoiced, unpreferred parts and celebrating natural processes. Violating taboos rather than bodies, Wittig nevertheless produces a physically disturbing text.

Barker, who often announces his intention to disrupt, works similarly. He foregrounds his text in semiotics and French feminist psychoanalysis. He cultivates ambivalence and openly "celebrates" perversity. From the start, in the outrageous (but semiotically accurate) title, *Books of Blood*, he employs "anti-horror" against conventional horror's misogyny. Taking on biological taboos "with a directness worthy of . . . David Cronenberg" (Campbell xii), Barker makes the wound his text's central metaphor and, through puns and ambiguities, its central issue. The issue becomes more problematic the longer we study it. Horror's victimization of women, epitomized in Alice Cooper's "Only Women Bleed," is revised by Barker in the *Books* epigraph to "*Every*body is a book of blood" [my italics]. According to the pun in the last line, reading (and writing) the body (as horror fiction does) means wounding (opening) it, just as wounding it inscribes it; "Wherever we're opened, we're red" (*Books* 1: ix). By bringing horror's psychoanalytic subtext (the female "wound") into the prominent position of text and the body, Barker changes the violent act of reading and writing the (female) body into the central problem of the series. Barker advertises the sadism of the text at the same time as he stresses its diagnostic necessity. Thus he makes his fictions "usefully dangerous" and useful for women. In their diagnosis of gender distress as well as their radical sexual openness, Barker's *Books of Blood* had less in common with Stephen King or splatter film than with contemporary Female Gothic writers who used the popular Gothic as a mode for expressing, in slightly disguised form, subversive ideas.

From 1982 through 1984, when he was writing the first three volumes of *Books of Blood*, slasher film violence against women was a primary issue in mass media and sexual politics. Barker kept the issue at the center of *Books of Blood* as he used the metaphor of the body as text to explore technologies of gender and desire. Barker's stories often position the reader as a woman; imagine female subjectivity with remarkable, if varying, degrees of success; and attempt to overturn misogynistic horror clichés, especially the "woman in peril" motif. His women are neither "mouthpieces for outraged feminism or cowering pretty things," Craig Burns remarks. They are, for example, "chubby cynics who work in rundown movie theaters trying (and failing) to imagine a better life" (101). In *Books of Blood*, Carrie, with her female power in the blood, grows up.

Burns describes Birdy, the protagonist of "Son of Celluloid" (*Books of Blood*, Volume III, 1984), a haunted theater story that satirizes horror and Hollywood film stereotypes. Birdy is a savvy version of Moers's persecuted victim-heroine who in facing down the monster, the male gaze, confronts her own fear of self. This fear is grounded in her ambivalent relationship with female body images. Like most of Barker's protagonists, Birdy is unconventional to begin with: she is intellectual but also resourceful; she is strong *and* overweight *and* agile.

Literally a tumor, the "Son of Celluloid" feeds on emotions invested in movies and seduces its victims by impersonating dead movie stars and clichés. To Lindi Lee, whom the Son assesses as "easy meat," it assumes the sentimental form of a Disney rabbit. The Son is also brilliant as John Wayne (male violence) and quickly dispatches Lindi's boyfriend Dean. But for the pseudo-intellectual, bisexual theater manager Ricky, who knows Wayne to be a "handful of lethal lies—about the glory of America's frontier origins, the morality of swift justice, the tenderness in the heart of brutes" (16), it must provide more potent seductions. As Marilyn Monroe the monster can tap directly into the male gaze. "I want you," she says, "I need your loving looks. I can't live without them" (26). Ricky is seduced by the scene from *The Seven-Year Itch*, in which Marilyn's dress billows up above her waist. He looks at "the dream of millions," at "the part of Marilyn he had never seen. . . . There was blood there. . . . As her muscles moved the bloody eyes she'd buried in her body shifted, and came to rest on him" (27). His glimpse of "monstrous" female subjectivity breaks the spell and almost saves him. But as a "pill-freak" and film buff, Ricky prefers the deadly, virtual Marilyn over real women, allowing the tumor to invade his body.

"Son of Celluloid" is like *Videodrome* in its attacks against the same visual pleasure that it exploits: the male gaze whose projection represents an elision of the female body. Assuming the form of a "single vast eye" that fills the doorway, or the male gaze and projection in one metaphor, the Son attempts to rape Birdy. Blinking "huge and wet and lazy, scanning the doll in front of it with the insolence of the One True God, the maker of celluloid Earth and celluloid Heaven" it jeers, "Here's looking at you, kid" ("Son" 30). Birdy weighs 225 pounds, and when it assaults her, she rolls over on it. Real flesh, unpreferred parts, and "good weight" triumph over body image, the literal and the feminine over the male symbolic.

Barker draws on his fringe theater experience here, interjecting farce—a bad fat-lady joke—into the scene in which Birdy rolls on the Son of Celluloid. The scene's ambivalence is strategic. The joke is positioned in a crucial way: while it stands on its own as a joke, on the one hand, it also is shown from Birdy's perspective as a heroic act (however mediated by her strong sense of irony). It is her joke rather than a joke on her. (In an earlier moment, her only weak one, Birdy relaxes her defenses in self-pity when images of Disney's Dumbo remind her of a cruel nickname from childhood.) Ultimately the Son forces her to confront her image of herself as abject, a "filthy thing, a tumor grown fat on wasted passion," bringing to mind "something aborted, a bucket case" ("Son" 35). In looking directly at the body, however, she recovers her own strength.

Instead of her prized weapon, a pipe wrench she calls Motherfucker, Birdy recovers the power of her body, reclaiming it from negative inscription. In the final section, titled "Censored Scenes," Birdy completes this process by tracking down Lindi Lee. Lindi is perhaps the ultimate literalization of the concept of the mass media stereotype—in her the Son of Celluloid has been born again, the celluloid Word Made Bimbo. The real tumor is the false ideal of female beauty projected by the heterosexual male gaze. In a parodic reversal of the *Phantom of the Opera*, Birdy pours acid on "tumor and human limb alike" (38). In this act, by creating a gap that the stereotype Lindi Lee once filled, Birdy also creates a space for herself. Her job done, she steps out into the street, confident in her "planning to live long after the credits for this particular comedy had rolled" (38).

The gaze and its images, hallucinations that we project or consent to, are the issues of "The Son of Celluloid," and the particular targets are mass media images of women. Birdy is in the female Gothic tradition of the persecuted victim who becomes a heroine by using her intelligence and sense of reality to hold her ground.

The protagonist of "Revelations" (Volume V, *The Inhuman Condition*), Virginia Gyer, is not only a persecuted victim-heroine but also the Female Gothic madwoman. From the beginning, however, the narrator shares Virginia's vision of ghosts in her room in the Cottonwood Motel, presenting that vision, together with the ghosts' point of view, in a broadly humorous deadpan. Clearly in Barker's world the psychics, psychotics, and women (including the ghost Sadie, electrocuted for killing her oafishly philandering husband Buck) are sane. Barker juxtaposes this perspective against the horrifically fantastic prophecies of the Book of Revelations, which Virginia's evangelist husband John (like Carrie White's mother) declaims every night in a frenzied and oppressive ritual: "he rose on a spiral of ever more awesome metaphor: from angels to dragons and thence to Babylon, the Mother of Harlots, sitting upon a scarlet-colored beast" (118). As Sadie first tells Virginia, these are "comic book terrors, fit to scare children with." The word of God is in turn "revealed" to be a misogynistic fantasy of doomsday violence. Sadie becomes Virginia's demonic advisor, assuming also the role of the perverse double. The ghost and the world of comic violence Sadie brings with her provide a sort of Bertha Mason to Virginia's Jane Eyre. Sadie speaks directly for Virginia's buried rage; moreover, her life's definitive act of shooting her husband (and remaining glad she did it) prefigures Virginia's final act. Reverend Gyer, who stands for patriarchy and logos, falls "like a toppled statue" (156). The story ends in high humor as Sadie counsels Virginia to plead insanity, counseling that "'you'll be notorious. That's worth living for, isn't it?' Virginia hadn't thought of that. The ghost of a smile illuminated her face" (156). Later, gazing at the moon, which represents the feminine as well as madness, and "putting on the craziest smile she could muster," Virginia tells the assembled crowd, "The Devil made me do it" (157).

The sensitive and muted "Coming to Grief," a story collected in Douglas Winter's anthology *Prime Evil* (1988),[3] focuses on the central issue of the modern Female Gothic, the female body as maternal legacy. Barker's protagonist Miriam Blessed, married and with a daughter, long ago disconnected herself from her mother in what seems to have been an act of disavowal. Miriam has been desperate not to be like her innocuous mother. Returning at her mother's death, Miriam must separate from the mother's body and experience the primary loss that is a biological and psychic necessity (Kristeva, *Black Sun* 79). In Kristeva's scenario, this means "coming to grief" in the sense of assuming the daughter's inheritance.

Miriam performs her funeral duties and feels very little: she returns to her mother's house, sorts through her things, views the body, reunites with a female friend, and visits the "Bogey Walk," the site of her childhood fear centering on a huge quarry haunted by a Bogeyman. And in one sense there is a real Bogeyman. A vine covered wall conceals a gap where the bricks are crumbling and which, at her weakest point, after the funeral, draws Miriam forward and invites her to stop to look down among the shadows.

Barker has made several statements about his refusal to exploit the "woman in peril" scenario. The Bogey, Miriam realizes, is no man. It is rather the absence of anything so patriarchal or simple: no "hook-handed men and secret lovers slaughtered in the act of love" (83), no hell, no heaven, no haunting. In his/its place Miriam finds her mother's ordinary face in death. The Bogey is the daughter's matricidal rage both projected and internalized. It has been displaced onto a mythical "man" and also swallowed, preserved within herself as anger against herself and as self-devouring inner emptiness: "Stone. Cold stone. Thinking about absence, about the disguise required by a thing that wished not to be seen, she turned into her mother's road" (85).

In the end, the death-bearing, devouring mother has an other side in "Judy's voice, Judy's hands" (104). Judy, her childhood friend, finds her, calls her back, and heals her with her presence. Having survived more drastic separations—the death of her father, a divorce, and a choice of lesbianism—Judy comforts Miriam through the night, and the next day Miriam returns to her husband and daughter.

"Coming to Grief" is a sign of Barker's considerable range. More characteristically, however, Barker's texts expose the wound, confronting readers with its potency, analyzing it as an unstable sign, and transposing it into a sign of female power. Thus he asks readers to reconstruct their perceptions of the monstrous feminine. "Jacqueline Ess: Her Will and Testament," "The Madonna," and "The Hellbound Heart" reconfigure the fatal woman archetype. In "Jacqueline Ess" (*Books of Blood*, Volume II), the lawyer and archetypal lover Oliver Vassi provides a testimony as a third of the text: "She was no lamia, no succubus. . . . She didn't bewitch me; that's a romantic lie to excuse rape. She was a sea: and I had to swim in her. . . . I'd lived my life on the shore, in the solid world of Law, and I was tired of it" ("Ess" 87).

Barker is drawing on the French feminist program that advocates a kind of feminist terrorism: the hysteric fully possesses her body and attains the power of the sorceress, Goddess, or Amazon. He uses the metaphor of the literal body to "realize" the feminine within the text as "absence" violently "striving to become a presence" (Gilbert,"Introduction" xviii). Cixous tells women they should write in literal milk or blood. Cixous, Wittig, and Du Plessis write marginal, polymorphous forms: prose poems, crosses between novel and essay, lyric and epic. In this way they reverse the equation in which the male word is made female flesh and so transcend the linear and inscribed to achieve a "no where into which we can fly in a tarantella of rage and desire . . . where the part of ourselves that longs to be free . . . can dream, can invent new worlds" (Gilbert, "Introduction" xviii). Subverting logos, French feminists celebrate the body perverse, the body as a book of blood.

Anne Sexton's poem "Consorting with Angels" comes close to projecting such a semiotic utopia. Tired of being a woman, the speaker has an ecstatic vision of transcending gender through a grotesque transformation—of being opened, made "all one skin, like a fish" (l. 39)—rendered in the cadences of the Song of Solomon. Barker's women often triumph through similar transformations of the flesh, reinventing themselves. They are also the powerful agents of male transformation. Jacqueline Ess, who finds herself powerless in the patriarchal world of Law, lacking access to the Word, reconfigures the male body in a quest for female power and identity. The text "Jacqueline Ess: Her Will and Testament," is a study of repressed anger and sexual power politics. It begins in the Cixousian myth of the hysteric who discovers the transforming rage of the sorceress within her body. Like Virginia Gyer (and Anne Sexton), Jacqueline is at first a mad housewife. Oppressed by "the boredom, the drudgery, the frustration" (75) of living as a woman, she attempts to succeed and fails. But precisely then, "from the deep trenches of her nature, faculties she had never known existed" swim up to the surface of her mind "like fish" up to the light.

She recovers these "faculties" through Medusan rage. Like the speaker in Adrienne Rich's "Phenomenology of Anger" (1968), who trains her hysteria into an image of pure "white acetylene" (57, line 59), Jacqueline first turns her hatred on her supercilious psychoanalyst Dr. Blandish, who refers to her "woman's problems" like an "All-knowing, all-seeing Father" (77). Feminism notwithstanding, Barker's special effects are derived from Brian De Palma (*Carrie*, *The Fury*) and Cronenberg (*Scanners*) as Jacqueline discovers her power to transform men's bodies. "Be a woman," she thinks, willing "his manly chest into making breasts" until the skin bursts and his pelvis expands until it fractures at the center (78). Dry mouthed with shock, Dr. Blandish loses the power to speak except from the body: "it was from between his legs that all the noise was coming; the splashing of his blood . . . on the carpet" (78).

Jacqueline next trains her mind on that relation between speech, power, and violence, specifically her husband's speeches that turn into justifications that become accusations, "assaults on her character," speeches that steal her space to be. Once again, she literalizes what we discover to be a violent metaphor. "Shut up," she thinks, telescoping him "into smaller and smaller space" until, when he is "shut up into a space the size of one of his fine leather suitcases," she thinks, "My God . . . this can't be my husband. He's never been as tidy as that" (81).

Jacqueline hopes to find freedom from male domination, female identity, and a voice in her newly born power. To learn mastery, she apprentices herself to Titus Pettifer, a crime boss, but discovers that such power can be another form of slavery. When Pettifer, who can neither live with her nor without her, begs her to kill him, calling her monster to inspire her rage, she turns him into a beast of "indeterminate species. Perhaps a crab, perhaps a dog, perhaps even a man. Whatever it was it had no power over itself" (109), not even the power to die. She moves from destroying men who pain her to using them as instruments for pleasure, but is unable to satisfy or even define her desire. "She'd gone through her life, it seemed, looking for a sign of herself, only able to define her nature by the look in others' eyes. Now she wanted an end to that" (98).

Jacqueline turns to several feminist fables of identity with ambivalent results. She writes her memoirs, but leaves off when she reaches her ninth year, "with the first realization of on-coming puberty" (103). But something shifts when she turns from the man and embraces her own monstrosity ("Monster he calls me: monster I am" [187]) by "writing" from her body. She finds that she can "will her body to ripple like the surface of a lake." Without sex, her body becomes "a mystery to her again," and she realizes the lesson of *Our Bodies, Ourselves*, "that physical love had been an exploration of that most intimate, and yet most unknown region of her being: her flesh" (102).

Then, however, Jacqueline finds that she must recover herself in relation to the Other. In Nancy Chodorow and Jessica Benjamin, women experience ego boundaries as fluid, in what Benjamin calls an "intersubjective space" (92). And so Jacqueline "understood herself best by embracing someone else; seen her own substance clearly only when another's lips were laid on it, adoring and gentle" (102). Conversely, in the language of power, destroying the Other means destroying herself.

By this time, engorged with power, Jacqueline concludes that she will be completely herself only when she destroys all witnesses to her power and becomes a whore who annihilates her clients. When Vassi, her one lover, comes to her in the conclusion, the story ends turning on a terrible paradox of human sexual dependence: Hell is Other People, especially people of the other sex; I am incomplete without the Other, and yet when completed in the Other, I am dead.

Jacqueline Ess's "Will and Testament" is a disturbing legacy. Its pessimism turns on problems raised in earlier Female Gothic narratives, many of which ended in death (George Eliot's *The Mill on the Floss*, Kate Chopin's *The Awakening*, and the lives of Sylvia Plath and Anne Sexton). Barker's narrative ends in a fiery lovedeath in which the masculine and feminine powers cancel each other out. At the same time, because it is composed of two texts, Jacqueline's story and Vassi's "Testimony," it is an ongoing dialogue, an open text.

If *Books of Blood* demonstrate and even celebrate body as a source of female subjectivity and power, they also, like Cronenberg's films, depict men encountering the feminine. Barker's texts similarly "instruct" male readers in the pleasure and pain of embodiment, regendering them. Vassi sees himself as a man speaking (testifying) to men about the truth of female power. "We cannot believe, we men, that power will ever reside happily in the body of a woman, unless that power is a male child. . . . . The power must be in male hands, god-given. That's what our fathers tell us, idiots that they are" (87). In "The Madonna," from Volume V of *Books of Blood*, entitled *In the Flesh* (1986), two men witness the power of parthenogenesis and undergo a literal sexual metamorphosis. Jerry Coloqhoun, a small-time grifter (who turns out to be the protagonist), interests an investor, Ezra Garvey, in renovating an abandoned bath-house. The obscure structure mystifies them both and they become separated in its darkness. In separate instances Jerry and Garvey, who has always been afraid of water and feels more comfortable within walls of institutions, are lured into the center of the pool complex by a naked girl. She teaches them a hard lesson: "The body does not need the mind. It has procedures aplenty, lungs to be filled and emptied, blood to be pumped and food profited from—none of which require the authority of thought." After fainting, Jerry becomes "aware of his body" as never before: "Its fragility was a trap; its shape, its size, its very gender was a trap. And there was no flying out of it; he was shackled to, or *in*, this wretchedness" ("Madonna" 167).

But Jerry's horror is just the beginning. As in "Jacqueline Ess," "Skins of the Fathers," and "Rawhead Rex," men who encounter the Anima or Mother undergo a sea-change in which they are released from the false consciousness of gender. Garvey and Jerry (subjectivized by the narrator's increasing use of his androgynous first name) have very different perceptions of the experience, both of which the reader is asked to consider. When Garvey finds himself changing, he blames Jerry and persecutes him in a display of retaliatory bravado. We follow his transformation through a subplot bearing on conflicts that develop between him and his lover Carole. In the beginning, mystified by the pools' architecture, Jerry shows a map to Carole, who sees that they are constructed on the principle of a labyrinth or spiral, which represents the intricate irrationalities of the feminine as perceived by the "linear" masculine mind. Then Jerry and Carole argue hotly over the merits of a French film that seems to Jerry "completely lacking in plot . . . a series of dialogues between characters discussing their traumas and their aspirations. . . . It left him feeling torpid" (150). When Jerry later finds his apartment vandalized by Garvey's thugs, he feels that his body has been invaded. To escape feelings of vulnerability, he forces himself on Carole and subsequently experiences paroxysms of guilt.

Barker makes the test of character a radical openness to the experience of the body, and in this story, that experience means literally turning into a woman. Garvey is horrified at the monstrosities he sees sprouting above and below his waist: "the bitches had worked this rapture upon him," he thinks as he slashes hysterically at the offending parts. Jerry is neither afraid nor "jubilant" but he learns to enjoy being a girl. He turns "his hands over to admire their newfound fineness, running his palms across his breasts." This biological transformation brings with it a spiritual one; Jerry is born again into pre-Oedipal innocence (and politically correct polymorphous perversity), accepting "this *fait accompli* as a baby accepts its condition" (178). In contrast to Garvey, Jerry experiences the revelations of the body fantastic: "There were miracles in the world! Forces that could turn flesh inside out without drawing blood; that could topple the tyranny of the real and make play in its rubble" (178).

The reader's experience, like Jerry's, involves a gradual (spiral-like) acceptance of the Madonna as Garvey, and even Carole (who is disgusted by the new Jerry), fall away, victims to their gendered preconceptions. Barker describes the Madonna at first in terms of her beautiful, naked "daughters," who at first seem to be conventional bathing beauties, then mermaids, and finally take on attributes of lamias, nursing strange, tentacled children—representing the prospect, under a matriarchy, of asexual reproduction. The Madonna herself, or the "eternal feminine," when finally revealed and demystified, is a vast fleshy mountain, a womb turned inside out. The narrator's description runs up and down the evolutionary ladder:

As the ripples of luminescence moved through the creature's physique, it revealed with every fresh pulsation some new and phenomenal configuration. . . . Mother? Jerry mouthed. . . . [S]wollen flesh

was opening; liquid light gushing. . . . The slit spasmed and delivered
the child—something between a squid and a shorn lamb—onto the
tiles. (168–69)

This fleshy revelation leaves Garvey paranoid and sick with confusion.
But by the end of the story, the narrator has transposed the terms and the
emotions associated with the abject mother into an evocation of the
sublime. As the whirlpool catches him, and like Tolstoy's Ivan Ilych (at
the moment of his death) or John Barth's spermatozoan on his erotic
"Night-Sea Journey," Jerry swims toward the light at the end of the tunnel.
From this new inner space, a womb's eye view,

> Death was no more certain than the dream of masculinity he'd lived
> these years. Terms of description fit only to be turned up and over
> and inside out. The earth was bright, wasn't it, and probably full of
> stars. He opened his mouth and shouted into the whirlpool, as the
> light grew and grew, an anthem in praise of paradox. (181)

The worship of the Madonna means not matriarchy but a "utopian dream
of a monstrous world without gender," such as Donna Haraway recom-
mends (223), a world open to change. Like Vassi ("Jacqueline Ess"), Jerry,
having lived his life on shore, in "the solid world," is tired of it. The
Madonna is "a sea" and he must learn to swim in her element. Also similar
is the way "The Madonna" ends in one of Barker's reversals of the
emotional dominant, which is usually horror, into its opposite.

   In all the stories previously mentioned, Barker offers a happy ending
that is also profoundly disturbing, or he establishes a tone of optimism in
the presence of uncertainty. Such shifts deny conventional pleasure and
conventional pain and are consequently provocative. As in absurdist
theater, the point is to disrupt our normal categories for processing
experience. Barker contrasts his position on physicality with David
Cronenberg's: "There is an argument that he's being repulsed by the flesh
he's writing [sic] about, whereas I tend to be having a good time with it.
'Long Live the New Flesh' would be a cry that would come from both our
lips" (Barker, "Tearing" 269). "Having a good time with it" means using
fantasy to shift aesthetic, moral, and political values lent to body images
and so changing the way we construct ourselves. The stories also desta-
bilize conventional emotional resonances and move the reader to experience gender in different terms.

   In the several stories that explore the conflict of male and female
principles, the spectrum of issues and dialogue of perspectives invites

the reader to participate. The titillation and semantic play lead to a more serious form of play in which images of gender are transposed and reconstructed. Barker often exposes orthodox belief systems, the church, the law, and psychology in particular for handing down misogynistic mythologies of the body. "Rawhead Rex" (*Books of Blood, Volume III*), is a splatter-movie version of the walking erection in "The Age of Desire" and another deconstruction of Lacan's Phallus, the Law of the Father. Rex is a monstrous materialization of the phallus running rampant, making its bloody way through the Welsh town of Zeal. The battle of Good and Evil as configured between Christ and the Anti-Christ is referred back to a much older allegorical struggle of masculine and feminine principles.

In the religious allegory, Rawhead Rex is the last of a race of child-de-vouring Titans that owned the land "Before Christ. Before civilization" (57) and that is uncovered from centuries of sleep by a farmer removing a huge stone in a field. Rex recalls perhaps the "rough beast" or Anti-Christ Yeats predicted in "The Second Coming." The spineless verger at the local Anglican church plays his John the Baptist, bowing to a "Lord of the Hardon" whose demands would be "plain, and real." "Raw Head. The name was an imperative. It evoked a skinned head. Its defenses peeled back, a thing close to bursting, no telling if it was pain or pleasure" (6). Rex acknowledges the verger's apostleship by urinating copiously on him. Orthodox zealots, Barker thereby suggests, are really motivated by the physiology of sex, and most especially pleasure in the hydraulics of ejaculation.

The most striking reversal is of the symbolism of blood, associated in the Church with the crucifixion and the power of resurrection into spiritual life. Like Anne Rice, Barker deconstructs the Judeo-Christian myths of blood, recovering its origins in more ancient fertility rites, cannibalism, and menstruation taboos. In the latter, the woman who was "born to bleed" but did not die was both abject victim and immortal monster. The Christian totem of the cross has suppressed the pagan taboo (and the taboo has elided female power) to the extent that the subject of menstruation was rarely broached in horror or any literature until Anne Sexton's "Menstruation at Forty."

In "Rawhead Rex," one of Barker's most violent stories, images associated traditionally with the female "abject" are reconfigured as symbols of life. Rather than eliding or exploiting the taboo, as Hanson has accused Stephen King of doing in *Carrie*, Barker allegorizes the issue. At first, Gwen's period comes on as a biological defense reflex: she "didn't see the giant, but her innards churned. Damn periods, she thought, rubbing her

lower belly in a slow circle. . . . This month she'd come on a day early"
(49). The body language comes from Rex's perspective as well: there was

> no way [Rex] could bring himself to touch this woman; not today.
> She had the blood cycle on her, he could taste its tang, and it sickened
> him. It was taboo, that blood, and he had never taken a woman
> poisoned by its presence. (49)

Barker describes menstruation as a horror specifically to the monster
Rex, thus foregrounding the issue in the primitive literalism of his perception. He is, after all, an embodiment of the phallus. Our reading of rape is
also foregrounded when Rex remembers the good old days when he and
his brothers had

> taken women into the woods, spread them out, spiked and loosed
> them again, bleeding but fertile. They would die having the children
> of those rapes. . . . That was the only revenge . . . on the big bellied
> sex. (69)

Rex's hypermasculinity masks a terrified womb envy. What finally
defeats him is the sign of the taboo raised on high as a totem, a stone icon
of Venus, sign of the "bleeding woman, her gaping hole eating seed and
spitting children. It was life, that hole, that woman, it was endless fecun-
dity." It is the power Hélène Cixous has described as the laugh of the
Medusa. When neither the police nor the crucifix (the sign of the bleeding
man) daunts him, the woman "terrifie[s] him" into submission (87), and
he is forced back into the hole from which he last emerged.

"Rawhead Rex" begins as what seems to be a celebration of male sexual
violence. But hard-ons don't last. At least half of the story is described
through Rex's perspective, to the extent that much of the pleasure of
reading it is designed with male action-movie lovers in mind. The narrator
delights with Rex in phallic power as he devours the entrails of babies and
urinates on the alternatingly groveling and ecstatic verger. But the story
increasingly reveals the limitations of this Law of the Father—that he is
the last of his breed, dooming his offspring (who kill their mothers as they
are born). In Barker's characteristic turn, we learn that Rex has "never been
a great thinker," that he lives in the eternal present of the instinctual
(49–50). In the last third of the story, the archeologist Ron Milton loses
his son to the phallic principle and becomes a hero when he screams: "The
scream had always belonged to the other sex, until that instant. Then,
watching the monster stand up and close its jaws around his son's head,

there was no sound appropriate but a scream" (78). "Dead sons," he discovers, "were the crux of the Church after all" (50). Thus "Rawhead Rex" turns the mythology of the Church into myths of gender and images of the body fantastic.

"In none of my fiction," Barker has said, "will you find any religious solution to a problem. Nobody ever whips out a crucifix and expects to keep a monster at bay with it. Those are old solutions. We have to find new solutions" (qtd. in Castaneda 59). In moving toward new solutions we should recover the artifacts buried under the altars, whose iconography is based in monstrous images of the body. Learning to see into these images, however, is merely the beginning. The goal is to re-imagine them and thereby re-invent ourselves.

Inevitably Barker's fiction returns to the idea of embracing the monstrous feminine in order to be fully human. And because the feminine is the marginal "sex which is not one" (Irigaray), it includes or implies androgyny. Barker's dialogues of gender suggest that within conventional constrictions, we are all misshapen fragments of whole people, or at best halves searching for the missing or possible Other. We are all seeking to re-imagine our present selves. Sexual metamorphosis is often positively self-transcending.

Barker's lively, myth-transforming "splatter prose" should be considered in a context that includes feminist artists Judy Chicago and Robert Mapplethorpe, who (while obviously quite different) have designed images of the body that make space for sexual difference. I am thinking of Chicago's *The Dinner Party*, a series of dinner plates designed to suggest the female genitalia in metamorphosis or flight and Mapplethorpe's reconstructions of the phallus. "The Madonna" and "Rawhead Rex" venture into revisionist mythmaking.

Feminist subtexts inform the discourses of the body that comprise Barker's six volumes. *Books of Blood* are fantastic voyages through the gendered body, with the male and female principles represented in images of its inner spaces. They show the extent to which psychoanalysis shifted its base in the mid-1980s, from the subject's mind-centered emphasis on consciousness to the bodymind or the body fantastic. *Books of Blood* are also dialogues in which gender may be transposed or transformed; they are re-genderings of the body.

In "Rawhead Rex," the perspective shifts from a randy phallocentrism toward gynocentrism, and turns from a splatter film into a dialogic text. "Jacqueline Ess" moves from female powerlessness to the monstrous feminine to the paradox of human sexual dependence. This paradox is embodied in a text in which Jacqueline's fatal and female "Will and

Testament," unwritten except in a fragment of a diary and the misshapen fragments of male flesh, is co-authored and made possible by Vassi, whose "Testimony" also represents a significantly revised version of the patriarchal law. Jacqueline's story proper provides a satirical mirror of the Word, and Vassi's passionate lyricism responds to and deflects Jacqueline's rage. Neither text would be complete without the other. The story, like the *Books* as a whole, becomes a collaborative text, a dialogue of positions, and a problem thrust on the reader.

As his move toward fantasy indicates, Barker's interest in essentialist concepts, including archetypal and psychoanalytic analysis, is superseded by what must be called his "faith" in change and his war against Blakean "mind-forged manacles." Barker attacks Freud, for example, in "The Body Politic," for fitting the mind in "neat classical compartments," and suggests that his own viewpoint is more Jungian. At the same time, Barker exposes the stereotyping tendencies of archetypal approaches, celebrating variegation.

In presenting a spectrum, *Books of Blood* are subversive in form as well as content: each story is composed of several counterpointing characters or voices, each volume consists of four to six such tales, each playing off the others, the dialogic play destabilizing the whole, reversing and revising stereotypes. Instead of closure, Barker offers heteroglossia and transformation, which make for humorously black, weirdly optimistic, or triumphantly paradoxical endings. The six volumes provide a Bakhtinian Carnival in which normally suppressed voices are heard "in the flesh" as transformation and intertextuality triumph over patriarchy and logos. At the same time, as violent texts, *Books of Blood* subvert political correctness itself, sliding into ambivalence.

"CELEBRATIONS OF PERVERSITY": BARKER'S FILMS

Transformation is the essential element in Barker's visual style, whatever the medium. This theme is perhaps most obvious in his films and screenplays. A case in point is *Hellraiser*, his enormously successful 1987 directorial debut, and an all-out, perversely dislocating splatter movie.[4] The film's focus is the deconstruction and gradual reconstruction of Frank Cotton from a bit of slime and ganglia on up.

Based on his novella *The Hellbound Heart* (1986), *Hellraiser* cross references *Faust*, *Frankenstein*, and *The Marriage of Heaven* and *Hell* and may draw on Barker's early Grand Guignol plays. Frank Cotton wishes to "redefine the parameters of sensation" and to release himself from "the dull round of desire, seduction and disappointment that ha[s] dogged him from late adolescence" (*Hellbound Heart* 187). By manipulating an exotic puzzle box, Frank summons the Cenobites, described in *The Hellbound Heart* as "theologians of the Order of the Gash" (187), masters of pleasure and pain and providers of private hells, imagined as a fleshy limbo. In the film these demons are visual puns, metaphors of sadomasochism—a head scored into perfect squares and studded with pins; a face trapped in a prison of flesh that covers all but the mouth and a set of chattering teeth. As Frank discovers, the Cenobites offer *jouissance* through ultimate sensational experience and physical transformation in exchange for his self. A flood, a "cacophony" of sensations is unleashed and "written on his cortex," until he feels "close to exploding" (*Hellbound Heart* 193), as indeed he is. In the film his body is ripped apart in a literalization of deconstruction. However, eternal *jouissance* is paradoxically a type of entrapment. There is no exit.[5] Julia, Frank's sister-in-law and lover, feels trapped in a conventional marriage and equally fractured into roles. Divining her lover's presence in the family house, she agrees to resurrect and literally raise him through a bloody ritual in which she seduces, bludgeons, and feeds a series of men to Frank's voracious remains.

In *Hellraiser*, the central image is Frank's radical dismemberment in the prologue and gradual reconstruction throughout the film in spectacular effects sequences. These reverse the traditional horror movie structure in which the monster is deconstructed and expelled at the end of the movie. The opening sequence concludes as fragments of the organs of his senses are displayed on hooks in artful tableaus in the style of Grand Guignol and Hieronymous Bosch. The reconstruction involves eight stages of clinically detailed effects that suggest the layered transparencies of a medical textbook.

In the transformation of Frank, Barker attempts to recreate the effect of the "very beautiful" sixteenth-century medical illustrations of the anatomist Andreas Vesallius, who portrayed "flayed men and women standing in classical poses or leaning against pillars. The whole atmosphere of these images is cool and elegant. . . . " With these etchings in mind, Barker and effects designer Bob Keene made Frank and the Cenobites "beautiful and repulsive simultaneously" (Barker, qtd. in Floyd, "Clive Barker" 313).

The resulting film is subversive, as Barker and Bob Keene, the effects technician, intended. Like Cronenberg's *Dead Ringers*, the effects reverse splatter film violence against the female and (perversely) flay, open up, and "feminize" the male. This skinless and continually "new" Frank is a walking wound, his anatomy his visible destiny. An excruciating reminder of our physiological limits, and thus Frankenstein's monster, Frank is alternately the body in pieces and the body in flux: "the map of his arteries and veins still being drawn anew," "puls[ing] with stolen life" (*Hellbound Heart* 238).

Hellraiser is erotic in sexually dislocating ways. At his most rapacious Frank is portrayed as a growing fetus nourished in the chamber of Julia's desire. Like Rawhead Rex, he is a penis—rising from the floorboards with the gasp/roar/cry of a beast/child/orgasm, the *mise-en-scène* bringing the sights and sounds of birth, predatory violence, and sex into disturbing juxtaposition. In an oddly painful and compelling scene, Frank, newly born from the pool of slime that he was, has a cigarette as he chats with his mistress. Conventional horror "portrays women as more squeamish than men" (*Women in Horror*), Barker has complained, and he plays against stereotype, generating perverse overtones. As Julia bathes in the blood of her victims and mates with the slime of Frank on the floor of the womblike room—as she embraces villainy and abjection—she becomes paradoxically more beautiful. (In the novella *The Hellbound Heart*, she also becomes perversely maternal: "she [f]orsak[es] the dregs of her distaste," touching the hair—"silken, like a baby's—and the shell of his skull beneath" [240]).

Equally dislocating is the film's "relativized morality," which Nigel Floyd calls a "cruel parody of the old liberal maxim, 'Everyone has their reasons' " ("Clive Barker" 313). Julia is no "fatal woman" stereotype, and she is especially sympathetic from a Female Gothic point of view. Seduced by Frank before her wedding to the kind but dull Rory, she nurses Frank back to life to give her pleasure. Like Jacqueline Ess, she chooses "masculine" knowledge, power, and creativity over traditional female roles and changes from a neurotic housewife to a woman possessed by desire. "She had made this man, or remade him, used her wit . . . to give him substance. The thrill she felt, touching this too vulnerable body, was the thrill of ownership," the novella tells us (Hellbound Heart 240). Julia relishes the Female Gothic experience of "unnatural" authorship (surrogate motherhood) to Shelleyian "hideous progeny." But as Nigel Floyd explains, viewers are torn between their sympathy for Frank and Julia and their "disorientation at being encouraged to identify with the forces of evil. Refused any single organizing moral point of view, the viewer is kept continually off-balance" (Floyd 318).

Hellraiser subverts the kind of certainty found in bourgeois horror films rooted in the nuclear family, whose purpose is to expel the monstrous. The film additionally tests the limits of the genre, using its conventions to unsettle viewers. Such reversals and paradoxes of *Hellraiser* defamiliarize splatter conventions and make viewers newly and uncomfortably conscious of the body as a process, as incessant transformation. Barker has explained that such "rearrangements of the flesh," as he calls them, only show what takes place "on a moment-to-moment basis," a process that he says is "kind of celebrated" in his fiction. In an interview with Morgan Gerard, Barker describes it in terms of "sitting together, growing old; our flesh minutely changing outside our control; our bodies responding to the alcohol we're taking in; our organs, for all we know, growing tumorous. The flesh can decide to get sick, to get upset, to make us desire" (qtd. in Gerard). Barker's images are confrontations with the wound that reveals change at the heart of things. This recognition Barker celebrates, paradoxically, because it requires (and also can free) us to re-imagine the world. The flux that is the body is ultimately a source of power.

Barker's drawings therefore portray characters who actively recreate themselves. Barker explains that they are "only just holding onto their coherence" (Burke 52), "exploding out of their condition into something else. Becoming" (Burke 38). We are "programmed socially, economically, emotionally, religiously," but the possibility of "throwing over . . . self-restrictions" taught by "priests, parents, and psychologists" is always present. "Can we not erupt?" he asks rhetorically. "We re-invent ourselves anyway, day-to-day, friend-to-friend, moment-to-moment—it's just that we don't really perceive that" (qtd. in Burke 44).

This concept of the self in flux Barker expressed early in "The Skins of the Fathers" (*Books of Blood* II), which re-dressed H. P. Lovecraft's "The Dunwich Horror" in a radical imagery derived from the fantastic painters. In the "cosmic horror" of Lovecraft's Cthulhu Mythos, the demons are oozy, huge, and malign. Like many of Poe's horrors, they are "unnameable" and refer to a feminine monstrosity. Barker turns Lovecraft's coding wrong side out by making his equally marginal demons the heroes, the "true" fathers of the human species. When the patriarchs of Welcome, Nebraska, first encounter the demons, they see only a procession of apparent celebrants, a "gorgeous array" of shapes, colors, sizes, wearing "headdresses and masks that [totter] well above human height," reeling "like drunkards, loping one moment, leaping the next, squirming, some of them, on the ground" (118–19). But these are not costumes, and the demons have reemerged, after several millennia, the last of their species, to celebrate the birth of their changeling son Aaron. Their "extraordinary anatomies, the dreaming spires of heads, the scales, the skirts" (153) and their empathic language (or is it song?) defy the townspeople's categories for body and gender types. (The denizens of Welcome call them "[d]irty, stinking, faceless fuckers" [155].) The demons dismantle biological norms and the larger natural order. When Aaron blossoms into the "soup of shapes" (154) of his/her truer form, an epic battle between authentic and false fathers and a grand apocalypse of a landslide ensues.

Barker explains that the "representatives of society, who, in most horror films, are figures of order and stability," are in his works "models of moral depravity." The fathers of Welcome are characterized as "fat white fists hot with guns" (147), and Aaron's human father abuses him for being a "sissy." In a reversal that few male writers in any genre would attempt, modern patriarchy is portrayed as a violent moment following a golden prehistory in which women had always existed as a "species to themselves," with the demons. "But they had wanted playmates: and together they had made men. What . . . a cataclysmic miscalculation. Within mere eons . . . the women were made slaves, the demons killed or driven underground" (147). The imagery links women further with the demons, associating them together with life-affirming plenitude, freakish diversity, and the Dionysian or Bakhtinian carnival. In the utopia Barker imagines, both "species" are sexually whole and embody a prehistoric version of pre-Oedipal polymorphous perversity. "Skins of the Fathers": sins, foreskins, forefathers. The demons are all of these. " 'See, them black-eyed sons of bitches don't have no fucking heads,' Eugene was screaming" (151). Their association with foreskins, reinforced by their appearances and their bisexual apparatus, is Barker's reconstruction of Judeo-Christian law in which the foreskin is considered unclean, tainted with the archaic Mother, and is removed from the son's penis. Aaron, the changeling son, looks like an ordinary boy—slender like the rod that prefigures him—until his real nature erupts in a manner that suggests both an erection and a polymorphous blossoming. In the typology of the symbolic, these skins more properly belong to "stinking, faceless mothers," to *This Sex Which Is Not One*, or "male and female in one indistinguishable congress."

Barker has described the natural world as "relentlessly beautiful, relentlessly inventive, relentlessly complex. And [in this respect] it celebrates the marginal in a way that human structure doesn't. . . . The Third Reich is the ultimate non-celebration of the marginal" (qtd. in Gracey-Whitman and Melia 412). "The Skins of the Fathers" displaces the phallic signifier here as part of the program to privilege the marginal as consistent with the variegation and transformation in nature. Although several stories tall, the demons cradle and croon to Aaron telepathically, surrounding him with a womb of sound and sensation. Alternately whimsical, exotic, awe inspiring, grotesque, and charming, "The Skins of the Fathers" is a hymn to diversity, asking readers to think about a world uninscribed by gender, culture, or species, and in which the human is disseminated rather than prefigured. As sands cover the demons and the Welcomers alike, the demons' song lingers over the "text" provided by the remnants of the Law: a head, a torso, a nose, and a mouth emerging from the sand. The story ends with a nod to Lovecraftian "cosmic" horror and awe as from the long perspective we view these "trivial forms," these "[l]ittle dots and commas of human pain" (122).

It is not surprising that Barker was quickly taken up by the adult comic book industry. Epic Comics illustrator McLaurin, who draws the *Hellraiser* and *Nightbreed* series, explains: the *Hellraiser* series is not the kind of horror "you'd expect from an EC comic, where a twist ending bundles up the plot in one bloody package." Unlike King, who deals in "everyday" horror, "Barker is set apart by his ability to create an entirely believable mythological universe, populating it with a menagerie of the monstrous" (Labbe 41).

After *Books of Blood*, *The Damnation Game* (1986), and *The Hellbound Heart* (in *Night Visions* series, No. 3, 1986), Barker moved away from splatter fiction and the iconographic toward the *fantastique*. This mode increasingly emphasizes variegation or creative diversification. Transformation becomes the subversive use of fantasy to re-imagine the self and the world, especially in *Weaveworld*, his "anti-fantasy" or meta-fantasy of 1988.

In emphasizing the social function of transformation and metamorphosis, Barker is in line not only with feminist revisionists but also with "magic realists" Gabriel Garcia Marquez, Jorge Louis Borges, and Italo Calvino. Like these writers, Barker believes that the cultural attitudes toward the flesh, toward difference, and toward other species need to change. Like them he celebrates the marginal.

Barker's Bakhtinian vision is overtly presented in his 1989 film *Nightbreed*, based on his novella *Cabal* (1988). In its world, as described by Maitland McDonagh, "every day is a carnival . . . real carnival, a no-holds-barred celebration of the grotesque and the inverse" (60). *Nightbreed* is not a successful film. It is a nearly incoherent film unless it is viewed in part as meta-film, "read against" horror conventions. The videotape, however, begins with a helpful prologue. Barker is shown sitting dressed in black on a dark sound stage and surrounded by the masks of the *Nightbreed* monsters. The faces, including Barker's, are bathed in an eerie glow. "I've always loved monsters," he announces. "A dark corner in all of us . . . envies their powers, . . . would love to . . . fly, or change shape at will." Monsters are our transgressive desires. Therefore Barker has created Midian, an underground city "peopled with creatures of our darkest fantasies" and where, consequently, "we can feel strangely at home." He invites "you" to join in "flipping all the conventions of the horror movies, plunging you to a world of insanity and miracles, where dead men can be heroes, monsters beautiful, and the only place of refuge is the most forbidding place on earth."

Like *Hellraiser*, *Nightbreed* undermines the categorical thinking behind concepts like *sadism*, *masochism*, and *necrophilia*, and "embraces the monstrous," but by means of plotting, characterization, and conventions more properly associated with the *fantastique*. Midian is threatened by the forces of order represented in Eigermann the fascist sheriff, Ashbery the masochistic priest, Decker the sadistic psychoanalyst, and even the hero-enlightener Aaron Boone. The film begins with the twist that would have provided the clincher for the conventional horror movie, one that foregrounds the character of Decker and his cohorts. Dr. Decker has convinced Boone, his patient and scapegoat, that he is a serial murderer, having programmed Boone with his own psychopathic memories. Decker is a type, Barker's satire on psychologists as terrorists of the imagination, so that his hollowness as a character, his lack of authenticity, history, or motivation, is the point. He is also characterized externally through casting and visual metaphor. In the crucial role is horror film director David Cronenberg, directly imported from the fantastic clinicism of *Dead Ringers* (1989).

Performed with the chilly detachment of one of Cronenberg's doctors, Cronenberg-as-Decker also represents *Dead Ringers*'s theme of "male horror and envy of female reproductive process" (Showalter 242), symbolized in "the breed" and their unruly proliferation of the fantastic. Cronenberg's presence at the extra-diagetic level interacts with the visual metaphor of Decker's alter ego, "The Mask" (as Decker addresses it in the novella), under whose authority he acts as a grim reaper. The Mask links Decker the psychologist unsettlingly with the icon for the teenage slasher movie, Jason's hockey mask. Decker's Mask is the cloth face of a sewing-box doll—"zipper for mouth, buttons for eyes, all sewn on white linen and tied around" With "the teeth . . . gleaming knives, their blades fine as grass blades" (Cabal 88). With these he accomplishes his mission of "sewing/sowing" culture. The construction of reality means the death of imagination, as represented in Barker's Carnival of shape shifters, freaks, and dark dreamers—the "children of the Moon."

As a visual metaphor, and as a sign of genre, Decker's mask presents the antithesis to the protagonists, who are fantasy images, grotesques inspired by Goya and Bosch. In an interview with Nigel Floyd, Barker explains that the film contains a "generic collision" between the world "of the fabulist and the world of iconographic images" and representing the larger one between the world of Midian and the world of Law. The latter is represented iconographically by Cronenberg/as Decker/as psychologist/as slasher/as mask and is equated with the modern horror movie at its most conventional. Decker is a "reductionist, cold-hearted and soulless thing" (Floyd, "Frights" 345). Decker portrays the modern horror tradition as being "about throwing the monster out, about the rejection of the marginal" says Barker. Within his metaphorical worlds, however, "it's not possible to throw the monster out and assume that one's house has been purged . . . because the monster is part of our internal workings" (Floyd, "Clive Barker: Hellraiser" 312).

In the *Nightbreed* characters, the grotesque is a sign of Dionysian energy, to Barker the equivalent of soul. More specifically, the grotesque represents the self with potential for transformation. The Nightbreed are, as opposed to any one image or type, shape shifters. The visual metaphor of the mask gives the concept of transformation psychological and physiological force. Narcisse, the protagonist's sidekick, is an icon of the "authentic" man-without-a-face. In the beginning, as one of Decker's patients, he is a madman tormented by dreams of utopia (Midian). As a way of seeking admission to the city of his dreams, Narcisse suicidally strips the skin from half of his face, rendering it a mask, thus transforming himself into a dualism and a paradox, a freak "worthy" of such a utopia. Like R. D. Laing and Michel Foucault, Barker sees madness as the name given to those whose vision might subvert the symbolic order. In contrast to Narcisse and thus portraying a different kind of madness, the hero Aaron Boone erupts, smoke pouring from all orifices, and transforms his human face (or public mask) into the powerfully beastlike Cabal, the savior-priest who is also Midian's "undoing." It is through the same deconstructive logic that Boone can fulfill his destiny only by dying and becoming a "beast," by losing his heroic name (to the signification "Cabal," from *cabala* and signifying magic) and by becoming Midian's unmaking. By causing the destruction of this refuge for Otherness, and however unwittingly, Boone forces Carnival back into the world where it can remain vitally subversive.

As Lisa Tuttle points out, *Cabal/Nightbreed* is *Weaveworld*, which she reads as a classic, "even archetypal, fantasy," in reverse. By "archetypal fantasy" she means

the longed-for Other Place. . . . This longing—desire—is the engine which drives fantasy, just as in the horror story the engine is fear. But that desire and fear might be inextricably linked is something not usually commented on or explored by writers in either genre. . . .

Perhaps now . . . artists are interested in exploring the nexus of fear and desire. (216)

The shape-shifting Children of the Moon, together with Baphomet, their "god and goddess in one body" (*Cabal* 207), embody that nexus. They represent the possibility inherent in unconstructed—quilled, tentacled, multi-textured, and rainbow-colored—life. In the novella, confronted with the "true Midian" for the first time, the heroine Lori feels a mixture of horror and fascination:

Was it simply disgust that made her stomach flip, seeing the stigmatic in full flood, with sharp-toothed adherents sucking noisily at her wounds? Or excitement, confronting the legend of the vampire in the flesh? And what was she to make of the man whose body broke into birds when he saw her watching? Or the dog-headed painter who turned from his fresco and beckoned her to join his apprentice mixing paint? (*Cabal* 112–13)

The Nightbreed are Jungian masks or faces of the unconstructed self, grotesques, and they stand for Barker's concept of transformation. "You call us monsters but when you dream you dream of flying, changing," one of the Children of the Moon explains to Lori. They also incarnate the modern view of life and death as relative conditions: some are predators (while others are not); some are alive and some are technically dead but "living" in the liminal state that Midian's underground space, otherwise signified as carnival, represents. Allusions to the classic film statements on carnival, to Tod Browning's *Freaks* and *Fellini Satyricon*, abound. Barker has explained the film as a hymn to variegation and in the *fantastique* tradition, including the paintings of Bosch, Goya, Blake, and Fuseli. The "generation of fresh imagery" is its purpose (Barker, qtd. in Floyd, "Frights" 343).

In Clive Barker's films, as in his fiction, the imagery of violence and the experience of pain are aspects of his metaphorics of transformation. Like Mapplethorpe's photography or Wittig's writing, his texts do violence to the body, opening it into a text, in order to shift the emphasis we call gender and articulate difference. Stephen King has said that horror "arises from a pervasive sense of disestablishment, that things are in the unmaking" (Introd. 22). But when Barker's anti-horror fantasy unmakes the world, he does so in part to open spaces, to appeal to the reader's or viewer's desire to recreate the world. People should "leave the moviehouse or put down the book knowing that they can begin to reinvent this," he says, tapping an empirical table, "and our relationship to this," he empha-sized recently. "Works of the imagination are finally tools for change" (Strauss, "New King" 94).

Chapter 5

Transfigured Vampires: Anne Rice

NO EXIT: *INTERVIEW WITH THE VAMPIRE*

"When I grow up I want to be a vampire," began twelve-year-old Jules, reading his composition entitled "My Ambition" in front of the seventh-grade class. This was 1951, in a story by Richard Matheson ("Drink My Blood" 214), and Jules's teacher and classmates were suitably shocked. By the barbaric 1980s, nurtured on Pac Man, Dungeons and Dragons, *The Terminator*, and Gothic rock, Jules's career goal no longer seemed un-usual. Characteristics that had once made the vampire supernatural and Evil incarnate now meant a superhero, a survivor, or the merely human. In the 1990s, with the wolf and wild woman, the vampire was revealed as Western culture's Shadow (in Tim Burton's darkly brooding *Batman*) or a sensitive New Age guy (especially in Coppola's new *Dracula*). While the vampire's physical enhancements have obvious appeals to a culture based in the body, the inversions of the Christian sacraments merely reminded us of the values we really live by. They are the body's: predation and symbiosis, blood or life consumed and given, biological immunity as a state of grace.

The modern sympathetic vampire emerged in the late 1960s with *Dark Shadows*' Barnabas Collins, soap opera hero and reluctant bloodsucker. The novelization initiated a series of Gothic romances by Marilyn (a.k.a. Dan) Ross. Then, around 1972, came the "discovery" of the historical Dracula by Raymond McNally and Radu Florescu, documented in their *In Search of Dracula*. McNally and Florescu traced the monster back to the fifteenth-century (1431–1476) Wallachian prince Vlad Dracul, known as Vlad Tepes ("the impaler"), named for his method of maintaining national order. These biographers offered Vlad up to "higher" criticism, presenting an enigma: was he a bloodthirsty monster or a great Machiavellian politician, the savior of his country? It didn't matter. By 1976, Romania had begun honoring him with a postage stamp ("Count Dracula"). Dracula was now approachable as a man—if a man of "immense capability, power, and violence" (Mascotti 114).[1]

Florescu and McNally also traced the legends surrounding Elizabeth of Bathory, a sixteenth-century (1560–1610) Hungarian Countess who tortured, cannibalized, and bathed in the blood of servant girls, which she believed rejuvenated her (McNally and Florescu 148–55). Bathory's story provided the key elements in the myth: membership in the predatory lower aristocracy, the bite, the use of blood to recover longer life, erotic pleasure, androgyny, and bisexuality or homosexuality.

Barnabas, the historicized Dracula, and the Countess emerged with the trend toward psychological horror started by *Psycho* (1960) and Norman Bates, the monster as the Terrible Mother's Boy. Psychological horror merged with the "nonfiction novel" to create the crime documentary from the killer's perspective. Truman Capote's *In Cold Blood* (1965) and Vincent Bugliosi's *Helter Skelter* (1974) were ancestors of today's serial killer testimonials. Various chronicles and "higher criticisms" of the relevant texts found sympathy with the Devil. Ink flowed more copiously than blood, and writers bent to the task of compiling, editing, and ghostwriting the documents, papers, tapes, and memoirs—from Raymond Rudorff's *The Dracula Archives* (1972), to Peter Tremayne's *Bloodright* (1980), to Chelsea Quinn Yarbro's Saint-Germain chronicles.

In Fred Saberhagen's *The Dracula Tape* (1975), the Count recounts and rebuts, scene-by-scene, the arguments of Stoker and the envious Van Helsing, who framed him for Lucy Westenra's murder (the result of the Professor's unmatched blood transfusions). He is the vampire as modern scientific rationalist and hero. The new vampire is undaunted by the vampire hunter's paraphernalia. "That is, how would you say today . . . bullshit?" (22). So Anne Rice's vampire Louis puts the matter in 1976 in what is now the modern vampire classic *Interview with the Vampire*. Louis is not harmed by crucifixes but keeps them around him as piquant reminders of an age of faith.

Louis was the first fully realized specimen of this new breed.[2] But Rice's revision of Stoker, her first published novel, was also an anguished confession and cover for Rice's own self-analysis. The dramatic situation, an interview conducted by a boy reporter, was seductive, and the novel became an immediate best seller. "I would like to tell you the story of my life," Louis began.

"Why did everything work for me when I introduced a character who is a vampire?" Rice asked herself in 1993. "Why did I suddenly start to be able to write about everything I felt?" (Diehl 61). The answers keep coming, in a recent biography and guide (to what are now *The Vampire Chronicles*, 4 volumes), in numerous radio and television appearances (ABC's *Day One*, A&E's *Ancient Mysteries* in 1993), interviews (*Playboy* [March 1993] and *Esquire* [March 1994]), and a video biography titled *Birth of the Vampire: A Biography of Anne Rice* (1994). The vampire Louis provided a mask for articulating the complex experience of growing up in New Orleans and the deaths of her mother (from alcoholism) and five-year-old daughter, Rice told Katherine Ramsland. As Louis, she was able "to touch painful realities. Through Louis's eyes, everything became accessible" (Ramsland, *Companion* 196).

The story of the writing of *Interview with the Vampire* has itself become the core of the myth of Anne Rice. Essential for serious readers is Rice's authorized biographer and chronicler, Katherine Ramsland, Ph.D. (philosophy), author of *Prism of the Night: A Biography of Anne Rice* (1991) and *The Vampire Companion: The Official Guide to Anne Rice's The Vampire Chronicles* (1993). Ramsland's biography is a "[r]evelatory, intimate . . . unusual" tale "as entertaining and unsettling as Rice's own fiction," reports *The Atlanta Journal and Constitution* and *The San Francisco Chronicle* (quoted on the front and back covers). She accounts for Rice's first novel through a patient interweaving of documents with analysis and extensive, revealing interviews with Rice and her family members.

Growing up in a large Irish Catholic family in "the only Catholic city in the United States," Rice was indoctrinated in original sin as the evil born of flesh and blood. She remembers the spiritual exercises of Saint Ignatius as lessons in masochistic body language. They encouraged her to identify with Christ "as they drove the nails through his hands" and provided "an approach to imagination that was entirely natural to me" (qtd. in Diehl 60). When she went to college in Texas in 1959, Rice suddenly found herself in "the modern world." "I ha[d] to know what's out there," she said. "I ha[d] to read Walter Kaufmann's books on existentialism. I ha[d] to see who Jean Paul Sartre [wa]s. But I wasn't supposed to read all this. It was a mortal sin. . . . That's when I broke with the church. It was astonishing" (Rice, qtd. in Diehl 61). A slow but "active" reader, Rice absorbed excerpts from Nietzsche, Kierkegaard, and Camus and styled herself as a Sartrean:

"I'd put on long black gloves, smoke Camel cigarettes and read Sartre. It felt terrific" (qtd. in Ramsland, *Prism* 69).

Existentialism provided a new myth, one that incorporated her experience of Catholicism, while its intrinsic theatricalism invested her with characters, masks, and pseudonyms. In the same way it inspired *Interview with the Vampire*.[3] Louis finds himself "made" a vampire with the same absurd abruptness as we all, according to Sartre, find ourselves "condemned" to life, freedom, and choice. Thus it is only as a vampire that Louis becomes fully alive and fully human: "I never knew what life was until it ran out in a red gush over my lips, my hands!" (*Interview* 82). Like Camus's anti-hero Mersault (in *The Stranger*), who is made aware of life's excruciating sweetness by his own death sentence (for killing another man), the doomed vampire throws into relief the absurd aspects of the embodied human condition.

Historically, Louis is a Romantic (born in 1791) who comes to vampiric maturity as an anguished late Victorian and mellows into an aesthete. (Rice first imagined him as a type of Oscar Wilde.) He represents the nineteenth-century's "broken heart." Louis's mentor Armand explains: "Your fall from grace and faith has been the fall of a century" (*Interview* 288). Yet Louis spoke equally for the human predicament in the last quarter of the twentieth century. No wonder that, in early 1994, as we recycled the 1970s and recapitulated the panic of the 1890s, *Interview With the Vampire* returned to the *New York Times* best-seller list for twenty-three-weeks.

As a Victorian and Modernist clinging to remnants of outmoded moral schemes, Louis is a failure in development, a nostalgic who longs to return to a childhood he imagines as innocent. As an adult (a vampire), he cannot come to terms with the body. The vampire is simultaneously "predator and victim of his own nature," as Jewelle Gomez explains. Condemned to a life of "constant craving," s/he "hungers for blood, hungers to be accepted into mortal society, hungers for the object of . . . passion."

In his craving for lost innocence, Louis becomes a self-flagellating masochist and pederast. When he finds a five-year-old waif crying beside the plague-infested body of her mother, he rationalizes that he should put the child out of her misery. But Lestat, hoping to keep Louis with him, makes her into a vampire (Claudia), and the purity and intensity of the child's hunger makes her the voracious, efficient killer Louis can never be. In contrast to the thoroughly adapted Lestat (who relishes the poignancy of "taking" young men in the prime of life), Louis remains a victim of the subject-object problem. Like Sartre's Roquentin or Kafka's artist-anorexic

("The Hunger Artist"), he is alienated from his physical processes and subsists, for a time, on rats' blood.

Sartrean existentialism begins in a similar alienation, or nausea, as the title of Sartre's novel *La Nausée* (1938) and an essay ("'Aminadab': Or the Fantastic Considered as a Language") explained. By the fantastic, he meant existence perceived in its true absurdity "in which things manifest a captive, tormented thought" that never manages to "express itself" purely:

> matter is never entirely matter, since it offers only a constantly frustrated attempt at determinism, and mind is never completely mind, because it has fallen into slavery and has been impregnated and dulled by matter. All is woe. Things suffer and tend toward inertia, without ever attaining it; the debased, enslaved mind unsuccessfully strives towards consciousness and freedom. (58)

Louis's nausea eventually refers through and beyond Sartre to our contemporary plague of eating and drinking disorders. He recalls the infant's pleasure in sucking, of body and mind fused and focused on "one vital source" (*Interview* 19). The back cover of Suzy McKee Charnas's *The Vampire Tapestry* (1980) sums up the predicament in this plaint: "no matter how modern his disguise, the vampire must still drink, and drink, and drink again." The vampire becomes, among other things, the yuppie, addict, and conscience-stricken consumer.

For Rice, *Interview* also reenacted at least two traumas: the death of her mother, of alcoholism, when Rice was fifteen, and the death of her five-year-old daughter Michele, of leukemia. If Louis represented her own disillusionment, desire, and confrontation with mortality, the book was a resurrection. It brought her daughter back to life, creating what Madeleine calls a "child who can't die" (*Interview* 268). Writing *Interview* was storytelling as therapy. Its audience included Rice herself or aspects of her "divided self." Writing was also an addiction. "[P]regnant" with the novel, Anne drank, wrote, and screamed, wrote her husband Stan in a poem: "Ten twelve fifteen beers, never enough" (qtd. in Ramsland, *Prism* 132–33). A vampire's "high," Rice explained later to Ramsland, is like a "drunken swoon. . . . It's like the golden moment of drinking when everything makes sense" (*Prism* 64).

The other side of her thirst was anorexia. In the weeks after Michele's death, it was difficult for Rice "to swallow food." She felt "a disgust for everything physical" and kept "thinking of her in the cemetery" (Diehl

64). Louis's disgust for the physical begins in guilt, grief, and nausea at the death of his brother, for which he feels indirect responsibility. He imagines his body "rotting in the coffin, and [cannot] bear it" (*Interview* 10).

Rice's nausea, like that of Sartre's Roquentin, was "cured" in the act of writing. In her novel, Claudia refuses her role as a child and attempts to kill Lestat, her vampire father. For Louis this means the death of God. He stumbles into a New Orleans cathedral and confesses to an incredulous priest, asking "Why, if God exists, does he suffer me to live?" (*Interview* 148). When he is answered only by the "lifeless profiles" and "frozen folds" of the statuary, he kills the priest as the sign of his recognition, with Nietzsche, the Victorian Aesthetes, and the Modernists, that these icons "gave an image to nothingness" (*Interview* 145). Like Roquentin, Louis sees into the nonsentient "thingness" of formerly spirit-filled objects and realizes that he is the only "supermortal" being in the place. In another vision of existential revolt, he ascends the altar steps and, seeing the Body of Christ, crumbles the wafers on the carpet, "giving Holy Communion to the dust." Through the ruins, Louis sees his destiny in a "waste land in all directions" and a procession of pale people dressed in black (*Interview* 145).

Rice has explained that her first novels "are concerned with the question of brotherhood" (Hebb 400), and Louis and Claudia are murderers of their vampire brother Lestat, who is also, perversely, their father and murderer. Together Lestat, Louis, and Claudia compose a parody of the nuclear family. Says Rice on this matter, "I am obsessed by the question of how we live [together] in our day and age when the faith in authority symbols is lost" (Hebb 400). The Modernist metaphor of the "heap of broken images" stood also for social and personality structures that included the bourgeois family and the ego. The novel becomes a journey initiated by Claudia, a quest for other vampires and, really, for themselves.

This leads them first to Eastern Europe, where they encounter the vampires of folklore, mindless revenants, themselves corpses in advanced stages of decomposition which, refusing to die, continue to feed on the living. Second, they go to *fin de siècle* Paris where they find a highly developed vampire "coven" at the Théâtre des Vampires, whose decadent culture Armand describes as a "fatuous . . . parody of the miraculous" (*Interview* 289). The two extremes are equally dehumanizing poles of consciousness and embodiment. As Donald Lawler explains, Rice's vampires are "a species torn between unacceptable life options": they are either "haunted" and tortured by the remnants of their humanity or become "so thoroughly vampirish" as to "lose the will to live altogether" (778).[4]

Joining the coven for lack of other options, Louis and Claudia learn of the monsters they will eventually become. Vampires get stronger with age and can become dormant indefinitely until stimulated into new life, but they can and do die, most often from ennui. The four-hundred-year-old elder Armand, whose boyish looks (like Dorian Gray's) belie his cynicism, claims that the average vampire burns out within three hundred years: he realizes one evening that whatever attracted him to immortality has disappeared, and that the act of killing is the only respite from despair. "And that vampire goes out [in the sun] to die" (*Interview* 285).

Louis concludes with Camus that if God doesn't exist, we alone understand the brevity and value of life and that Evil is "the taking of a single human life" (*Interview* 238). Death is the enemy. But the vampire *is* Death—death subsisting on human life, God, father, brother, murderer, a figure of Cain, Faust, and Hamlet. We are condemned to predation and alienation. Hell is Other people who are alternately and paradoxically our reason for being—the context in which we find our meaning and purpose—and our food.

Rice's *Vampire Chronicles* (as she came to call them) reflected a predatory consumer culture, one seduced by idealizations of youth yet exhausted by future shock. The vampire now referred to the allure and anguish of life without meaning or closure: no exit. The book expressed existential nausea with a difference. In a world where medical technology had alienated us from meaningful death by a philosophy of prevention, by making physical immortality the object of life, nausea was the reaction to the possibility of an undying sensational existence, an indefinitely protracted living death.

But that world was changing. With the coming crisis over AIDS, the gay rights movement, feminism, and Rice's own success, even the "new" vampire had to adapt or be destroyed.

TWILIGHT OF THE GODS: *THE VAMPIRE LESTAT* (1985)

By 1985, when she published *The Vampire Lestat*, the second of *The Vampire Chronicles*, Anne Rice herself had the near-mythic status of the cult author. She had given birth to the "new" vampire and a flourishing subgenre. Mainstream and literary writers such as George R. Martin, Tanith Lee, Angela Carter, Whitley Strieber, and Joyce Carol Oates discovered vampirism as a metaphor. Anthologies of vampire stories multiplied, acquired class, and were soon being circulated by the major book clubs. In Alan Ryan's *Vampires* (1987), *Blood is Not Enough* (1989), and *A Whisper of Blood* (1991), sophisticated boundary-extending stories edited by Ellen Datlow, in the novels of Nancy Collins, Dan Simmons, and Poppy Z. Brite, vampirism became the dominant metaphor for ways we live now: the ambivalence of intimate relations and dangerous sex, gender and power politics, the compulsion to consume, the struggle to survive, X-generation angst and alienation.

At the same time, with the exception perhaps of George Romero's *Martin* (1977), a disturbing case study of an adolescent who thinks he is a vampire, the vampire film remained relatively convention bound. The most notable difference was its mainstreaming from grade B to a slick B plus or A minus, from Hammer Studios to Hollywood, in movies starring increasingly beautiful people: from "sophisticates" like George Hamilton, David Niven, and Louis Jourdan, to pretty-faced Frank Langella (and the craggy-faced but famous Jack Palance) to androgynous rock star David Bowie and the fashion models Catherine Deneuve, Lauren Hutton, and Grace Jones. The film adaptation of *Interview With the Vampire* (1994), directed by Neil Jordan (fresh from *The Crying Game* [1992]), would cap this trend with its bevy of Hollywood hunks: with Tom Cruise as Lestat, Brad Pitt as Louis, Antonio Banderas as Armand, and Christian Slater as the reporter.

With Langella's *Dracula* (1979), the vampire became a softly seductive, androgynous anti-hero who offered his bride, a New Woman, a preferable alternative to the Victorian era. This new Dracula, together with surrealistic fantasy sequences in red, with lush, throbbing orchestration, would have been unthinkable before Rice. Rice had an even greater impact on the other side. According to *Esquire*'s Jennet Conant, Coppola's superstar-studded remake of 1992 was so influenced by Rice that it transformed Stoker's "bloodsucker into a lonely monster, as much in search of redemption as of revenge" (72).

Gary Oldman, like Klaus Kinski, was a passionate actor who played the vampire as a tortured Romantic. Kinski's Dracula (in Werner Herzog's 1979 *Nosferatu*) was entrapped in bestiality. He spoke to Lucy as a pathetically disembodied head, while "play[ing] against his appendages— his long claws, his pointed fangs." "My vampire," commented Herzog, is "so suffering, so human, so sad, so desperately longing for love that you don't see [his fangs] any more" (qtd. in Blume). Oldman's Dracula descended from Cocteau's *Beauty and the Beast* (by way of the 1980s TV series and the animated feature of 1991) and Neil Jordan's classy adaptation of Angela Carter's revisionist fairy tale *The Company of Wolves*.

In Whitley Strieber's *The Hunger* (1982), adapted to film by Tony Scott (1983), the vampire represented the pathos of aging, complicated by the impossibility (under modern medical technology) of death as simple closure. The mates of the powerful Queen vampire Miriam do not die, but after two hundred years begin to decompose, living on in a state of Tithonus-like decrepitude and finally laid to a hideous eternal unrest. In one scene, the current consort, John Blaylock (David Bowie), seeking a cure and sitting in a gerontologist's waiting room, ages two hundred years, into a pathetic, stumbling shell too weak to kill. Like Rice's Louis, weakened by his guilt and revulsion, Blaylock resorts to feeding on a twelve-year old girl who has come to Miriam's Manhattan East Side apartment for a music lesson. In post-Rice films, vampires experienced pain, nausea, and remorse, and stasis, and the reluctant vampire's initiation, subsequent conflict, and alienation was the emotional center of several films—in Joel Schumacher's *The Lost Boys* (1987), Katherine Bigelow's *Near Dark* (1987), Jimmy Huston's *My Best Friend Is a Vampire* (1988), the (new) *Dark Shadows* television series (1990–91), *Bloodstone: Subspecies 2* (1992), John Landis's *Innocent Blood* (1992), and *Bram Stoker's Dracula* (1992).

Vampire films, while continuing to be geared to a teenage audience, took up increasingly adult issues. The vampire became a metaphor for dangerous sex, sexual responsibility or irresponsibility, homosexuality, and the power of the horror medium itself. In *Fright Night* (1985), *The Lost Boys*, and *Near Dark* vampires were products and causes of dysfunctional families, and vampire gangs (drug using "alternative families") stole teenagers and children away from their parents. While vampires were projections of AIDS panic and homophobia on one level, the horror classics—*Bram Stoker's Dracula*, for instance—became sacred texts. In the quasi-metafictional *Fright Night* and *Fright Night 2*, Schlock Theatre host Roddy McDowell (imitating Vincent Price) was the modern Van Helsing as mentor to teenage protagonists, and late-night television is the source of enlightenment. The vampire hunter and the vampire increasingly shared characteristics. The blurring of distinctions between roles admitted, however obliquely, that they were masks or aspects of a modern divided self. In Tim Burton's *Batman* (1989) and *Batman Returns* (1991), the protagonist's dark, brooding rage and alienation are barely sublimated in his role of crime fighter, as his bat suit, a visual metaphor, visibly suggests. This vampire protagonist as resistance movement or political subversive began appearing as early as a 1985 episode of *Twilight Zone* called "Red Snow." Siberian peasants, the descendants of a vampire race, formed an underground resistance against the "truer" bloodsucker, the State.

In *The Rocky Horror Picture Show* (1978), many of these themes had converged as Tim Curry, Susan Sarandon, Meat Loaf and company vamped and sang their way through their metafictional "rocky horror science fiction picture show." Now S. P. Somtow's *Vampire Junction* (1984) and John Skipp and Craig Spector's *The Light at the End* (1986) asserted more or less directly that the world of heavy metal was intrinsically vampiric. Collaborations between film and rock music featured the connection. *The Hunger*, starring rock star David Bowie, opened as Gothic rock group Bauhaus chanted "Bela Lugosi's Dead," with a quick cut to a rhesus monkey attacking and consuming its mate. *The Rocky Horror Picture Show* and Michael Jackson's *Thriller* had set precedents taken up by Prince, Ozzie Ozborne, and Alice Cooper, in which rock performance was trans-sexual vamping, "monstrous" performance, and incantation. Acting, spectacle, psychodrama, and savage rite became indistinguishable. Ozzie Osborne bit the heads off bats on-stage, Alice Cooper welcomed the audience to his nightmare and sang of dead babies, staging songs as Caligariesque horror movies. Monsters, especially vampires, had become required mascots or totems for heavy metal groups that simultaneously protested and gloried in the savage lifestyle of the 1980s. Media-produced body images derived from rock culture reflected and demanded a lifestyle of aggressive consumption.

When the rock stars of the 1970s grew middle aged in the 1980s, they continued to resemble vampires. Instead of settling into lines of "character," their faces smoothed into glossy photogenic surfaces. Cher's face suddenly bloomed luscious red lips. In Neverland, the ranch where he invited children, Michael Jackson grew pale, thin-lipped, and hollow-cheeked.

At the fringes of the rock subculture of the early 1980s were groups of practicing vampires or "Gothics," devoted to a pantheistic-Druidic worship that included drinking the blood of "soul mates" (Skal 342). Beyond the mainstream, Rice became priestess of a cult following that appealed to lapsed Catholics, sadomasochists, gays and lesbians, and women.

But from the late 1970s through the early 1980s, as the world turned more overtly vampiric, Rice had turned to writing historical novels that gave her a sense of documenting the struggles of unvoiced people, outsiders beyond ethnicity or gender, freaks of culture rather than nature. *The Feast of All Saints* focuses on the experiences of the some 18,000 *gens de couloeur libre*, blacks who lived as free people in New Orleans before the American Civil War and were pulled in different directions by lines of race, class, and culture. *Cry to Heaven* (1982), set in eighteenth-century Venice, portrays the experience of the Italian castrati, boys who were castrated to preserve their soprano voices and who made careers as well of their polymorphic perversity. Tonio, the protagonist, is both trapped in and liberated by his body.

Writing for Rice became a matter of role playing—of finding a character and a voice for unspoken aspects of herself. In 1982, as feminists demonstrated against pornography's violation of women's civil rights, Rice wrote sadomasochistic pornography almost defiantly, proclaiming it "for women"—if under the pseudonyms of A. N. Roquelaure (*The Claiming of Sleeping Beauty*, 1983; *Beauty's Punishment*, 1984; *Beauty's Release*, 1985) and Anne Rampling (*Exit to Eden*, 1985; *Belinda*, 1987). As Roquelaure, she began revising the fairy tale in the discourse of the body. Rewriting gendered cultural myths as sadomasochistic fantasies allowed her to explore liminal areas of experience that could not be articulated in conventional literature, extant pornography, or politically correct discourse. Finding contemporary "California" voices (as she called them) for another novel, *Exit to Eden*, one female (Lisa) and one male (Elliot), she explored alternating male and female perspectives, voicing what she has called her "animus" over her "feminine" side (Ramsland, *Prism* 234). Like the erotic scenes in *Interview*, the pornography emphasized what was perhaps now the ultimate taboo for women, masochism. Tactile rather than visual, celebrating "tenderness and cruelty" (subtitle), her work appealed to gay and lesbian sadomasochists as well as heterosexuals. When her friends and neighbors began dying of AIDS, however, Rice abandoned erotica and gave her books away to use as fund-raisers (Ramsland, *Prism* 243). When she returned to the sequel to *Interview*, *The Vampire Lestat*, she called it the second of what would be *The Vampire Chronicles*. And she revised Lestat, who had been shadowy in *Interview*, into a new protagonist, one who would appeal to all her audiences.

The negative Eros that informed Louis's masochism and narcissism shifted poles and went in 1985 into the "positive" character of Lestat, an eighteenth-century vampire with an open, postmodern sensibility and text, an "intimate, warm-blooded man" (qtd. in Ramsland, *Prism* 245). Lestat's conversion begins not in a loss of faith (Lestat has none) or the deaths of parents (his father is blind and his mother unconventional) but in an immediate, visceral confrontation with his own mortality: "We'll just be gone, dead, dead, dead without ever knowing! . . . 'Oh,' I said. . . . 'Oh!' and then I said it louder and louder. . . . 'Oh, oh, oh!' . . . like a great hiccuping that I couldn't stop" (*Vampire Lestat* 55–56).

Lestat's reaction, provoked by his wholehearted love of life in all its guises, is like that of Camus's hero Sisyphus, who hopes to defy the gods and live forever. "One must," Camus tells us, "imagine Sisyphus happy" (*Myth* 91) even as he pushes his rock. *Interview* is a relic of the Waste Land; Lestat's tales within tales are eclectic, extroverted, forward looking.

Rice's style, lush and decadent in *Interview*, changed to accommodate her burgeoning characters and her expanding cosmos.

Louis's voice had been literary, Wildean, self-consciously freighted with his decadent past. *Interview* had the quality of a period piece and, like the twenty-five-year-old body of its narrator, seemed frozen in time. While Louis's quest is linear and dead ended, Lestat leaps between prehistory to the barbaric, postliterate present of the San Francisco Cow Palace. The contemporary vernacular "California" voice of *Exit to Eden*'s Elliot, chastened and "feminized" by Lisa, became Lestat's. Rice attempted to write "a novel that sounds spoken," she explained, "with the kind of freedom of a narrator who just steps in at any moment and talks about his characters" (qtd. in Ramsland, *Prism* 225). Lestat admits talking like "a cross between a flatboatman and . . . Sam Spade" and hopes readers will understand when he occasionally blows the eighteenth-century atmosphere "to smithereens" (*Vampire Lestat* 4). In *Interview*, Louis "confessed" in violation of every rule for vampires; Lestat goes on to challenge not only the authority of that text but of text itself.

In short, Lestat was the vampire for a world in which distinctions between history and reality have collapsed. It is the cultural phenomenon that brings him to life. Awakened by reverberations from a heavy metal band called Satan's Night Out, Lestat introduces himself to the group and is greeted with their scornful laughter. Someone throws him a copy of *Interview With the Vampire*, and he becomes attuned to the power of the media. Soon he is a rock star. There is "something vampiric" about rock music, he notes; it must have sounded "supernatural" even to unbelievers (*Vampire Lestat* 6). Conversely "You can imagine a vampire becoming a rock star with everyone just totally accepting it. They can get on the stage and do anything they want, and everyone would think it was just special effects," Rice explained in a 1985 National Public Radio interview.

Lestat becomes "realized" in the self-referential, multi-media phenomenon The Vampire Lestat, the name he gives to a series of records, music, video clips, an autobiography, and a network of bars called The Vampire Connection. Each Vampire Chronicle provokes another, and as context interacts with text to provoke a sequel, the "vampire network" is created and the text proclaims itself prophecy. *The Vampire Lestat* becomes inseparable from the cult phenomenon that it refers back to and completes, and is equated finally with the reader's experience of it. *The Vampire Lestat* thus pretends to postmodern performance art, a collection of narratives, each a revision of the vampire myth, and radical intertextual exchange. The currently thriving Gothic subculture, including a group called Lestat, is evidence of the efficacy of this phenomenon.

Lestat emerges from the ashes of the old vampire's mythic identity, adopting the "beguilingly androgynous," "barbaric and cerebral" style of the late twentieth century (6). Rice was tired of writing about people searching for themselves and made Lestat a character who "already *was* something, with more humor, less darkness," one who had never had a mentor and never complained of the lack (Ramsland, *Prism* 246). Louis is a divided self who fights his vampire nature and wants to be "good"; Lestat focuses his energies on becoming a good vampire. He embodies Nietzschean innocence (the absence of illusions), the will to power, and transvaluation. A natural performer who stages happenings and forges new roles for himself, he is a rule breaker. In Part I, he tells how he was born the earnest, adventurous third son of an eighteenth-century Marquis and ran away with a theatre troupe to become an actor. He is noticed by Magnus, who makes him a vampire (against his will) and abandons him to become his successor. In Part III, Lestat makes his dying mother Gabrielle a vampire. In Part IV, he encounters the coven at Les Innocents, where the vampires cower ghoulishly in their inversion of Judeo-Christian faith, declaring themselves condemned to serve Satan and shunning life, the Church, and all holy icons with pious religiosity. Lestat takes on the role of their Zarathustra, liberating them from what Marius would call the "dark and evil systems of thought" within themselves (381).

Whereas Louis's quest was for absolutes—innocence, God, or damnation—Lestat undertakes his to recover the roots of the vampire myth in the mythmaking process itself, as exemplified in the dialogue of his tales within tales. Armand, the leader of the coven vampires, tells Lestat in Part V of his creation by Marius, a Roman who informs him of vampires' Egyptian ancestry and introduces him to Akasha and Enkil (VII), the parents of the vampire species, now in a state of suspended animation. Marius then tells Lestat his own story of encountering the ancient Druid priest-god Mael.

Lestat's quest articulated a cultural need for self-creative myth making. Continuing the search for Dracula, and like many of her readers in the 1970s and early 1980s, Rice rediscovered James Frazer's *The Golden Bough* through Joseph Campbell's applications of Frazer and Carl Jung to myth. She had Lestat similarly recover the vampire's origins in the pre-Christian vegetation gods and Goddess worship; her vampires essentially perform a Druidic-Egyptian fertility ritual. Rice inverted the Christian tradition, discovered in the saints the remnants of an older polytheism, and found the figure of the dying and reviving priest-god in stories of the devouring Mother goddess, collapsing the god and goddess in one figure. She restored and validated Eros, polytheism, substance, the primary knowledge of the senses, and an aesthetic based in desire and the body. The rock concert of the "Epilogue," a self-deconstructing performance, repeats the burning of the Théâtre des Vampires in the first novel and completes Lestat's demystification. Lestat becomes the Osirian, Dionysian, or Orphean figure torn apart, deconstructed and internalized, reconstituted in his worshippers. Like Elvis or Christ, he is performer, priest, scapegoat, and sacrament. He is the sin eater who is himself eaten.

As rock star, Dionysian Stranger God, and vampire, Lestat is one of our "symbolic outsiders" who takes on "the burden of all our irrational drives and help us act all of that out," says Rice (qtd. in Wiater and Anker 15). Lestat marvels that "This god Osiris was the god of wine to the Egyptians, the one later called Dionysus by the Greeks. And Dionysus was the 'dark god' of the theater, the devil god whom Nicki described to me when we were boys at home. And now we had the theater full of vampires in Paris. O, it was too rich" (*Vampire Lestat* 33). The novel ends as in the "Epilogue" Lestat proclaims a *Götterdämerung* and calls for a complete naturalization, a dropping of all masks: "This is the Age of Innocence/True innocence/All your Demons are visible . . . material/Call them Pain/Call them Hunger/Call them War/Mythic evil you don't need anymore" (*Vampire Lestat* 541). The gods are dead, and he has found in the twentieth century a vigorous secular morality that motivated even the simplest people (*Vampire Lestat* 9). In the postliterate primitivism of the mass-mediated present, a throwback to the Savage Garden of preliterate, pre-Christian times, Lestat is at home.

The vampire was a very old idea, a myth of an immortality through the body in the simplest of senses, reinvented for the present. In the 1970s, it suggested monstrous polymorphic sexuality, and increasingly in the 1980s it implied dangerous sex, sex as death—and sex after death, sex in spite of (or after) AIDS, transcendence of the body through the homeopathic cure of the body fantastic. Armed with Freud and feminism, Campbell and Jung, Rice constructed a mythos invested in the primacy of the senses and the body, salvaged from the ravages of time and process, the body fantastic.

In returning to the polytheism of the old gods, Rice reclaimed Eros as necessarily "perverse" desire. Vampires, like homosexuals in particular, freed Eros from its purely reproductive function. Her vampires represented the interconnection of love and death, Eros and Thanatos as related aspects or masks of god. The vampire was our cultural Shadow, the sphinxlike beast of Yeats's "The Second Coming" that "Slouch[ed] toward Bethlehem to be born" (line 22), its time having come. "My work is filled with these moments," says Rice, "when people are scattered and broken and have to reinvent themselves. . . . As religion loses its hold on people in a magical way, people have to reinvent themselves in terms of new ideas" (qtd. in Ramsland, *Companion* 434–35).

HOCUS POCUS: POWER IN THE BLOOD

Blood has always been invested with power. There is power in blood as life and family bloodlines, in the Christian tradition, in Christ's blood. In Roman Catholic doctrine, Christ sacrificed his blood and body, which the process of transubstantiation sacramentally restores in sanctified wine and the Eucharist. Vampires perform this alchemy in reverse, taking the blood of others and transforming it into their own "preternatural" energy. *Hoc est corpus* becomes bio-power, power in the blood. Rice's vampires can also give mortals their "Dark Gift," whose power comes from the Great Mother Akasha much as Christ's comes from God and the Holy Ghost. (Thus Akasha's blood is empowered by the spirit Amel, named for an ancient Middle Eastern word for evil, that has invaded Akasha's body through her wounds.) Giving the Dark Gift costs Lestat an agony like "molten metal" coursing through "every sinew and limb," as a numbness comes over him "with the pulling burning through the numbness, and [his] heart thundering against it, feeding the pain" with every beat (*Vampire Lestat* 158–59). As their victim-beneficiaries drink their blood, vampires are imitations of the martyred and transubstantiated Christ. The Christian communion becomes the equally sacred cannibalism of the vampire's feast.

In the *Vampire Chronicles*, the body provides the structural principle for the self, shaping character, and forming identity or soul. Even spirits in Rice's cosmology are biological (not supernatural) wonders. They are amoral, powerful "whirling bodies of energy." They share the same DNA as humans but have ninety-two chromosomes, providing them with infallible immune systems (Ramsland, *Companion* 393). The blood is quite literally the life. Our Bodies, Ourselves.

Transcending nature in Lestat's perspective therefore means reclaiming nature in this potent, elemental form, and returning to the aesthetic law of the Savage Garden, Lestat's term for the pre-Christian Eden. "The whole thing [about the transformation] is to learn your nature. It's to look at a tree until you see its true self" (qtd. in Ramsland, *Companion* 433). Vampires return to preternatural innocence, to the purity of experience of the child or savage. Louis recognizes this when he is first "made" a vampire, and it is as if he has just "been able to see colors and shapes for the first time" and heard Lestat's heart beating like a drum (*Interview* 20).

In his sensory confusion, each sound runs into the next, and Lestat's laughter sounds like bells reverberating, the sounds overlapping, yet "each soft and distinct, increasing but discrete. . . . I became so enamored with [the moon] that I must have spent an hour there" (*Interview* 20). The vampire undergoes a breakdown of the ego in which his empty human beliefs and structures dissolve and he becomes what he sees, hears, touches. These "awakened senses" mean a heightened capacity for experiencing pain as well as pleasure, which makes Louis's death throes especially memorable. Death is a purgation of the human from the body: "All my human fluids were being forced out of me." Dying as a human while coming into life as a vampire, he must simultaneously experience and oversee the death of his body with "discomfort and, then finally, fear" (*Interview* 21).

The agony brings aesthetic transcendence. Soon Louis is burning, a gemlike flame, his viscera quite literally "consumed away." Like Yeats's poet in "Sailing to Byzantium" or Sylvia Plath's suicide-artist, he is purged into art. As seen by his interrogator, Louis appears to be "sculpted from bleached bone" and "inanimate as a statue." His white face moves with "the infinitely flexible but minimal lines of a cartoon" (*Interview* 3). Thus the dust jacket of the hard cover edition of *The Tale of the Body Thief* is a photograph of Giovanni da Bologna's sculpture *The Rape of the Sabines*. Vampires are "perfected"—their cells growing thinner, the body becoming harder, yet more resilient—as the centuries stretch on. They achieve the semi-transparency of marble, the permanence of art. As Louis adapts he finds consolation in art, literature, and the doll-like beauty of Claudia. Vampire experience realized the values of the *fin de siècle* and the Modernists, a life lived through art or preferably, as in the case of Lestat, living as an art. In the Théâtre des Vampires, foreshadowed in Louis's vision in the New Orleans Cathedral, is a world of frescoes by Bosch, Traini, and Dürer, and dominated by Breughel's *The Triumph of Death* painted as a massive mural (*Interview* 229).

Vampires are the body aesthetic. Part 2 of *Tale of the Body Thief* begins with Yeats's "The Dolls," a poem about the perfection of dolls protesting the mess and noise of children, birth, and life (and featuring a doll maker and his unhappy wife). Since writing *Interview*, Rice has collected dolls, which are often featured in her publicity photographs and interviews. Jennet Conant describes "the whole house, with its ghostly mirrors and statues, staring porcelain dolls, and eerie memorabilia" as being like a shrine (Conant 74). Interviewed on A&E's *Ancient Mysteries*, "The Origin of the Vampires" (1994), Rice was shown sitting next to a large, elaborately curled and dressed Victorian doll. Just behind it, on a table, was the smaller but equally overdressed figure of an angel. Like angels and dolls, cousins to the Terminator and the Soloflex man, Rice's vampires don't reproduce or defecate. Yet, like Christ, they weep blood. They are beasts who also have the healing power of bleeding statues.

Since seeing Boris Karloff in *The Mummy* (1932), which terrified her as a child, the mummy has been Rice's monster of preference (Ramsland, *Prism* 33–34). For the myth of origins in *The Vampire Lestat* (1985), Rice quite naturally went to the tombs of the Pharaohs and the myths of Isis and Osiris, and derived from them the vampire ancestors Akasha and Enkil, who are in a state of suspended animation. Dressed in the finest linen and jewelry like King Tut and Nefertiti and referred to as "Those Who Must Be Kept," they are glorified mummies, in effect having become their own sarcophagi. The coffin, central to all vampire lore, serves as womblike receptacle or chrysalis, a poetic space for transmutation from mortal body to eternal substance. Through consuming the life of other bodies, their bodies have hardened into chitinous shells. The Great Mother and Father of all vampires have in effect become statuary; catatonic, they are guarded for centuries in a crèche. To Lestat, they are "perfect Egyptian figures," with every eyelash in place and a fine lacquered surface, living as an art. Yet they better fit Camille Paglia's description of Egyptian art as "Apollonian objects [created] out of chthonian fear" (64), as a protest against natural process. Reviewing Neil Jordan's 1994 film adaptation of *Interview with the Vampire*, Kathleen Murphy comments: "Artifice and solipsism abound; no biological *nostalgie de la boue* afflicts Lestat and his Adams and Eves—soil never sullies their luxurious coffin-beds" (13–14).

William Butler Yeats's "Sailing to Byzantium," with its yearning for immortal substance—a body "out of nature," like the birds made by Grecian goldsmiths out of "gold and gold enameling," provides the epigraph to *The Tale of the Body Thief* (1993), the fourth Vampire Chronicle. (*Once Out of Nature* was Rice's original title.) As Rice recently explained to *Playboy*'s Digby Diehl, her vampire books are about "being trapped in the flesh when you have a mind that can soar. It's the human dilemma. What does Yeats say in the poem? 'Consume my heart away: sick with desire/And fastened to a dying animal'" (qtd. in Diehl 64). As such a body myth, *The Vampire Chronicles* had much to offer Anne Rice herself. Additionally they had poignant specific meanings for two of Rice's most loyal groups of readers, meanings outlined in the next two sections of this chapter. Predictably, one was a mainstream market dominated by women. The other was the gay community, for whom *The Vampire Chronicles* offered on the one hand a bisexual and homoerotic utopia and coping ritual for our plague years.

GAY SCIENCE

In his 1983 book on the "Blood Countess of Transylvania," Countess Elizabeth of Bathory, Dracula specialist Raymond McNally suggested *Dracula Was a Woman*, and scholars increasingly agree that Stoker's count was originally and subtextually "as much vamp as vampire" (Kaye). Bathory, whose life seems to have been the model for Dracula's more truly vampiric characteristics, and whose Aunt Klara was a well-known lesbian, preyed exclusively on women, had at least two female cohorts in her crimes, and enjoyed dressing in men's clothes and playing men's games (McNally 32–92). The one-page outline Stoker wrote five years before his novel suggests that in his original conception Dracula had a taste for same-sex victims, driving his "brides" away from Harker with the command "This man belongs to me!" followed by the declaration, "I want him" (qtd. in Kaye).[5] Stoker converted most of the homoerotic connotations of this passage into the heterosexual terrors and misogynistic overtones we are familiar with. Rice brought Stoker's vamp out of the closet.

A covert theme in *Interview* concerned the homosexual coming to terms with his sexuality, as Louis's affections shifted from Claudia to Armand, and as Claudia in turn chose Madeline as her ideal and coffin mate. Lestat, especially in *The Vampire Lestat*, appears to have been born with the drag queen's theatricalism. The gay accent reflected Rice's move in 1980 to San Francisco's Castro District. At that time a Mecca for creative outsiders, the Castro area "seemed like heaven" (Rice, qtd. in Ramsland, *Prism* 195). Rice's gay inflection has continued to the present. In a *Time* review of *The Tale of the Body Thief*, John Skow notes "The mannered dress and behavior, the private recognitions and ironies, the tireless naughtiness, the forbidden seductions and ultimate sterility . . . carried over unchanged to the vampire world" and the "pervasive and undisguised homoeroticism" (71).

The project had begun as early as Rice's unpublished *Nicholas and Jean* (1963), a gay version of Nabokov's *Lolita* (Ramsland, *Prism* 90–93), and an early short story in which the vampire was modeled on Oscar Wilde (Ramsland, *Prism* 143). The gay resonances are sustained in the opening scene as Louis speaks intimately to a young reporter who has approached him in a bar in San Francisco's Castro district, where his difference goes unnoticed.

As a child, Rice had identified with the androgynous figures in the church, "huge marble statues that look like both men and women combined" (Ramsland, *Companion* 17). In college in the 1960s she felt a similar admiration for and identity with homosexuals, whose "excessive-ness" she found exciting, associating it with the extreme sensibilities of the saints. She idealized homosexuals especially for showing "courage in the face of prejudice" (Ramsland, *Prism* 115). Gays were authentic in existential terms: they defied patriarchal standards of masculinity and refused anatomy as their sexual destiny. Gays reinvented themselves socially as well as physically, constructing new models for relationships. As they created a coherent civil rights movement, they seemed to represent Rice's own needs as a woman who did not identify with "being a woman" as stereotypically defined.

In the late 1960s, after reading Gogol's story "The Nose," about one man's stealing the nose of another, Rice wrote about seeing an attractive gay man in a park and exclaiming, "That man has my body!" (qtd. in Ramsland, *Prism* 105). Homosexuals combined male freedom with female sensibilities and reminded her of Church iconography based in "feminine-looking males, and males who weep over and over again" (qtd. in Ramsland, *Companion* 17). Rice envied the male body and fantasized being a man free to admire another male body. Gays subverted and circumvented the negative aspects of gender while exhibiting, passionately, the erotic. And a person who transcended gender, she felt, could achieve clarity and wholeness (Ramsland, *Prism* 105). Lestat provided Rice with an animus, an active "male" principle that allowed her to transcend her female body. *The Vampire Chronicles* also provided a gay utopia.

Becoming a vampire in Rice's novels means transcending socially constructed sexuality to realize one's sexual nature completely. The vampire had always covertly implied a perverse or displaced sexuality—that is, displaced from the genital to the oral stage, and combining phallic penetration with "feminine" orality and nurturing. Because vampires do not procreate genitally, vampire sex is polymorphously perverse, associated with the energy and wise innocence of pregender childhood. It is nothing short of having it all. Thus, when Claudia asks Louis what sex as a mortal was like, he describes it as linear, one-dimensional, "hurried". . . something acute that was quickly lost . . . the pale shadow of killing" (*Interview* 210). In the Chronicles, sex, which consists of killing and being killed (rape) and also the consensual sharing of blood between vampires, combines male intensity and female intimacy, domination and sharing. The kill engages the give and take of gay and lesbian sexuality or of symbiosis. As Louis drains his victim to the point of death, he feels the heartbeat "in perfect rhythm with the drumbeat of [his] own heart, the two resounding in every fiber of [his] being" (*Interview* 29). Lestat falls in love with his victims as he drains them, whether they be one-night stands or his best friend Nikki. Killing one's lover is the first step toward giving, in bestowing the "Dark Gift," and implies a revision of the horror of mother love (Johnson 78). Lestat's preternatural senses enhance not only his predatory skills but also his capacity for empathy. He is blessed and cursed to know his victims, to see what they see, feel what they feel. And if he feeds on the vital experience contained in their cells, he also undergoes their pain. Watching his mother Gabrielle die of tuberculosis, he can feel the "dull throb" of her aching (*Vampire Lestat* 152). When he can bear it no longer he makes her a vampire.

Male-female bonds in *The Vampire Chronicles*, however, are the exceptions, while male-male bonds are the most intense and erotic: Louis-Lestat, Louis-Armand, Lestat-Marius, Lestat-David Talbot, Lestat-Armand. Attracted to Armand, a narrow-waisted young boy in Paris, it seems that "this [act is] saving us, and the vast untasted horror of my own immortality [does] not lie before me, and we [are] navigating calm seas with familiar beacons, and it [is] time to be in each other's arms" as he feels "the two hot shafts driven hard through my neck and down to my soul" (*Vampire Lestat* 276). And as this passage suggests, with its combination of erotic intensity, danger, and denial, Rice is conscious already in 1985 of writing about and for homosexuals in the age of AIDS. *The Vampire Chronicles* would become a sort of journal of the plague years.

After all, parallels to AIDS "must resonate in every contemporary version, whether or not the director intends them," claims Elaine Showalter, who sees *The Lost Boys* (1987) as a film about adolescent homophobia. Coppola's film's discussion of sexually transmitted diseases and screen-engulfing shots of blood cells and transfusions caused *New York Times* critic, Frank Rich, to read *Bram Stoker's Dracula* "as an allegory of AIDS" (Showalter, "Bloodsell").

It seems clear that as early as 1984, when she quit writing pornography and returned to *The Vampire Lestat*, Rice was aware of *The Vampire Chronicles'* potential both as gay fantasy and for causing homophobic reactions. Adept at bending gender stereotypes, Rice had her greatest challenge thus far. Homophobes have long viewed homosexuals as cannibalistic predators. From the 1890s to the present, the connection between vamping, homosexuality, and lesbianism had been based partly in the association of sexual irregularity with "bad blood," sexually transmitted disease, and drug addiction. In folklores around the world vampires were metaphors for plague. As Rice explained to *Esquire* in March of 1994, "One reason the fifteen or so scripts of *Interview* hadn't worked was that people tended to make Lestat a stereotype of a horrible gay person" (qtd. in Hess 75).

On the other side, Rice has the example provided by the gay community, which has established a tradition of employing gay and lesbian stereotypes against themselves, acting out and reversing negative stereotypes. For instance, David Thompson, with the film adaptation of *Interview with the Vampire* in mind, comments on Halloween in San Francisco, where gays create a "fearsome vampire street theater in which the comedy and terror are inseparable—real lovers. It's a kind of defiance" (29). Similarly Rice uses the symbolism of vampires and vamping to transpose values, transmitting messages both to and beyond the gay community. In this respect her work resembles poet Judy Grahn's *Edward the Dyke* of 1969 (whose title speaks for itself) or Judy Chicago's *Holocaust Project* of 1994 (which uses the symbolism of a pink triangle and a background of pansies to commemorate homosexual victims of the Nazis).

The Vampire Chronicles flaunted their homoeroticism and alluded directly to gay and lesbian rights, homophobia, the battle of the sexes, genocide, and AIDS. In *Queen of the Damned* (1987) Akasha, Queen of the Vampires and a living abstraction for six millennia, comes out of her trance to effect her plan to eradicate all males (except for a number of breeders), whom she holds responsible for human violence. Rice meant to evoke an image of AIDS's devastation of the gay community (Ramsland, *Prism* 301) and AIDS panic as well—referring to fundamentalist and neo-Nazi gay-bashing. Akasha is the Third Reich, Jerry Falwell, *and* Andrea Dworkin and Catherine McKinnon rolled into one abstraction that even Lestat worships for a time.

In *The Tale of the Body Thief* (1992), Lestat once again questions and comes to terms with his vampire nature, attempting suicide and trading bodies with mortals. The novel performs a twist on the Frank Capra film *It's a Wonderful Life*, in which the angel Clarence Oddbody reveals to the suicidal George Bailey the value of his life, and the angel, killing, guarding, and ministering to mortals, is its presiding metaphor. The vampire embodies death and invulnerability to death simultaneously, and the species is the product of a blood-transmitted "virus" whose curse, like a chance mutation, brings with it great opportunities for risk taking and marvelous powers. This vampire has been transfigured as an androgynous and preternaturally embodied Christ figure for the Age of AIDS.

Rice enhances her protagonists' powers, book by book. Even by 1985 (*The Vampire Lestat*), vampire "burnout" is no longer a real issue. Immortality is time rendered into potential, "poetic" space. Armand's claim of being the oldest vampire is shown to be false when Lestat meets ancestors from Roman, Druid, and Egyptian cultures. In fact, as vampires age they become more powerful, as Magnus, Marius, and Those Who Must Be Kept progressively reveal. Akasha and Enkil watch over their vampire "children" and provide an image of constancy and immutability. Lestat exults in his powers: he has been destroyed and resurrected like Dionysus, he can fly, is telepathic, and has such regenerative capability that in *The Tale of the Body Thief* he spends days in the Gobi desert attempting to die and is defeated by his body, which becomes tempered and stronger as it burns.

Rice's vampires transfigure the fear of AIDS into a myth of healing bio-power in the blood, as signified by the vampire body's immunity to death, demonstrated by its ability to heal itself. Lestat, drained and torn after bestowing the Dark Gift on his friend David Talbot, feels confidence in his "heart pumping lustily" and knows "no more than a sick mortal as to why I was healing. . . . But some dark engine inside me was working busily and silently upon my restoration, as if this fine killing machine must be cured of all weakness so that it may hunt again" (*Tale* 419).

It is no wonder that, in the 1980s, vampire novels—Rice's in particular—became best sellers at gay book stores.[6] *The Vampire Chronicles* tell a story of gender transcendence and dangerous sex. Grouped together on pages 71 and 72 of the 23 November 1992 *Time* magazine are reviews of Rice's *The Tale of the Body Thief*, Francis Ford Coppola's *Bram Stoker's Dracula* (a film that "powerfully reimagines [the] Victorian myth for the age of AIDS" [Corliss, "A Vampire"]), and Tony Kushner's Tony Award-winning *Angels in America* ("An AIDS epic" drama that "dazzlingly blends sitcom, the supernatural and the ghost of Roy Cohn" [Henry III]). These items comment wryly on one another and on all that is spoken and unspoken in contemporary pop culture. Rice's *Vampire Chronicles* voice the several messages linking gays and AIDS but, unlikely as it might seem, subordinate fear of difference and death to an emphasis on desire and bonding.

In Camus's *The Plague* (1947), the plague bacillus lies dormant in all of us. When death is a common denominator of the human, it becomes the basis for human solidarity. Having death-driven vampire blood similarly means being hooked telepathically into the "network" that interconnects the global subculture and an instant link to others like oneself. In Rice's *Vampire Chronicles*, Camus moves into cyberspace. Paul West, reviewing Rice's *Lasher* (1993), the sequel to *The Witching Hour* (1990), complains with justification of "the monofilamentous, monotone rambling about this or that branch of the Mayfair family tree, and every witch bird roosted in it" and notes that Rice "repeats herself . . . to confirm some kind of ritual, to tell readers they have been here before." The *Vampire Chronicles* have a similar ritualistic quality and purpose. In the final pages of *The Tale of the Body Thief*, Lestat's meditations return to Louis, Maharet and Mekare,

Eric and Mael and Khayman, old friends and enemies. "Then I saw
Gabrielle, my beloved mother" (395), Pandora, Santino, "My old enemy
and friend Armand," Marius,

> the great ancient master who had made Armand in love and tender-
> ness so many centuries ago . . . who had led me down into the depths
> of our meaningless history and bid me worship at the shrine of Those
> Who Must Be Kept. . . . Dead and gone as was Claudia. For kings
> and queens among us can perish as surely as tender childlike fledg-
> lings. Yet I go on. I am here. I am strong. (396)

Like soap operas, the Chronicles must repeat themselves, must "go on,"
for they function as an extended family. Their opulent surfaces lend
pageantry and semblance of meaning to an otherwise "meaningless history." As Lestat tells us in *The Tale of the Body Thief*,

> my dark soul is happy again, because it does not know how to be
> anything else for very long, and because the pain is a deep dark sea
> in which I would drown if I did not sail my little craft steadily over
> the surface, steadily towards a sun which will never rise. (394)

Skal suggests that Rice's novels convey "a complicated healing message
to a community that . . . suffer[s] a concentrated level of human loss
unprecedented outside of wartime—or medieval plague" (346). As for the
larger aging population, the Chronicles have provisions more comforting
than Medicare. In *The Queen of the Damned* Rice invented the Talamasca
(meaning "animal mask"), an organization originally of witches and
shamans that tracks paranormal phenomena. "Like a Catholic religious
order, the Talamasca took care of its old and infirm. To die within the order
was . . . to spend your last moments the way you wanted, alone in your
bed, or with other members near you. . . . A great gathering . . . witnessed
each burial" (*Queen* 157). Together with Maharet's tapestry and the
matrilineal family tree, the Talamasca provides a lineage, a coherent
mythology, with its goddess and gods, its sacred texts and sacred days, its
organizations, rituals, and "Motherhouse," a coping mechanism.

Interview was in the nostalgic tradition of the confession and psychoanalysis. The novel presumed a Freudian ego and the bourgeois family,
noted its breakdown, and mourned its loss. In *The Vampire Lestat*, *The
Queen of the Damned*, and *The Tale of the Body Thief*, we see only the
vestiges of these structures as a Nietzschean Gay Science—transvaluation—takes over. Lestat's is a world in which subjects are responsible for

creating themselves and restructuring relationships and bonds, a post-Nietzschean, post-feminist, "cyberqueer" (Morton) utopia of transsexual myth making.

Rice's Chronicles appeal to subcultures beyond the gay community, as her book sales indicate. Among the fans are lesbians, renegade feminists, and sadomasochists. But her books are also (and primarily) directed to a far larger mainstream market dominated by middle-class, middle aged, primarily heterosexual women—perhaps the very women to whom she directed (with only partial success) her pornography. For these various groups, Rice functions as a sort of New Age priestess, psychoanalyst, and storyteller. And in writing about gay men, she writes covertly in the masked and self-divided tradition of the Female Gothic—about women, about her divided self.

POST-FEMINIST FAIRY TALES

Named Howard Allen O'Brien for her father, "Anne" Rice readily admits she has "always felt very uncomfortable in the role of being a woman" (qtd. in Ramsland, *Prism* 234). A child of the "sexual revolution," she identified with gay rights and projected her sense of sexual difference onto idealized homosexual types. Until recently she has been able to recover a sense of the feminine as power, as positive energy, only when wearing a male mask. Her vampires are transsexual bodies, experiments in identity beyond gender. Thus in 1983 she published *The Claiming of Sleeping Beauty*, "an erotic novel of tenderness and cruelty for the enjoyment of men and women" (cover), as the genderless (but therefore masculinized) A. N. Roquelaure. *Roquelaure* means "cloak," allowing the seductive French word to reveal the fact that it pretends to conceal—"Anne's cloak."

By the mid-1980s Rice was speaking of her work as "the divided self" (qtd. in Ramsland, *Prism* 225). In fact, she had required three different pseudonyms: A. N. Roquelaure, who wrote the hard-core *Sleeping Beauty* trilogy; Anne Rampling, who wrote the softer *Exit to Eden* and *Belinda*; and Anne Rice, who wrote *The Vampire Chronicles* and historical *Bildungsromans*. The self-division and the pornography were by-products of her experience of growing up female in a Church that sublimated her sensuality in devotional forms and gender norms that inscribed the female body as evil. The sadomasochistic books explored her Roman Catholic revulsion against the feminine—against nature, the chthonian, and the female fact of embodiment. More problematically, female masochism had become taboo in the post-feminist 1980s, as male masochism had always been. Thus together with the subversive adult fairy tales of Angela Carter and Joyce Carol Oates (to whom several attributed the *Beauty* books), Tanith Lee, Joanna Russ, Fay Weldon, and Jane Yolen, Rice's pornography defiantly indulged, flaunted, exploited, and examined her distinctively female sadomasochism.

Believing with Jung that all of us have masculine and feminine aspects, Rice explains that "I feel like my intellect is masculine or androgynous. Perhaps in my writing I go to my secret side" (qtd. in Ramsland, *Companion* 17). Lestat became the "man" in Anne Rice (as for Gabrielle), the character who did things she longed to do. "Lestat is my hero. He is the male I would like to be," Rice told John Hockenberry in an ABC television interview. "He is my dream self" (*World*). *The Vampire Chronicles* provide a poetic space ("out of nature") for this "dream self," whose male body's hardness and resilience resembles the "gold and gold enameling" of Yeats's bird. Lestat is the body fantastic in the sense of Art and Decadence, Oscar Wilde over Andrea Dworkin, the androgynous (male configured) angels over the Virgin/Madonna. In the blueprint with which she was furnished as a girl, the feminine ideal was the "female eunuch," or nothing. Angels, derived from the concept of the universal subject as male, transcended the human issue of gender altogether. Thus in Rice, as in Paglia's *Sexual Personae* and Ellis's *American Psycho*, the "hardbodies" tend to win. Female vampires stand for women as "the sex" and are vestiges of the patriarchal gender system.

At the same time, male bonds are based in feminine values of intimacy and nurturing. These vampires spend their long nights bonding with one another: touching, weeping, discussing philosophy and ethics, but in terms of their desires, roles, connections, relations, and roots (through The Great Family Tree). The Savage Garden is ultimately Dionysian, feminine, and matriarchal in the larger scheme. Vampire psychosexuality is overwhelmingly feminine and potentially lesbian. So in spite of Rice's alienation from the mother, the Chronicles privilege the feminine.

Louis is a woman trapped in a man's predatory sexuality, an inversion of Rice as she viewed herself—as a man trapped in a female body. Made a Female Gothic victim by Lestat, he transcends his condition through suffering, sensitivity, and earnestness, and becomes a victim-heroine. The human qualities that haunt him are conventionally feminine ones: empathy, the desire to connect and nurture, shrinking from violence, self-contempt, submissiveness. He experiences his transformation into a vampire in forms of female and lesbian sexuality. He remembers how the movements of Lestat's lips raised the hair all over his body, a shock of sensation like "the pleasure of passion" (*Interview* 188).[7] And in the way that Rice views writing as an "assault on the senses" (qtd. in Wiater, "Anne Rice" 43), thus privileging the "female" body and the feelings, *The Vampire Chronicles* subvert patriarchal values. As in French feminism, writing expresses the subject's experience of the body.

Rice's transfiguration of Christian into erotic myth is similar to that of Madonna, another divided self, self-advertised lapsed Catholic, and the only person to whom she says she would "sell the video or film rights to the *Beauty* books." Madonna, she says, exists because "there are certain people whose function is to outrage us" (qtd. in Diehl 59). As Madonna panted and sang of how sex made her feel "Like a Virgin"—reborn into radical innocence—Rice's vampire tells us how being killed and killing are divine communion. Both transvalue the Church's polarization of sexuality and virginity, death and life, the demonic and the angelic. Ultimately Rice's iconography, like Madonna's, expresses her ambivalence toward the female body as inscribed by Roman Catholicism—which made it potent with sacrilege and evil—and her ambivalence toward Church dogma.

Vampires are finally associated with the archetypal feminine elements, with darkness, the earth, the abyss, the moon, blood, with Dionysian substance, androgyny, and transformation. Shunning the sun and the Apollonian, masculine principle, male vampires are androgynous while female vampires like Akasha and Maharet are intensely powerful (Ramsland, *Companion* 443). From 1985 on, Rice's revampings of the myth exposed its origins in the body of the Goddess as opposed to male monotheism. *The Vampire Chronicles* therefore carried on the agenda Rice began in her twenties when writing pornography that she declared was "for women." The vampire expressed the feminine repressed in Western culture and was an early (1970s–1980s) covert form for what Estes (following up the success of Robert Bly's "wild man" Iron John) would proclaim the "wild woman" archetype.

If the male vampires provided an animus for female desire that would otherwise have gone unvoiced, Rice's female vampires before *Queen of the Damned* (1988) are invariably "dark." Rice admits as much, claiming she does not know why. Perhaps, she says, "the feminine side of me is suffering and the masculine side is always the one with the sense of humor. The women invariably turn out like Claudia" (qtd. in Ramsland, *Prism* 234), the character most directly inspired by Rice's reaction to the deaths of her mother and daughter. Claudia is "the embodiment of my failure to deal with the feminine, a woman trapped in a child's body," Rice has admitted. "She's the person robbed of power" (qtd. in Ramsland, *Prism* 154). If the male vampire's hard body is powerful and flexible, the female vampire is a living doll—fixed, passive, infantile—an explicitly female metaphor for the horror of embodiment. Claudia is as fiendishly voracious as she is tiny and beautiful and must seduce her victims by pretending to be a helpless child.

The two males "make" her after having been smitten with her doll-like appearance, play with her "as if she were a magnificent doll" (*Interview* 100), and give her dolls when she is past forty, reinforcing her stereotype as the Victorian child-bride. Claudia's rage, "rising like some dormant beast in her, looking out through her eyes," expresses Rice's own rage: "Snatching me from mortal hands like grim monsters in a fairy tale, you idle, blind parents! Fathers! . . . To give me immortality in this . . . helpless form!" (*Interview* 263–64). Increasingly frustrated, she chooses a doll maker named Madeleine who makes the same doll over and over in an attempt to recreate the daughter that she has lost. Conversely, Claudia asks Madeleine to make her a "lady doll" that gives an image both to her dead mother and the woman she might have become. Claudia, Madeleine, and the dolls are finally a comment on the traditional Mother-Daughter relationship as self-replicating, narcissistic, and destructive. Claudia desires Madeleine much as Madeleine desires her, not as a mother or a lover but as an image to complete the self. The replication comments on the Female Gothic world of enclosure, weak reflections, half-lives, replicas, and substitutions. Madeleine is in perpetual mourning for her dead daughter, and Claudia for her absent mother. Thus for all her rage and brilliance, Claudia must die, and Madeleine, who replicates the concept of female anatomy as social destiny, is already in effect dead. Unable to grow into friends or lovers, the two women are finally driven by the coven into an air shaft to burn up in the sun. However liberated from sexual functions and hence from the feminine as defined by patriarchy, Rice's female vampires stand for anatomy as a destiny that is socially inscribed. The coven's exclusion and destruction of Claudia and Madeleine, the one female "couple" in the novel, sets Louis free to love Armand. As in *Frankenstein*, female bonds are sacrificed. Perhaps in these entrapped, "born-dead" female characters, Rice destroyed early on and in one stroke her dead mother, her dead child, and her dead self.

Thus patriarchy is most despicable in Armand's coven, whose abstract Law rigidly enforces outmoded human customs and Biblical prohibitions in the name of social order. As a metaphor for bad faith, or conformity, the coven is most visible in its females. The coven vampires believe their destiny is to embody evil—much as women bear the curse of childbirth, death, and pain—and they consequently shun all trappings of religion and goodness. Like Dracula's brides or "groupies," they hover around Armand or cluster and whisper among themselves. Two have the nearly reversible names of Estelle and Celeste, with Estelle explaining that vampires must wear black and that Claudia's pastels are inappropriate. "We blend with the night," she says (*Interview* 246). Believing that their destiny is to embody Evil, condemned to carry out its law, they are also the female body as absence. It is their passive-collective will that effectively shuts out Claudia and Madeleine, sealing their fate.

The Vampire Lestat was where Rice recovered the active male principle or animus, and it was equally a turning point in her dealing with the feminine: a revision of the story of Claudia and Madeleine (Ramsland, *Prism* 247–48). When Lestat makes Gabrielle a vampire, he experiences what Freud thought the primary male fantasy: the memories of childhood

> wove their shroud around us . . . the sense of her before words . . .
> the smell of her all around me and her voice silencing my crying . . .
> and the terror of her and her complexity. . . . And jetting up into the
> current came the thirst, not obliterating but heating every concept of
> her, until she was flesh and blood, and mother and lover and . . .
> everything I had ever desired. (*The Vampire Lestat* 157)

When Rice's friend Andy Brumer asked if "that kind of bonding" might be "paid for with a loss of the self," she replied that with eternity "you can work out anything, even an Oedipal complex" (qtd. in Ramsland, *Prism* 253). *The Vampire Chronicles* provided a poetic space in which to transcend or, rather, transfigure gender. Rice was first inspired by her desire to resurrect her own mother. "Gabrielle was a real turning point for me," Rice said, for she had decided that the mother "was not going to die again" (qtd. in Ramsland, *Prism* 253). In giving her mother an escape, she also gave herself another life and reconstructed her relation to the female body. For the first time she was consciously liberating a woman from gender. In the novel's prologue, Lestat, after observing the brave new world of 1984, remarks that women were possibly for the first time in history "as strong and as interesting as men" (*The Vampire Lestat* 7).

Gabrielle was also the beginning of her breakdown of the symbolic order and sacred gender, family, and class codes. Made a vampire by her son Lestat, Gabrielle dies to her tuberculosis-ravaged body and to the children who "devoured her and abandoned her" (158) into a person who can now live for herself. She is transfigured, her inscription as mother, woman, countess, having smoothed into a masklike and almost geometrical abstraction and comprising a page on which she will overwrite a new life. Her age lines have become fewer and deeper, with the "barest fold of extra flesh remain[ing] to each eyelid," heightening "the sense of triangles in her face" and giving her the crystalline delicacy of a diamond (160). Although quite literally the body inscribed by a complex of genetic and social codes—she is also freed as a vampire to construct a new identity. As a "fledgling," Gabrielle reinvents herself as a young man, cutting her hair, dressing in men's clothes, and choosing a man's sarcophagus. Lacking an iconography other than the phallic, she remakes herself in the image of her son. Once completely "out of nature," however, she disrupts the gender system, becoming adventurous, practical, androgynous. As Lestat becomes more intimate with mortals ("feminized"), she becomes distant, disappearing like a male adventurer for centuries at a time. For Gabrielle, who must cut her hair every evening, gender is performance, choice, and intertextual discourse. Taking what Sandy Stone, in "The Empire Strikes Back: A Posttranssexual Manifesto," calls a "transgendered positionality" (168), Gabrielle "embodies a sense of freedom that even Lestat cannot grasp," as Ramsland puts it—from gender, familial, and social roles and from the contingencies of relationships (*Companion* 150).

Gabrielle discards the identity trappings associated with bourgeois patriarchy. Vampire social groups reflect the transformations of the family in our time, the weakening of a sense of a biological, gender-specific family, and the shift to constructed, provisional, gender-unspecific bonds and groups. Rice's novels suggest that breaking down gender does not destroy masculine and feminine distinctions but instead subverts gender oppression and divisiveness. *The Vampire Chronicles* reconstruct the nuclear family, turning the Freudian myth that epitomized it in the direction of Jungian individuation, myth making, and storytelling as self-exploration and transfiguration.

As mortals, Rice's characters are the constructs of dysfunctional families. Louis experiences the classic symptoms of sibling rivalry, guilt, grief, and despair over his brother's death, and appreciates him only when he is dead. Gabrielle is fundamentally at odds with her female roles—despises feminine occupations, forbids her children to call her "Mother," and (much like Rice's mother) spends most of her time alone reading. As mother and son, Gabrielle and Lestat are bonded by their alienation, their hatred of class attitudes and family roles, but when he makes her a vampire (in effect becoming *her* mother) and the "silence" falls between them, she quickly severs most ties.

As a mortal woman, Gabrielle lived through books and sons, telling Lestat he was the organ for her "which women do not really have" (Ramsland, *Prism* 245). But for vampires (as for Osiris, who had been dismembered, "feminized," and resurrected as the god of Death) phalluses are irrelevant. When she realizes she no longer covets the phallus, Gabrielle no longer needs Lestat, who in making her a vampire has given her the means to become herself. She outgrows her human identity, and the vampire network offers her a gender-unspecific space in which to construct new bases for relationships. This myth has enormous appeal to women who have turned away from patriarchal models to reconstruct their lives.

The silence that falls between vampire and child, like a generation gap or gender conflict, forces the fledgling vampire to become his or her own parent and child. "We live in an age," Rice claims, "where technology, warfare, and science have reached a point [at which] parents can't give answers anymore. The parents can't guide us" (Ramsland, *Companion* 313). Each Chronicle is a quest for answers in history, parents, or law that ends in failure as paradigms shift.

In the vampire world, the patrilineal bourgeois family is a paradigm evoked to be tested, found wanting, and reconstructed. In *Interview with the Vampire*, the relationship of Lestat, Louis, and Claudia parodies the "incestuous" nuclear family, with Lestat as heavy father, Louis as mother, and Claudia as child. Lestat loves the "figure we cut, the three of us," and Louis relives his human childhood by instructing her in the beauty of the human world, in poetry, music, and the arts (100). But this experiment, we learn later, began in Lestat's failed attempt, based in nostalgia, to recover an outmoded human social structure. No simple recovery is ever possible, and Lestat finds that traditional structures adapted to the vampire "life" only imprison, provoke violent revolt, and finally kill. (Claudia attempts to kill Lestat and is later destroyed in part for this ultimate violation of the vampire code.) In The *Vampire Lestat*, the patrilineal family is replaced by the matrilineal Great Family Tree whose source resides in Akasha. Yet even that matrilineal paradigm becomes destructive and is itself destroyed.

A similar reactionary structure and a revolution occur within the Great Family of the species in *The Queen of the Damned* (1988) when Akasha plans to use her matriarchal power to eradicate "male" violence. She hopes to totalize her concept of the family as woman's community, creating a New Eden. But in so doing she will reinstate the Church in an inverted form, replacing the Kingdom of God with a Kingdom of Woman, a theocracy based in the worship of the Mother Goddess, and like Dostoevsky's Grand Inquisitor, relieving subjects of free choice. Her argument is as abstract and (ironically) phallic as Akasha herself.

Opposing her and balancing the anti-feminist satire are the powerful, positive twins Mekare and Maharet, who represent a productive dialectic of opposite temperaments. Witches from a Palestinian tribal culture that practiced omophagia, the ritual of eating parts of their ancestors' bodies to preserve their bodies in their offspring, they are positive images of the feminine and the Mother archetype. In an act of sacred cannibalism, an assertion of substance over Akasha's abstraction, they destroy her reign while assimilating her powers (and saving the vampire species) by eating her brain and her heart. As Akasha is fascist, a (literally) flat character who attempts to eliminate conflict, and a too-obvious type of Kali, Maharet is vital substance and action. Her form of sacred cannibalism inverts the Devouring Mother archetype into a nurturing, communal model. Internalizing Akasha's knowledge and power, Maharet becomes the new keeper of the *Chronicles* and genealogist of the Great Family Tree.

The Queen of the Damned is Rice's critique of feminism and also her analysis of her own misogyny, reflected in the *Chronicles'* constant displacement of the feminine. Akasha is Claudia frozen to a pedestal, enshrined, and perversely empowered. Through Lestat, whom she manipulates (as Claudia manipulated Louis), she unleashes "Claudia's" pent-up rage in the form of a fiery apocalypse. This sort of writing from the body is as self-destructive as that of Clive Barker's Jacqueline Ess.

As much as the twins oppose and balance Akasha in *The Queen of the Damned*, the *Chronicles* continued to reveal Rice's discomfort with traditional female roles, female bodies, and female power and her preference for "gay science" over feminism. Positive female bonds, lesbian relationships for example, are exceptions. (An interlude between Jessie and Mekare is brief and perfunctory.) Indeed, perhaps the only female in Rice's books who is truly wise, without reservation, is Belinda (in the novel of 1986), a nubile eighteen-year-old who teaches her male lover, a middle-aged children's writer, the arts of living and loving. Belinda is a Lolita figure and the child as Mother of the man. Until *Queen of the Damned*, where Maharet and her descendent Jessie represent recoveries of Madeleine and Claudia, of the feminine, female vampires remain haunted by their past constructions. (Only Louis, who is really a woman, Rice herself, and Lestat's beloved Nikki, are as haunted by their past lives.) For Rice, even after all is said and done, woman is still "the sex."

Yet, as in the case of homosexuality, Rice reflects the world around her. In *Feminism Without Women*, Tania Modleski examines "postfeminist" phenomena from Pee Wee Herman to *Three Men and a Baby*, arguing that under the pretext of gender studies and the deconstruction of manhood, popular culture, and criticism have co-opted territory gained earlier by feminists. (She might similarly account for Clive Barker who, uncomfortable with conventional masculine roles, identified with and found power by impersonating female embodiment in the 1980s.) Rice's novels provide another, perhaps more positive, face of this trend. Like Camille Paglia,

Rice has been outspoken in her criticism of radical feminists. But, as we have seen, she has also made the story of her self-alienation public myth. Uncomfortable in "woman's role" as it had been presented to her, openly divided against her female self, Rice seems to have found her way to the feminine only first through a complicated masquerade, by identifying with homosexuals and transsexuals in their equally self-divided gender switching. On the one hand, Rice can be seen as an almost Victorian case of "anxiety of authorship" such as Gilbert and Gubar describe in *The Madwoman in the Attic* (1979). As in Linda Hamilton's hardbodied film heroine Sara Connor or Jodie Foster's Clarice Starling, women empowered are women in drag. Bodies are discursive territories, and when Gabrielle or Rice wear the stolen male body, they steal the language that goes with it. In the meantime, Rice provided a trans-gendered myth for men who were uncomfortable in the role of a man before the "sensitive" man was fashionable. Still a woman who is a divided self, Rice speaks for many divided persons, for whom physical transformation is a metaphor of self-reinvention and trans-figuration (Ramsland, *Companion* 434).

"[W]hen I work with these comic-book vampire characters, these fantasy characters," Rice explains, "I can touch reality" (Diehl 64). For her fans, the *Chronicles* or Vampire Bible and apocrypha (*The Mummy*, *The Witching Hour*, *Lasher*, the historical novels, and the pornography), together with their authorized concordance (*The Vampire Companion*) and biography (*The Prism of the Night*) constitute a kind of sacred canon, with its creed, metaphysics, commandments, saints' lives, gods (plural), and rituals, but based, as Rice as a woman apparently felt it to be, in substance. Just as Louis's story was the story of a century, so apparently was Rice's. Instead of the Word Made Flesh, and much as Barker does, Rice offers books of blood, celebrations of perversity.

As William Gibson suggests, Rice also uses horror as an "exploratory probe, a conscious technique" owing as much to speculative fiction as to the Gothic tradition (xvi), as much to male science as to female romance. Mary Shelley similarly "found" a voice through male narrators engaged in making monsters. In *Frankenstein*, Victor and his androgynous monster speak for Shelley as monstrous mother and monstrous child, while the female characters are silent, trapped in their roles of letter recipient, (dead) mother, (waiting) fiancee, and monster's bride (torn to pieces and thrown in the sea). Similarly Anne Rice seems to have found the most divided form of the Female Gothic, the androgynous or trans-sexual vision, her mode. Anxiety of authorship continues to infect Rice's texts.

In *The Witching Hour* (1990) and *Lasher* (1993), she had begun a new series and constructed a mythic apparatus that directly addressed the feminine as an issue. In these novels she explores its powers as well as its horrors, its endless creativity, ambition, and capacity for monstrous births. Rowan Mayfair, the female protagonist, a brain surgeon from an ancient family of powerful witches, employs reproductive technology to "raise" a demon lover from her own body. She mates patriarchal science (Victor Frankenstein) with matriarchal witchcraft (midwifery) and gives birth to her brainchild Lasher (a fantasy figure of masturbation). The resulting creature is the monstrous shape of Rowan's desire—male and female, lover and child, spirit and matter—but essentially clone, the product of a matrilineal line of descent.

Far more than Frankenstein, who is disgusted by "the workshop of filthy creation," Rowan finds biology erotic. Like Cronenberg's Nola Carveth or Clive Barker's Julia, she is "in love with the cells of th[e] thing" (*Witching Hour* 1030). As *The Vampire Chronicles* are Rice's *Dracula*, the Mayfair-Lasher saga is her *Frankenstein*. Paul West thinks *Lasher* poor Gothic romance but compelling science fiction:

> Poignant images begin to form: Rowan breast-feeding her mutant, getting into X-ray departments to run a brain scan on him, hemorrhaging time and again and scraping up the "tiny gelatinous mass at the core. . . . There was something here, and it had limbs!"

Like Victor, Rowan dreams—of a keyhole-shaped door she first entered as a girl when, like Eve, she became fascinated with the mysteries of science. But Rowan is doomed like Milton's Sin who, in the aftermath of Eve's act, gave birth to Death, who immediately raped her.

The fear of women's creativity, based in womb envy, as Marie-Hélène Huet argues, suggests that the unnatural thoughts of women produce monstrous births. For Rice, as for many men and women, the (woman's) body is still a Dark (and hence fascinating) Continent. Although Rowan is her strongest, most sympathetic woman to date, it is Rowan's consort Michael (a sensitive New Age romance hero who looks like his namesake, the archangel), who is allowed some righteousness.

Rice herself suggests that her work is the ongoing process of a "divided self" seeking fuller articulation, her very shortcomings therapeutic for her readers as well as herself. Like Clarissa Pinkola Estes, she provides a personal case history that implies a therapeutic method and framework. Estes, who practiced Jungian analysis for twenty-two years before she became an author-cantadora, comments on how her book struck a chord with so many readers: "We all wait for a mirror to show us who we are, to validate us. When we hear something about ourselves that we have never heard before, it feels like a blessing and it gives power. [By writing the book] I have given a voice to that mirror" (qtd. in Crocker 17). Rice's *Vampire Chronicles* function similarly for her audiences.[8]

Afterword

"A society without stories to show the dark side of life" as well as its "righteous pathways," says Clarissa Pinkola Estes, "will collapse of its own unconsciousness" (qtd. in Roberts 19). Horror fiction has thus figured in the current cultural project to reclaim the body, and with it, Thanatos, the Other, and the feminine, for consciousness and language.

As Anne Rice's iconic status began to compare with that of Stephen King, she began dressing for the occasion. Before 1990, she looked like a cross between Vampira and a Catholic schoolgirl: with waist-length black hair and short pleated skirts. Just before her fiftieth birthday, she cut her hair to just below the chin. Soon she was coming out for television interviews in black velvet three-piece suits, cultivating the style of androgyny Lestat had inspired in the 1990s Gothic subculture.

The vampire subgenre had entered a new phase. In January 1992 Elaine Showalter had noted that the "weekly New York digest of the Romanian TV news begins with a montage of national heroes including . . . Vlad." The last weekend in May 1995 Bucharest hosted the First World Dracula Congress. Regardless of their politics, vampires were politically correct. Thus, in *Mad Forest*, Caryl Churchill's play about the Romanian revolution of 1989, Dracula is "a sleek aristocrat desperately courted by a starving dog, in an allegory of a poor country's cringing susceptibility to tyrants" (Showalter, "Bloodsell"). In Dan Simmons' *Children of the Night* (1992), set in post-Communist Romania, Dracula joins the fight against AIDS. (Some vampires were just plain political, as when in January 1994, 1,000 Rice fans gathered in front of Houston's Crossroads Market & Bookstore to protest the casting of Tom Cruise as Lestat in the film of *Interview with the Vampire* [Conant 72]).

The "most offbeat genre" at the 1995 Sundance Film Festival was the "black-and-white, Lower Manhatten-set, revisionist vampire flick," represented by two films, Abel Ferrara's *The Addiction* and Michael Almereyda's *Nadja*, each centered in a female performance (Hoberman 45). But the hit film of Sundance and Cannes was Larry Clark's *Kids*, scripted by 19-year-old Harmony Korine. *Kids* had a plot "familiar to any Dracula fan," says Richard Corliss. Telly specializes in virgins as "safe" sex. When Jennie (who has been only with Telly) tests HIV positive, she must prevent him from infecting Darcy. "Telly is the vampire, pestilent and possessed; Darcy is Mina, his virginal victim-to-be; and Jennie is both Lucy, the walking dead with the fatal love bite, and Van Helsing, the fearless vampire killer" (Corliss, "Festival" 69). All three films seem inspired not only by Rice but by Poppy Z. Brite, whose vampire novels capture teen angst.

On *The X-Files* ("3," June 16, 1995) "real" vampires raid blood banks and cruise clubs. On the Internet, the alt.books.anne-rice newsgroup (376 entries on May 23, 1995), is dominated by the storytelling game *Vampire: The Masquerade*, based on *The Vampire Chronicles* and dedicated to Czech Republic President Vaclav Havel. Some other "Thinkers" acknowledged are Albert Camus, Herman Hesse, Carl Jung, and Joseph Campbell—via (of course) Lestat. The alt.books.gothic newsgroup, some 700 strong, announces that the band Lestat will appear Saturday June 24 at the Club Noir in Chicago to promote their *Vision of Sorrows* release in conjunction with the Convergence Gothic Festival. Correspondents debate distinctions between Gothic, New Gothic, and the European Dark Wave. Others discuss the relative merits of Love is Colder than Death, Necrophilistic Angel, and The Dead Can Dance.

Lending mythical coherence to this frenzy of Thanatopsis are Anne Rice, *The Vampire Chronicles*, and Lestat. The current gothic subculture attempts to live out an androgynous lifestyle whose primary ideology is a refusal of traditional bifurcations of male and female, good and evil, life and death (Melton 369). Overlapping with Rice's *Chronicles* the androgynous Gothic subculture, lesbian feminists have re-visioned vampires to reflect their sexuality and have projected utopias based on symbiosis rather than domination—for instance, in Karen Marie Christa Minns's *Virago* (1990), Elaine Bergstrom's *Daughter of the Night* (1992), and Jewelle Gomez's *Gilda Stories* (1991).[1]

The left-wing reclamation of the vampire capped the larger trend. In the 1950s, horror had been a "low" (and clearly homophobic) entertainment embraced by the baby boomers, and was developed by independent writers and filmmakers into a marginal, at times subversive, language in the 1970s and 1980s, when it entered and then infiltrated the mainstream. By the 1993 Christmas season, for instance, the major chains had given their central aisles over to mountains of copies of Rice's *Tale of the Body Thief*, King's *Dolores Claiborne*, and Estes' *Women Who Run With the Wolves*. In 1995, thanks in part to "postliterate prose," there has been a burgeoning of chain-run book and multimedia emporiums run by Barnes and Noble, Borders, and Media Play. There you can cuddle up with *Interview with the Vampire* and a cappuccino, listen to it on tape, watch a videotape of the film, or all of the above.

As the monsters, books, and movies achieved mythic and low-classic status, name directors made revisionist adaptations—for instance, Coppola's *Bram Stoker's Dracula* (1992), Mike Nichols' *Wolf* (1994), and Kenneth Branagh's *Mary Shelley's Frankenstein* (1994). Jordan's *Interview with the Vampire* was "less a horror movie than a luxurious reverie on horror-movie themes" and "vampire mores," noted Terrence Rafferty, and Rice's screenplay traded conventional suspense for a seductive "fairy-tale darkness" that mingled pleasure and danger (Rafferty, "Blood Lust" 127, 199). In a similar spirit, writers with literary aspirations rewrote the horror classics from the Other's point of view. Valerie Martin's *Mary Reilly* (1990), which tells the story of Dr. Jekyll and Mr. Hyde from the maidservant's point of view, was inspired by Margaret Atwood's feminist costume gothic (*Lady Oracle*) and science fiction (*The Handmaid's Tale*); and the book has been adapted to an "art" film by writer Christopher Hampton and director Stephen Frears (*Dangerous Liaisons*). The most recent book by erstwhile social historian Theodore Roszak, *The Memoirs of Elizabeth Frankenstein* (1995), gives Victor Frankenstein's ill-fated bride a voice.

In presuming to recover lost female voices by writing from the body, Roszak joins Clive Barker and the "reformed" Stephen King, who has shared his personal rediscovery of the "alternative" Louisa May Alcott in the September 10, 1995 *New York Times Book Review*. "One wonders," King speculates, "what kind of a writer she might have been had she been able to cast the malignantly conventional spirit of Professor Bhaer from her, and to take her thrillers as seriously as her feminist editors and elucidators do today" ("Blood and Thunder" 20). Meanwhile, literary authors like Margaret Atwood, Toni Morrison (*Beloved*, 1987), Doris Lessing (*The Fifth Child*, 1988), E. L. Doctorow (*The Waterworks*, 1994), Peter Ackroyd (*The Trail of Elizabeth Cree: A Novel of the Limehouse Murders*, 1995), Andrei Codrescu (*The Blood Countess*, 1995), and Joyce Carol Oates (*Zombie*, 1995) go on finding Gothic and pop horror clichés useful to their revisionism and social commentary.

In its annual nod to "literature" for June 1994, *USA Weekend*'s Summer Fiction Series led off with "Animal Life," a charming ecological cautionary tale by Clive Barker, about "A man and his dog in the rubble of post-earthquake L.A." (4–5). The story also engages in feminist myth making. Barker pictured the earthquake as a wakeup call from the Goddess, who speaks through the narrator's dog. His *Everville* (1994) is a featured alternative of the Quality Paperback Book Club, a quasi-intellectual, New Age reading crowd. The first three volumes of Barker's *Books of Blood* are advertised by QPBC in a special one-volume edition. They are thus pronounced contemporary horror classics.

Candyman (1992), Bernard Rose's film based on Barker's story "The Forbidden" (*In the Flesh*), had a literate script, a haunting choral score by Philip Glass, and Shakespearean actor Tony Todd in the title role, and managed to scare Roger Ebert "with ideas and gore, instead of simply with gore." Barker's story of the hook-handed bogey, set in a London slum, concerned the power of myth to assert itself in the lives of its believers. Transporting the story to a setting of immediate social urgency, Chicago's Cabrini Green housing project, Rose envisioned Barker's Candyman as a slave's son lynched for having an affair with a white girl. The real horror was not Candyman's splitting victims from end to end but the specters of racism, black on black violence, the hopelessness and fatalism of the hood, the myth in which black men fatally desire white women and vice versa, male violence against women, women as victims and the monstrous feminine, and the perverse power of legend or myth itself. Actor Tony Todd, who does community work with gang members in his home state of Connecticut, knows numerous black fans of Candyman, who represents "empowerment" to the "disenfranchised" (French, "Candyman" 42).

Barker's postmodern splatter prose has left a legacy, as suggested by the Abyss line of cutting-edge horror fiction. Abyss features authors like Dennis Etchison (*Shadowman*, 1994; *California Gothic*, 1995), Melanie Tem (*Wilding*, 1993), Nancy Holder (*Dead in the Water*, 1993), Poppy Z. Brite (*Lost Souls*, 1992), Tanith Lee (*Dark Dance*, 1992), Kathe Koja (*Bad Brains*, 1992; *Skin*, 1993; *Strange Angels*, 1994). The group is dominated by women inspired by the literate and perverse body politics of Barker and Rice, by feminist science fiction, and by mainstream literature by women such as Joyce Carol Oates (recently, *Hauntings*, 1994), and Cathy Acker (*Blood and Guts in High School*, 1978). Paul Sammon's *Splatterpunks II* (1995) boasts about its domination by twelve "intrepid femmes" (2).

The September 2, 1994, issue of *The Times Literary Supplement* disparages the current trend in British fiction that seems to imitate "violent Hollywood blockbusters" and Stephen King (Shone 5). Note the following culprits: McGrath's *Dr. Haggard's Disease*, Ada Mar-Jones's *The Waters of Thirst* (kidney disease), Martin Amis's *Other People*, William Boyd's *The Blue Afternoon*, and Michael Ignatieff's *Scar Tissue*. Thanks to these "New Bodysnatchers," novelists are "sliding into position behind the surgeon" (Shone 5). As an issue, the Splatterpunks may have come and, largely, gone, but their brutal clinicism, derived from splatter film, medical writing, and the hard-boiled prose of Raymond Chandler and Mickey Spillane, has not. They have bequeathed their documentary mode, which gave the carnage legitimacy, to serial killer fiction, biography, autobiography, and crosses between these. A serial killer book club offers five books for a dollar to new members.

The cultural diagnosis of "excessive sex and violence in the media" may be short sighted. Thanatos, repressed in part by violence itself, had returned with a vengeance. Behind the popularity of the Fox TV show *The X-Files* is "yuppie morbidity" (Wollcott 99). In one form or another, as attested by this summer's *Die Hard With a Vengeance* and *Casper the Friendly Ghost*, which brings a dead TV cartoon series from a dead comic strip about a dead child back to life, Thanatos was entrenched for the 1990s. "We don't know why, but every time we go to the bookstore, there's another new book about death," quipped R. E. Neu in "What to Read Until the Undertaker Comes" (20). "Death Becomes Us," announced a feature article by Christopher Lehmann-Haupt of the *New York Times News Service* in May 1994. Books on assisted suicide (such as Derek Humphry's do-it-yourself manual *Final Exit*, 1991) were bestsellers in the early 1990s. Soon, for aging baby boomers, near-death became the new frontier. Dannion Brinkley's *Saved by the Light* (introduced by Raymond Moody, M.D.), and Betty J. Eadie's *Embraced by the Light* (with a foreword by Melvin Mose, M.D.) have held on to the top of the best-seller lists for over a year.

"It may not be such a far cry from medicine to literature," says Miller (9). What seemed like an unlikely best seller by Sherwin Nuland, *How We Die: Reflections on Life's Final Chapter* (1994), deconstructed the myth of the dignified death in a series of graphic case histories. On the popular fiction front, Michael Palmer (*Extreme Measures*, *Natural Causes*) competes with Robin Cook for the medical thriller market, and ex-physician Michael Crichton (*Jurassic Park*, *Disclosure*), is republishing medical thrillers he wrote in the 1960s under the pseudonym of Jeffrey Hudson. *A Case of Need* (1968) is described on the title page as "intensely timely."

Infectious diseases once obsolete—including tuberculosis and the bubonic plague—have resurrected in resistant forms, and as the emergence and spread of newly discovered diseases (such as the Ebola and hantavirus) become ever more probable, the "age of antibiotics is giving way to an age of anxiety about disease." It is no wonder that Stephen King's *The Stand* "earned some of the year's [1994's] highest ratings" (Lemonick 66). The miniseries led off ABC's May sweeps in the summer of 1994, airing on Mother's Day, a ritual repeated this summer with *Stephen King's The Langoliers*. The "Stephen King film," once a target of scorn, is considered Academy Award material (*The Shawshank Redemption, Dolores Claiborne*).[2]

The King of "white soul" goes on performing much of his cultural work in the old style. In contrast to Anne Rice, he looks like "a middle aged Bart Simpson" (Applebome). A story in *The* [Nashville] *Tennessean Showcase* publicizes a May 28, 1993, performance of the Rock Bottom Remainders, King's band, a group of authors who see themselves as "failed musicians." "Take, for example, Amy Tan (*The Kitchen God's Wife*), Robert Fulghum (*All I Really Need To Know I Learned in Kindergarten*), or Stephen King (you know who he is)." "This is not going to be a literary experience," said Roy Blount, Jr., as he introduced the event. "In a literary experience, you don't even move your lips." Dave Barry, playing lead guitar, improvised crowd pleasing couplets: "Lord, I only want just one thing, / To sell as many books as Stephen King." King's songs included "Last Kiss": "When I woke up the rain was everywhere / I wiped her eyeball out of my hair" (Mansfield, "Stephen King").

More than ever, in this culture of naturalized vampires, mythologized serial killers, physician writers, medicine women, and men who run with the wolves—in a world whose mythologies increasingly concern the problem and meaning of the body—the sin eaters have their work cut out for them.

Notes

INTRODUCTION

1. For an overview of recent books of criticism on the modern horror genre, see my book, *Film, Horror, and the Body Fantastic* (Westport, CT: Greenwood Press, 1995).

CHAPTER 1

Some of the material in this chapter was published in a considerably different form in my article "Movie Grue and Books of Blood," in *Consumable Goods*, ed. David K. Vaughan (Orono, Maine: The National Poetry Foundation, 1986), 63–73.

1. See *Film, Horror, and the Body Fantastic*, chapter 1, for a considerably fuller discussion of the issues, concepts, and listings in this chapter.

2. Moers outlines three versions of the female Gothic. In Ann Radcliffe's *The Mysteries of Udolpho*, it is a variation on the woman-in-peril formula: "The central figure is a young woman who is simultaneously persecuted victim and courageous heroine" (Moers 91). With Mary Shelley's tale of "hideous progeny," the modern Female Gothic was born in a myth about the horrors and powers of maternity (92–93). Later feminists focused on the "reproduction of mothering" (Chodorow's term) in the "maternal legacy" of the female body (Showalter, *Sister's Choice* 128), seen as antagonistic to the sense of self, as Other or monstrous. The female Gothic is thus a body language in giving "visual form to the fear of self," holding "anxiety up to the Gothic mirror of the imagination" (Moers 107). The Gothic heroine is thus a hysteric who expresses through her body what cannot be articulated in conventional language.

CHAPTER 2

Some of the material in this chapter was published under the titles "Love and Death in the American Car: Stephen King's Auto-erotic Horror," in *The Gothic World of Stephen King: Landscape of Nightmare*, eds. Gary Hoppenstand and Ray Brown (Bowling Green, Ohio: Popular Press, 1987), pp. 84–94; and "Stephen King," volume 4 of *Critical Survey of Long Fiction*, revised edition, ed. Frank N. Magill. Copyright, 1991, by Salem Press, Inc., pp. 1883–1897.

1. Erik Hedegard, "Mentors," *Rolling Stone College Papers*, April 15, 1982: 52; qtd. in Winter, *Stephen King* 22.

2. Tony Magistrale (*Landscape*) and David G. Hartwell (Introd., *Dark Descent* 690) have also noted the similarity between King and Dickens.

3. I have grouped Ong's eighteen or so devices into more general categories for purposes of this analogy.

4. The relations of Stephen King's fiction with the electronic media are many and complex. All of his full-length novels through 1993 (with the exception of *Thinner*, *The Talisman*, *Gerald's Game* and *Rose Madder*) have been made into or sold as films, most have been profitable, several exceptionally so (*Carrie*, *Stand by Me*, *Pet Sematary*, *The Running Man*), and several have been critically acclaimed (*Carrie*, *The Shining*, *Misery*, *The Dead Zone*, *Christine*, *The Shawshank Redemption*, *Dolores Claiborne*). He has written numerous screenplays and directed the film *Maximum Overdrive* (1986). His collaborations with filmmakers are well known. His co-writing with George Romero on *Creepshow* (1982), a film anthology inspired by E. C. Comics' blend of camp and gore and television series such as *The Twilight Zone*, *The Outer Limits*, and *Night Gallery*, in turn inspired dozens of horror and fantasy anthologies and series such as HBO's *Tales from the Crypt*, which turned the cinematic version of the tale of terror into a showplace for the work of first-time and well-known directors alike.

As a video image King is familiar from American Express commercials, talk shows, and parodies. He has hosted and chatted with fans in a series of television specials called *The Horror World of Stephen King*. The ABC-TV miniseries adaptation of *It* (1990) signaled recognition of King's commercial appeal by network television. Rob Reiner's Castle Rock company produced *Stand By Me* (1986) based on "The Body" (1982), *Misery* (1990), and *Needful Things* (1993), all directed by Reiner. King wrote the original screenplays for the ABC series *Stephen King's Golden Years* (1990) and the film *Sleepwalkers* (1992). Richard Corliss in *Time* magazine most recently reports twenty-one Stephen King films. Since then, *Pet Sematary 2* (1991), the television miniseries *The Tommyknockers* (1993), George Romero's *The Dark Half* (1993), Rob Reiner's *Needful Things* (1993), Mick Garris's ABC miniseries *Stephen King's The Stand* (May 1994), Frank Darabant's *The Shawshank Redemption* (1994), Taylor Hackford's *Dolores Claiborne* (1995), and the ABC miniseries *Stephen King's The Langoliers* (May 1995) have appeared. See the Filmography, Jeff Conner's *Stephen King Goes to*

Hollywood and Ann Lloyd's *The Films of Stephen King* for a more complete listing.

The "Master Storyteller" is also widely available on audio cassette, notably as narrator of his own *Dark Tower* cycle.

5. For three weeks, November 17–31, 1985, and January 12–18, 1986, King had five simultaneous entries on the bestseller lists (Twitchell, *Preposterous* 106).

6. Twitchell's general point about the appeal of violence to adolescents, however, is supported by the boom in the adolescent niche market for horror and thrillers. Stephen King may have had something to do with this trend. See Paul Gray, "Carnage: An Open Book," *Time* 2 August 1993: 54.

7. "When the weekly newsmagazines account for King's success, they betray their bourgeois bias and his talent. *Time* considers him under the rubric Show Business, while . . . *Newsweek* settles for Business," reports James Twitchell. In *Forbes*'s special issue on "entertainment's biggest earners" for 1986, King ranked with actors, singers, and producers and was the only author on the list (Twitchell, *Preposterous* 106). In a June 1993 feature, "What People Earn," *Parade Magazine* ranks "Stephen King, 46, Author, Bangor, Maine," at $15 million a year (VerMeuelen 4).

8. King's most recent effort is *The Green Mile*, published in six Dickens-style installments.

CHAPTER 3

Some of the material in this chapter was published under the titles "Love and Death in the American Car: Stephen King's Auto-erotic Horror," in *The Gothic World of Stephen King: Landscape of Nightmare*, eds. Gary Hoppenstand and Ray Brown (Bowling Green, Ohio: Popular Press, 1987), pp. 84–94; and "Stephen King," volume 4 of *Critical Survey of Long Fiction*, revised edition, ed. Frank N. Magill. Copyright, 1991, by Salem Press, Inc., pp. 1883–1897.

1. *Pet Sematary*, which he called "too horrible to be published," was based on a cluster of incidents in 1979, while he was a writer in residence at the University of Maine at Orono. See Winter, *Stephen King* (129–31).

2. On Halloween, Norma has a heart attack; at Thanksgiving, Church dies; on Christmas, "Frankencat" leaves a dead bird on the doorstep; around Passover, Gage dies and shortly thereafter, in passages of increasing disjunction, he rises from the dead.

3. See Robert Coover, "Hyperfiction: Novels for the Computer," *New York Times Book Review* 29 August 1993: 1, 8–12.

4. King originally submitted *The Dark Half* as a collaboration of King and Bachman, but Viking was afraid this idea would confuse people (Magistrale 166, n. 13).

5. See Pharr, Keesey, and Bosky.

6. Recent films by horror film directors such as *Wes Craven's New Nightmare* (1994) and John Carpenter's *In the Mouth of Madness* (1995) play off

different levels of reality and have a similarly ambivalent effect and purpose. Carpenter's film clearly has Stephen King in mind and alludes to the uncanny way the things King wrote about decades ago seem to be coming to pass. Based on an H. P. Lovecraft story, the film is about a horror writer (Sutter Caine) whose books are used by an ancient alien race to destroy the human species and overrun the earth.

CHAPTER 4

1. See Rockett on horror as *Theater of Cruelty*.

2. Asked in an interview with G. Dair if he were confident in his *own* sexuality, Barker answered discreetly: "I'm confident in my own complexity and that really interests me, because of the ambiguities of sexuality, the ambiguities of metaphysics, and the metaphysics of sexuality are things which hugely influence what I write" (393). Unlike Stephen King (who maintains the image of a family man who *can* make his private life common knowledge and would publish his laundry list if he thought it would sell) or Anne Rice (who has a listed phone number and publishes her sexual fantasies for all the world to see), Barker has until very recently steered clear of the subject of his private life, intellectualizing the issue or referring back to his work. But this past year, after the manuscript of this book was complete, Barker spoke "as an openly gay man for the first time" in *Out* magazine ("The 1995 *Out* 100," *Out* Dec.–Jan. 1996: 90). Featured in *Genre*'s "Men We Love" section (Dec.–Jan. 1996), he says he is "first and foremost a gay man who imagines. How important the gay part is depends on the medium, but I can't imagine making art without some form of sexual content" (50).

3. "Coming to Grief" was also published in *Good Housekeeping* (Oct. 1988) in the United Kingdom.

4. *Hellraiser* won the Grand Prix De La Section Peur at the 16th Annual Avoriaz Fantasy Film Festival in France in 1989 and was the number one box-office hit in Europe in 1988.

5. *Lord of Illusions*, Barker's 1995 film, was released in October 1995, after I completed the manuscript for this book.

CHAPTER 5

1. See McNally and Florescu, Margaret Carter, and Mascetti (114–51) for more extensive information on Vlad Tepes.

2. For bibliographies of modern vampire fiction, see Frost, Margaret Carter, Melton, and Auerbach's *Our Vampires, Ourselves* (Chicago, 1995), published just after this book was completed.

3. Ramsland, Copeland, and Waxman have noted the existentialism in *Interview with the Vampire*.

4. The two groups of vampires reflect the vampires of folklore and literature, respectively. In European folklore, a vampire is a revenant, a corpse which feeds on human blood. Feral and mindless, it is popularly recognized as the primal horde in Richard Matheson's *I Am Legend*, Stephen King's *'Salem's Lot*, George Romero's zombie movies, and numerous stories of plagues. The Byronic vampire, who descends from literature—from Romantic poetry ("Lamia," "Christobel") and prose fiction (beginning in English with John Polidori's *The Vampyre*, 1919)—is cultivated and willful.

5. Recent scholars have begun to emphasize the feminine in Dracula's lineage and claim that "he" is essentially a bisexual or androgynous metaphor through which the conventionally Victorian, homophobic Stoker expressed his most potent fears and desires. See McNally, Keesey, Dijkstra, and Creed, *The Monstrous Feminine*, 62–66.

6. Unicorn Books in West Hollywood told David Skal that "all its best-selling titles for a period during 1991 were vampire titles, with Anne Rice topping the list" (Skal 346).

7. Louis's femininity is suggested in Rice's models. *Bram Stoker's Dracula* she found "beastlike" and never finished the novel and read Sheridan Le Fanu's *Carmilla* instead. She was profoundly influenced by Gloria Holden in *Dracula's Daughter* (1936). She sympathized with the "tragic figure" of Dracula's daughter as "articulate and intelligent" and also "regretful": she "didn't want to kill" but was the victim of an erotic obsession (qtd. in Ramsland, *Prism* 41).

One plan for a film of the novel included a screenplay in which Armand, Louis's lover, was a woman and Claudia a girl of eighteen. Rice proposed making Louis a woman instead. "It works. It's all the same passivity, the same philosophical ideas, the same inability to fight Lestat's domination. It's fine for Louis to be a woman because he is a woman—he's really me" (qtd. in Ramsland 269). She had Cher or Meryl Streep in mind as stars who could play Louis as a transvestite, transgendered female, a fighter much like Gabrielle.

8. *Memnoch the Devil*, Rice's fifth Vampire Chronicle, was published after the manuscript for this book was completed.

AFTERWORD

1. See Johnson, Gordon, and Keesey.

2. In July 1995 in Lanark County, Ontario, public schools, however, King became the center of a hot literary controversy. English department heads selected his collection of novellas *Different Seasons* for the standard senior high school reading list, partly on the basis of its appeal to "reluctant readers," and the board of trustees voted to remove the book from the list (Egain A1). Unruffled by it all and perhaps savoring his short-lived status as a "banned" classic, King had free copies distributed to interested students.

Selected Bibliography

Applebome, Peter. "TV Gets a New Poltergeist: Stephen King." *The Tennessean Showcase* [Nashville] 14 July 1991: 4.

Arlen, Michael J. "The Cold, Bright Charms of Immortality." *The View from Highway 1*. By Michael J. Arlen. New York: Farrar, Straus and Giroux, 1974. Rpt. *The Contemporary Essay*. Ed. Donald Hall. New York: St. Martin's, 1984. 273–80.

Ashton-Haiste, Anthony. "Bleedful Kings." *Fangoria* Aug. 1991: 30.

Atwood, David. "The Summer Main Selection: Stephen King, *Rose Madder*." *The Book of the Month Club News* Summer 1995: 2–3.

Auerbach, Nina. "Engorging the Patriarchy." *Feminist Issues in Literary Scholarship*. Ed. Shari Benstock. Bloomington and Indianapolis: Indiana UP, 1987. 150–60.

———. "Not With a Bang but an EEEOOOOARRRHMM!" Rev. of *The Tommyknockers*. By Stephen King. *New York Times Book Review* 20 Dec. 1987: 8.

Bachelard, Gaston. *The Poetics of Space*. Trans. Maria Jolas. Boston: Beacon, 1964.

Badley, Linda. *Film, Horror, and the Body Fantastic*. Westport, CT: Greenwood Press, 1995.

Barker, Clive. "The Age of Desire." Barker, *Inhuman Condition* 194–220.

———. "Big Chills." Jones 263–69.

———. "The Body Politic." Barker, *Inhuman Condition* 57–102.

———. "The Book of Blood." Barker, *Books of Blood I* 1–16.

———. *Books of Blood Volume I*. 1984. New York: Berkeley, 1986.

———. *Books of Blood Volume II*. 1984. New York: Berkeley, 1986.

———. *Books of Blood Volume III*. 1984. New York: Berkeley, 1986.

———. *Cabal.* Rpt. in *Cabal* (including *Books of Blood Volume VI.*) New York: Simon & Schuster-Pocket, 1988. 1–218.

———. "Coming to Grief." Winter, *Prime Evil* 83–105.

———. *The Damnation Game.* 1985. New York: Putnam, 1987.

———. "The Forbidden." Barker, *In the Flesh* 75–127.

———. *The Hellbound Heart. Night Visions: The Hellbound Heart.* Ed. George R. R. Martin. 1986. New York: Berkeley, 1988. 183–278.

———. *Imagica.* New York: Harper Collins, 1991.

——— . *The Inhuman Condition: Tales of Terror.* Vol. 4 of *Books of Blood.* 6 vols. 1986. New York: Simon & Schuster-Poseidon, 1986.

———. *In the Flesh: Tales of Terror.* Vol. 5 of *Books of Blood.* 6 vols. 1986. New York: Simon & Schuster-Poseidon, 1986.

———. "In the Hills, the Cities." Barker, *Books I* 172–210.

———. "Jacqueline Ess: Her Will and Testament." Barker, *Books II* 75–116.

———. "The Life of Death." Barker, *Books VI, Cabal* 219–61.

———. "The Madonna." Barker, *In the Flesh* 129–81.

———. "The Midnight Meat Train." Barker, *Books I* 17–52.

———. "New Fiction by Clive Barker: Animal Life." *USA Weekend* 24–26 June 1994: 4–7.

———. "Rawhead Rex." Barker, *Books III* 39–88.

———. "Revelations." Barker, *Inhuman Condition* 104–57.

———. "The Skins of the Fathers." Barker, *Books II* 117–57.

———. "Son of Celluloid." Barker, *Books III* 1–38.

———. "Stephen King: Surviving the Ride." Underwood & Miller, *Kingdom of Fear* 55–63.

———. "Tearing Your Soul Apart." *Your Worst Fears Confirmed.* Nov. 1988. Jones 269.

———. *Weaveworld: A Novel.* New York: Poseidon, 1987.

Barth, John. *Lost in the Funhouse: Fiction for Print, Tape, Live Voice.* 1968. New York: Doubleday, 1988.

Barthes, Roland. "The Death of the Author." *Image/Music/Text.* Trans. Stephen Heath. New York: Hill & Wang, 1977. 142–48.

———. *The Pleasure of the Text.* Trans. Richard Miller. New York: Hill & Wang, 1975.

———. *Writing Degree Zero.* Trans. Annette Lavers and Colin Smith. New York: Hill & Wang, 1977.

Baudrillard, Jean. "The Ecstasy of Communication." *The Anti-Aesthetic: Essays on Postmodern Culture.* Ed. Hal Foster. Port Townsend: Bay Press Books, 1983. 126–34.

Beahm, George, ed. *The Stephen King Companion.* Kansas City: Andrews and McMeel, 1989.

Becker, Ernest. *The Denial of Death.* New York: Free Press, 1973.

Benjamin, Jessica. *The Bonds of Love: Psychoanalysis, Feminism, and the Problem of Domination.* New York: Pantheon, 1988.

Bernheimer, Charles and Claire Kahane, eds. *In Dora's Case: Freud—Hysteria—Feminism*. New York: Columbia UP, 1985.

Bettelheim, Bruno. *The Uses of Enchantment: The Meaning and Importance of Fairy Tales*. 1975. New York: Vintage, 1977.

Biddle, Arthur W. "The Mythic Journey in 'The Body.'" Magistrale, *Dark Descent* 83–97.

Blatty, William Peter. *The Exorcist*. New York: Harper & Row, 1971.

Bolotin, Susan. "Don't Turn Your Back on This Book." Rev. of *Skeleton Crew*, by Stephen King. *New York Times Book Review* 9 June 1985: 11.

Booe, Martin. "Deliciously Terrifying." Interview with Clive Barker. *USA Weekend* 26–28 Jan. 1990: 8.

Bosky, Bernadette Lynn. "Playing the Heavy: Weight, Appetite, and Embodiment in Three Novels by Stephen King." Magistrale, *Dark Descent* 137–56.

Boss, Pete. "Vile Bodies and Bad Medicine." *Screen* 27 (Jan.–Feb. 1986): 14–24.

Brite, Poppy Z. *Lost Souls*. New York: Abyss-Dell, 1992.

Brophy, Philip. "Horrality—The Textuality of Contemporary Horror Films." *Screen* 27 (Jan.–Feb. 1986): 2–13.

Burke, Fred. *Clive Barker Illustrator*. Ed. Steve Niles. Introd. Stephen R. Bissette. Forrestville, CA: Arcane-Eclipse, 1990.

Burns, Cliff. "Naughty Bits." Van Hise 95–102.

Burns, Craig William. "It's That Time of the Month: Representations of the Goddess in the Work of Clive Barker." *Journal of Popular Culture* 27.3 (Winter 1993): 35–40.

Campbell, Ramsey. "Introduction." Barker, *Books I* xi–xiii.

Carter, Angela. *Nights at the Circus*. 1984. New York: Viking-Penguin, 1985.

———. *The Sadeian Woman and the Ideology of Pornography*. New York: Pantheon, 1979.

Carter, Margaret, ed. *Dracula: The Vampire and the Critics*. Ann Arbor, MI: UMI Research Press, 1988.

———. *Vampirism in Literature: The First Comprehensive Bibliography*. Ann Arbor, MI: UMI Research Press, 1989.

Casebeer, Edwin F. "The Ecological System of Stephen King's 'The Dark Half.'" *Journal of the Fantastic in the Arts* [Double Issue: *The Doppelganger in Contemporary Literature, Film, and Art*] 6.2&3 (1994): 126–42.

Castaneda, Laura. "Britain's Clive Barker: Future King of Horror." *The Tennessean Showcase* [Nashville] 24 Aug. 1986: 58–59.

Charnas, Suzy McKee. *The Vampire Tapestry*. New York: Pocket, 1980.

Cixous, Hélène. "The Laugh of the Medusa." Trans. Keith Cohen and Paula Cohen. *Signs* 1 (Summer 1976). Rpt. *New French Feminisms*. Eds. Elaine Marks and Isabelle de Courtivron. New York: Schhocken, 1981. 245–64.

Clover, Carol. *Men, Women, and Chain Saws: Gender in the Modern Horror Film*. Princeton: Princeton UP, 1992.

Codrescu, Andrei. *The Blood Countess*. New York: Simon & Schuster, 1995.

Collings, Michael R. *The Stephen King Phenomenon*. Mercer Island, WA: Starmont House, 1987.

Collins, Philip. Introd. *Sikes and Nancy and Other Public Readings*. By Charles Dickens. Oxford: Oxford UP, 1983. vii–xx.

Conant, Jennet. "Lestat, C'est Moi." *Esquire* March 1994: 71–75.

Conner, Jeff. *Stephen King Goes to Hollywood*. New York: New American Library, 1987.

Coover, Robert. "Hyperfiction: Novels for the Computer." *New York Times Book Review* 29 August 1993: 1, 8–12.

Copeland, Dawn. "Anne Rice's Existential Quest: Louis' Search for Meaning." Thesis. Middle Tennessee State U, 1993.

Corliss, Richard. "By the Book." *Film Comment* March–April 1991: 37–38, 40–41, 44–46.

———. "Festival of Lost Children." Rev. of *Kids*. *Time* 5 June 1995: 69.

———. "A Terminal Case of Brotherly Love." Rev. of *Dead Ringers*. *Time* 26 Sept. 1988: 84.

Creed, Barbara. *The Monstrous-Feminine: Film, Feminism, Psychoanalysis*. London and New York: Routledge, 1993.

Crosland, Margaret. "Introduction." *The Lesbian Body*. By Monique Wittig. New York: Avon, 1978. v–viii.

Dair, G. "Eroticizing the World." *Cut* Oct. 1987. Rpt. in Jones 393–95.

Dangerous World. By Douglas Bradley and Oliver Parker. Dir. Clive Barker. Program notes. Rpt. in Jones 137.

Daniels, Les. *Citizen Vampire*. New York: Charles Scribner's, 1981.

Datlow, Ellen, ed. *Blood Is Not Enough*. New York: Berkeley, 1989.

———, ed. *A Whisper of Blood*. New York: William Morrow, 1991.

Day, William Patrick. *In the Circles of Fear and Desire: A Study of Gothic Fantasy*. Chicago: Chicago UP, 1985.

Deleuze, Gilles, and Félix Guattari. *Anti-Oedipus: Capitalism and Schizophrenia*. Trans. Robert Hurley, Mark Seem, and Helen R. Lane. Minneapolis: U of Minnesota P, 1983.

Diehl, Digby. "Playboy Interview: Anne Rice." *Playboy* March 1993: 53–64.

Dijkstra, Bram. *Idols of Perversity: Fantasies of Feminine Evil in Fin de Siècle Culture*. New York: Oxford UP, 1987.

Docherty, Brian, ed. *American Horror Fiction: From Brockden Brown to Stephen King*. New York: St. Martin's, 1990.

Doniger, Wendy. "Shackeled to the Past." Rev. of *Gerald's Game*, by Stephen King. *New York Times Book Review* 16 Aug. 1992: 3.

Ebert, Roger. "*Candyman*." *Roger Ebert's Video Companion*. 1994. *Microsoft Cinemania '95*. CD-ROM. Redmond: Microsoft, 1995. CD 194–052V1995.

Egain, Kelly. "King Books Not Fit to Teach, Board Says." *The Ottowa Citizen* 18 July 1995: A1, 2.

Ehrenreich, Barbara. "The Morality of Muscle Tone." *Lear's* Sept. 1990. Rpt. in *Utne Reader* May–June 1992: 65–68.

——— . "The Ultimate Chic." Editorial. *Nation* 6 Dec. 1993: 681, 695.

——— . "Why Don't We Like the Human Body?" *Time* 1 July 1991: 80.

Eisenstein, Sergei. "Dickens, Griffith, and the Film Today." In *Film Form: Essays in Film Theory and The Film Sense*. Trans. Jay Leyda. New York: Meridian, 1957. 195–255.

Ellis, Brett Easton. *American Psycho*. New York: Vintage, 1991.

Ellison, Harlan. "Two Selections from 'Harlan Ellison's Watching'." *The Magazine of Fantasy and Science Fiction* (1984). Rpt. in Underwood and Miller, *Kingdom of Fear* 67–80.

Estes, Clarissa Pinkola. *Women Who Run With the Wolves: Myths and Stories of the Wild Woman Archetype*. New York: Ballantine, 1992.

Etchison, Dennis. *California Gothic*. New York: Dell-Abyss. 1995.

——— , ed. *Metahorror*. New York: Dell-Random House, 1992.

——— . *Shadowman*. New York: Dell-Abyss, 1994.

Ewen, Stuart. *All Consuming Images: The Politics of Style in Contemporary Culture*. New York: Basic Books, 1988.

Fiedler, Leslie. *Love and Death in the American Novel*. Rev. Ed. New York: Stein & Day, 1975.

——— . *Freaks: Myths and Legends of the Secret Self*. New York: Simon & Schuster, 1978.

Fleenor, Juliann, ed. *The Female Gothic*. London: Eden, 1983.

Florescu, Radu, and Raymond McNally. *In Search of Dracula*. Greenwich, CT: New York Graphic Society, 1972.

Floyd, Nigel. "Clive Barker: Hellraiser." *20/20* May 1989. Rpt. in Jones 309–317.

——— . "Frights of Fancy." Jones 341–46.

Foucault, Michel. *The Birth of the Clinic: An Archaeology of Medical Perception*. Trans. A. M. Sheridan-Smith. New York: Vintage-Random House, 1975.

——— . *Discipline and Punish: The Birth of the Prison*. Trans. Alan Sheridan. New York: Vintage-Random House, 1979.

——— . *A History of Sexuality. Volume I: An Introduction*. Trans. Robert Hurley. New York: Vintage-Random House, 1990.

——— . *Madness and Civilization: A History of Insanity in the Age of Reason*. Trans. Richard Howard. New York: Pantheon, 1964.

Frazier, Tom. "Everybody Has One: Stephen King and the Jungian Shadow." Diss. Middle Tennessee State U, 1994.

French, Todd. "A 'Books of Blood' Sequel: Clive Barker's *Candyman 2*." *Cinefantastique* Feb. 1995: 8–9; April 1995: 40–41, 43.

——— . "Candyman: Interview with the Monster." *Cinefantastique* April 1994: 42.

Freud, Sigmund. *Beyond the Pleasure Principle* (1920). Freud, *Standard Edition* 18: 1–64.

————. *The Standard Edition of the Complete Psychological Works of Sigmund Freud.* Ed. James Strachey. 24 vols. London: Hogarth, 1964.

————. *Totem and Taboo* (1913). Freud, *Standard Edition* 13: vii–162.

————. "The 'Uncanny'" (1919). Freud, *Standard Edition* 17: 219–52.

Frost, Brian J. *The Monster with a Thousand Faces: Guises of the Vampire in Myth and Literature.* Bowling Green, OH: Popular Press, 1989.

Gaylin, Willard. "Harvesting the Dead." *Harper's* Sept. 1974: 23–24, 26–30.

Gerard, Morgan. "Clive Barker The Horror!" *Graffiti* Jan. 1988. Rpt. (as excerpt) in Jones 157.

Gibson, William. "Foreword: Strange Attractors." *Alien Sex: 19 Tales by the Masters of Science Fiction and Dark Fantasy.* Ed. Ellen Datlow. New York: Dutton, 1990. xv–xvi.

Gilbert, Sandra M. "Introduction: A Tarantella of Theory." *The Newly Born Woman.* By Katherine Clement and Hélène Cixous. Trans. Betsy Wing. Theory and History of Literature #24. Minneapolis: U of Minnesota P, 1986. ix–xviii.

Gilbert, Sandra, and Susan Gubar. *The Madwoman in the Attic: The Woman Writer and the Nineteenth-Century Literary Imagination.* New Haven, CT: Yale UP, 1979.

Gomez, Jewelle. *The Gilda Stories.* Ithaca: Firebrand Books, 1991.

————. "Vamps and Victims." *Village Voice* 15 December 1992: 72.

————. "Writing Vampire Stories: Recasting the Mythology." *Hot Wire* Nov. 1987: 42–43, 60.

Gordon, Joan. "Rehabilitating Revenants, or Sympathetic Vampires in Recent Fiction." *Extrapolation* 29.3 (Fall 1988): 227–34.

Gracey-Whitman, Lionel, and Don Melia. "Beneath the Blanket of Banality." *Heartbreak Hotel* July–Aug. 1988. Rpt. Jones 403–23.

Grant, Charles L. "Many Years Ago, When We All Lived in the Forest. . . ." Rev. of *Shadowland*, by Peter Straub. *Shadowings.* Ed. Douglas Winter. Mercer Island, WA: Starmont House, 1983. 30–32.

Gray, Paul. "Stephen King: Master of Postliterate Prose." *Time* 30 Aug. 1982: 87.

Green, Lee. "The Sound of Success." *American Way* 1 August 1993: 40, 42–43.

Gross, Louis. *Redefining the American Gothic: From Wieland to the Day of the Dead.* Ann Arbor: UMI Research Press, 1989.

Hanson, Clare. "Stephen King: Powers of Horror." *Docherty* 135–54.

Haraway, Donna. *Simians, Cyborgs, and Women: The Reinvention of Nature.* New York: Routledge, 1991.

Hartwell, David G. Introduction. *The Dark Descent: The Evolution of Horror.* Ed. David G. Hartwell. New York: Tor, 1987. 1–11.

————. Introduction. *Foundations of Fear: An Exploration of Horror.* Ed. David G. Hartwell. New York: Tor, 1992. 1–11.

Hassan, Ihab. *The Dismemberment of Orpheus: Toward a Postmodern Literature.* New York: Oxford, 1971.

Havelock, Eric. *The Muse Learns to Write: Reflections on Orality and Literacy from Antiquity to the Present.* New Haven, CT: Yale UP, 1986.

Hebb, Nancy. "Rice, Anne." *Contemporary Authors.* New Revision Series. 1981. 399–400.

Heldreth, Leonard G. "Viewing 'The Body.' " *The Gothic World of Stephen King: Landscape of Nightmare.* Ed. Gary Hoppenstand and Ray B. Brown. Bowling Green, OH: Popular Press, 1987. 64–74.

Henry, William A., III. "Celebrating Gay Anger." Rev. of *Angels in America. Time* 23 Nov. 1992: 72–73.

Herron, Don. "King: The Good, the Bad and the Academic." Underwood and Miller, *Kingdom of Fear* 129–57.

Hillman, James. *Revisioning Psychology.* New York: Harper & Row, 1975.

Hobermann, J. "Bloodsuckers Invade Sundance." *Premiere* (June 1995): 45, 47.

Hoffmann, E.T.A. "The Sandman." *Tales of E.T.A. Hoffmann.* Ed. and trans. Leonard J. Kent and Elizabeth C. Knight. Chicago: U of Chicago P, 1969. 93–125.

Hughes, Dave. "Clive Barker in the Flesh." *Skeleton Crew* 3–4 (1988). Rpt. in Jones 391.

Indick, Ben P. "King as a Writer for Children." Underwood and Miller, *Kingdom of Fear* 189–205.

Irigaray, Luce. *This Sex Which Is Not One.* Trans. Catherine Porter. Ithaca, NY: Cornell UP, 1985.

Jackson, Rosemary. *Fantasy: The Literature of Subversion.* New Accents series. London and New York: Methuen, 1981.

Jameson, Fredric. "Postmodernism and Consumer Society." *The Anti-Aesthetic.* Ed. Hal Foster. Port Townsend, WA: Bay Press, 1983. 111–25.

Jardine, Alice. *Gynesis: Configurations of Woman and Modernity.* Ithaca, NY: Cornell UP, 1985.

Jarvis, Jeff. "The Couch Critic." Rev. of *Stephen King's The Stand* (miniseries). *TV Guide* 7 May 1994: 7.

Johnson, Judith E. "Women and Vampires: Nightmare or Utopia?" *Kenyon Review* 15.1 (Winter 1993): 72–80.

Jones, Stephen, ed. *Clive Barker's Shadows in Eden.* Lancaster, PA: Underwood-Miller, 1991.

Jung, Carl G. *The Collected Works of C. G. Jung.* Eds. Sir Herbert Head, Michael Fordham, and Gerard Adler. 20 vols. New York: Pantheon, 1953–79.

Kahane, Claire. "The Gothic Mirror." *The (M)Other Tongue: Essays in Feminist Psychoanalytic Interpretation.* Eds. Shirley Nelson Garner, Claire Kahane, and Madelon Sprengnether. Ithaca, NY: Cornell UP, 1985. 335–51.

Kanfer, Stefan. "King of Horror." Cover story. *Time* 6 Oct. 1986: 74–78, 80, 83.

Kaye, Richard. "Out of the Coffin." *Village Voice* 15 Dec. 1992: 72.

Keesey, Douglas. "'The Face of Mr. Flip': Homophobia in the Horror of Stephen King." Magistrale, *Dark Descent* 187–202.

Keesey, Pam, ed. *Daughters of Darkness: Lesbian Vampire Stories.* Pittsburgh and San Francisco: Cleis Press, 1993.

Kendrick, Walter. *The Thrill of Fear: 250 Years of Scary Entertainment.* New York: Grove-Weidenfeld, 1991.

Kiely, Robert. "Armageddon, Complete and Uncut." Rev. of *The Stand,* by Stephen King. *New York Times Book Review* 13 May 1990: 3.

Kilgore, Michael. "Interview with Stephen King." Underwood and Miller, *Bare Bones* 101–11.

Kimbrell, Andrew. "Body Wars." *Utne Reader* May–June 1992: 52–64.

King, Stephen. "Afterword." King, *Different Seasons* 499–507.

——— . *The Bachman Books: Four Early Novels by Stephen King.* New York: New American Library-Signet, 1985.

——— . "Blood and Thunder in Concord." Rev. of *A Long Fatal Love Chase,* By Louisa May Alcott. *New York Times Book Review* 10 Sept. 1995: 17–18, 20.

——— . "The Body." King, *Different Seasons* 289– 433.

——— . "The Breathing Method." King, *Different Seasons* 437–97.

——— . *Carrie.* New York: New American Library, 1974.

——— . *Christine.* 1983. New York: New American Library-Signet, 1984.

——— . *Danse Macabre.* New York: Everest, 1981.

——— . *The Dark Half.* New York: Viking, 1989.

——— . *The Dark Tower: The Gunslinger.* 1984. New York: New American Library, 1988.

——— . *The Dead Zone.* 1979. New York: New American Library-Signet, 1980.

——— . *Different Seasons.* 1982. New York: New American Library-Signet, 1983.

——— . *Dolores Claiborne.* New York: Viking, 1993.

——— . "An Evening with Stephen King at the Billerica, Massachusetts Public Library." Lecture, 1983. Rpt. as "An Evening at the Billerica," in Underwood and Miller, *Bare Bones* 1–24.

——— . *The Eyes of the Dragon.* New York: Viking, 1987.

——— . *Firestarter.* New York: Viking, 1980.

——— . Foreword. King, *Night Shift* xi–xxii.

——— . *Four Past Midnight.* New York: Viking 1990.

——— . *Gerald's Game.* New York: Viking, 1992.

——— . "Imagery and the Third Eye." *The Writer* Oct. 1980: 11–14.

——— . *Insomnia.* New York: Viking, 1994.

——— . Introduction. *The Arbor House Treasury of Horror and the Supernatural.* Compiled by Bill Pronzini, Barry Malzberg, and Martin H. Greenberg. New York: Arbor House, 1981. 11–19.

——— . *It.* New York: Viking, 1986.

——— . *Misery.* New York: Viking, 1987.

——— . "The Mist." King, *Skeleton Crew* 24–154.

——— . *Needful Things.* New York: Viking, 1991.

————. *Night Shift.* 1976. New York: New American Library, 1979.

————. "On Becoming a Brand Name." Underwood and Miller, *Fear Itself* 14–42.

————. *Pet Sematary.* 1983. Harmondsworth: Penguin, 1984.

————. "The Raft." King, *Skeleton Crew* 278–306.

————. "Rage." King, *The Bachman Books* 1–207.

————. "The Reach." King, *Skeleton Crew* 546–66.

————. "Rita Hayworth and the Shawshank Redemption." King, *Different Seasons* 15–16.

————. *Rose Madder.* New York: Viking, 1995.

————. *'Salem's Lot.* 1975. New York: New American Library-Signet, 1976.

————. "Secret Window, Secret Garden." King, *Four Past Midnight* 247–405.

————. *The Shining.* New York: New American Library, 1977.

————. *Skeleton Crew.* New York: New American Library, 1985.

————. *The Stand.* Garden City, NY: Doubleday, 1978.

————. *The Stand: The Complete and Uncut Edition.* New York: Doubleday, 1990.

————. "Survivor Type." King, *Skeleton Crew* 407–26.

————. *Thinner.* By Stephen King Writing as Richard Bachman. 1984. New York: New American Library-Signet, 1985.

————. "Trucks." King, *Night Shift* 127–42.

————. "Two Past Midnight: A Note on 'Secret Window, Secret Garden.'" King, *Four Past Midnight* 249–51.

————. "Why I Was Bachman." Introd. King, *The Bachman Books* v–xiii.

———— and f-stop Fitzgerald. *Nightmares in the Sky: Gargoyles and Grotesques.* New York: Viking Studio Books, 1988.

Koja, Kathe. *Skin.* 1993. New York: Dell, 1994.

————. *Strange Angels.* New York: Delacorte, 1994.

Kristeva, Julia. "Approaching Abjection." Trans. John Lechte. *Oxford Literary Review* 5.1–2 (1982): 125–49.

————. *Black Sun: Depression and Melancholia.* Trans. Leon S. Roudiez. European Perspectives. New York: Columbia UP, 1989.

————. *Powers of Horror: An Essay on Abjection.* Trans. Leon S. Roudiez. European Perspectives. New York: Columbia UP, 1982.

Kübler-Ross, Elizabeth. *On Death and Dying.* New York: McMillan, 1965.

Lawler, Donald L. "*Interview With the Vampire.*" *Magill's Survey of Modern Fantasy Literature.* Ed. Frank N. Magill. 5 vols. Englewood Cliffs, NJ: Salem Press, 1983. 776–80.

Lee, Tanith. *Dark Dance.* New York: Dell-Abyss, 1992.

Le Fanu, Sheridan. *Carmilla.* Keesey 27–87.

Lehmann-Haupt, Christopher. "Death Becomes Us." *The Tennessean* [Nashville] 8 May 1994: F1, 4.

Lemonick, Michael D. "The Killers All Abound." *Time* 12 Sept. 1994: 62–69.

Levin, Ira. *Rosemary's Baby: A Novel.* New York: Random House, 1967.

Lieberman, David. "Horrors!" *TV Guide* 27 Oct. 1990: 3–7.

Lloyd, Ann. *The Films of Stephen King*. New York: St. Martin's, 1993.

Magistrale, Tony, ed. *The Dark Descent: Essays Defining Stephen King's Horrorscape*. Westport, CT: Greenwood Press, 1992.

―――― . *Landscape of Fear: Stephen King's American Gothic*. Bowling Green, OH: The Popular Press, 1988.

―――― . *Stephen King: The Second Decade*. New York: Twayne, 1992.

Mansfield, Brian. "Singing Authors Open the Book on Rock 'n' Roll." *The Tennessean Showcase* [Nashville]. 23 May 1993: 6.

―――― . "Stephen King Buries Horror-ble Rock Show." *The Tennessean* [Nashville] 29 May 1993: 5D.

Mascetti, Manuela Dunn. *Vampire: The Complete Guide to the World of the Undead*. Harmondsworth: Penguin-Viking Studio Books, 1992.

Matheson, Richard. "Drink My Blood." Rpt. in *Ryan* 362–70.

May, Lee. "It's a Book about Life, There's No Question about That." Interview with Sherwin B. Nuland. *The Tennessean* [Nashville] 4 May 1994: F4.

McDonagh, Maitland. "Future Shock: Clive Barker and William Gibson." *Film Comment* Jan–Feb. 1990: 60–63.

McDowell, Michael. "The Unexpected and the Inevitable." Underwood and Miller, *Kingdom* 83–95.

McGrath, Patrick. *Blood and Water and Other Tales*. New York: Poseidon, 1988.

McNally, Raymond T. *Dracula Was a Woman: In Search of the Blood Countess of Transylvania*. New York: McGraw-Hiill, 1983.

Melton, J. Gordon. *The Vampire Book: The Encyclopedia of the Undead*. Detroit: Gale-Visible Ink, 1994.

"Mexicans Howling over Halloween." *The Tennessean* [Nashville] 1 Nov. 1992: 7A.

Michie, Helena. *The Flesh Made Word: Female Figures and Women's Bodies*. 1987. New York and Oxford: Oxford UP, 1989.

Middleton, Joyce Irene. "Orality, Literacy, and Memory in Toni Morrison's *Song of Solomon*." *College English* 55.1 (January 1993): 64–75.

Miller, Michael Vincent. "The Stranger in My Hospital Bed." Rev. of *Raising the Dead*, by Richard Seltzer. *New York Times Book Review* 20 Feb. 1994: 9.

Minns, Karen Marie Christa. *Virago*. Tallahassee, FL: Naiad, 1990.

Mitford, Jessica. *The American Way of Death*. New York: Simon and Schuster, 1963.

Modderno, Craig. "Topic, Horrors!" *USA Today* 10 May 1985. Rpt. in Underwood and Miller, *Bare Bones* 142–45.

Modleski, Tania. *Feminism Without Women: Culture and Criticism in a "Postfeminist" Age*. New York: Routledge, 1991.

―――― , ed. *Studies in Entertainment: Critical Approaches to Mass Culture*. Bloomington: Indiana UP, 1986.

Moers, Ellen. *Literary Women: The Great Writers.* New York: Doubleday, 1976.

Moore, Thomas. *Care of the Soul: A Guide for Cultivating Depth and Sacredness in Everyday Life.* New York: Harper-Collins, 1992.

Morrison, Michael A. "The Delights of Dread: Clive Barker's First Three *Books of Blood.*" Jones 157–169.

———. "Monster, Miracles, and Revelations: Clive Barker's Tales of Transformation." Jones 173–83.

Morrison, Toni. "Rootedness: The Ancestor as Foundation." Rpt. in *Literature in the Modern World.* Ed. Dennis Walder. New York: Oxford UP, 1992. 326–32.

Morton, Donald. "Birth of the Cyberqueer." *PMLA* 110.3 (May 1995): 369–81.

Murphy, Kathleen. "Nativity Scenes." Rev. of *Interview with the Vampire* and *Anchoress. Film Comment* Jan.–Feb. 1995: 13–16.

Mussell, Kay. *Fantasy and Reconciliation: Contemporary Formulas of Women's Romance Fiction.* Westport, CT: Greenwood, 1984.

Norden, Eric. "*Playboy* Interview: Stephen King." *Playboy* July 1983. Rpt. in Underwood and Miller, *Bare Bones* 24–56.

"The Novelist [Stephen King] Sounds Off." *Time* 6 Oct. 1986: 80.

Nuland, Sherwin B. *How We Die: Reflections on Life's Final Chapter.* New York: Knopf, 1994.

Nutman, Philip. "Douglas E. Winter on Splatterpunk and 'Anti-Horror'." *The Twilight Zone Magazine* Oct. 1988: 85.

———. "Inside the New Horror." *The Twilight Zone Magazine* Oct. 1988: 24–29, 85.

———. "The Man Who Collected Lovecraft." *Fangoria* Dec. 1986: 34–38, 67.

———. "Putting the Hell in *Hellraiser.*" *Fangoria* Aug. 1987: 28–31.

——— and Stefan Jaworzyn. "Meet Clive Barker." *Fangoria* Jan. 1986. Rpt. in Jones, 185–89.

Ong, Walter J. *Orality and Literacy: The Technologizing of the Word.* New Accents. London and New York: Methuen, 1982.

Origin of the Vampire. Ancient Mysteries. Prod. and Dir. J. Charles Stein. Voyagers Group/Arts and Entertainment Networks. 1994.

Paglia, Camille. *Sexual Personae: Art and Decadence from Nefertiti to Emily Dickinson.* 1990. New York: Vintage, 1991.

Peck, Abe. "Stephen King's Court of Horror." *Rolling Stone College Papers* Winter 1980. Rpt. in Underwood and Miller, *Bare Bones* 93–101.

Pharr, Mary. "Partners in the *Danse*: Women in Stephen King's Fiction." Magistrale, *Dark Descent* 19–32.

Poe, Edgar Allan. *The Complete Works of Edgar Allan Poe.* Ed. James A. Harrison. Virginia Ed. 17 vols. New York: AMS, 1965.

———. "The Facts in the Case of M. Valdemar." Poe, *Complete Works*, 6: 154–66.

———. "The Fall of the House of Usher." Poe, *Complete Works*, 3: 273–97.

————. "The Philosophy of Composition." Poe, *Complete Works*, 14: 193–208.

Rafferty, Terrence. "Bad Blood." Rev. of *The Dark Half*, dir. George Romero. *New Yorker* 3 May 1993: 105–6, 107.

————. "Under a Cloud." Rev. of *Dolores Claiborne* and *Martha and I*. *New Yorker* 3 April 1995: 93–95.

Rampling, Anne [Anne Rice]. *Belinda*. New York: Jove-Arbor House, 1986.

————. *Exit to Eden*. New York: Dell, 1986.

Ramsland, Katherine. *Prism of the Night: A Biography of Anne Rice*. 1991. New York: Penguin-Plume, 1992.

————. *The Vampire Companion: The Official Guide to Anne Rice's The Vampire Chronicles*. New York: Ballantine, 1993.

Reed, Susan. "Reading, Writing, Murder." *People* 14 June 1993: 44.

Rein-Hagen, Mark. *Vampire: The Masquerade*. Stone Mountain, GA: White Wolf, 1992.

Reino, Joseph. *Stephen King: The First Decade, Carrie to Pet Sematary*. Boston: Twayne, 1988.

Rice, Anne. *Beauty's Punishment*. New York: Dutton, 1984.

————. *Beauty's Release*. New York: Dutton, 1985.

————. *Interview With the Vampire*. 1976. New York: Ballantine, 1977.

————. *Lasher*. New York: Knopf, 1993.

————. *Queen of the Damned*. New York: Knopf, 1988.

————. *The Tale of the Body Thief*. New York: Knopf, 1992.

————. *The Vampire Lestat*. New York: Knopf, 1985.

————. *The Witching Hour*. New York: Knopf, 1990.

Rich, Adrienne. *Adrienne Rich's Poetry and Prose: Poems, Prose, Reviews and Criticism*. Ed. Barbara Charlesworth Gelpi and Albert Gelpi. New York: Norton, 1993.

Roberts, Susan. "The Battle for Your Soul." *USA Weekend* 21–23 Oct. 1994: 18–19.

Rockett, Will H. *Devouring Whirlwind: Terror and Transcendence in the Cinema of Cruelty*. Westport, CT: Greenwood Press, 1988.

Roquelaure, A. N. [Anne Rice]. *The Claiming of Sleeping Beauty*. New York: Dutton, 1983.

Roszak, Theodore. *The Memoirs of Elizabeth Frankenstein*. New York: Random House, 1995.

Ryan, Alan, ed. *Vampires: Two Centuries of Great Vampire Stories*. New York: Doubleday, 1987.

Saberhagen, Fred. *The Dracula Tape*. New York: Warner, 1975.

————. *The Holmes-Dracula File*. New York: Ace, 1978.

————. *Thorn*. New York: Ace, 1979.

"Sacred or for Sale? The Human Body in the Age of Biotechnology." A forum with Jack Hitt, Lori Andrews, Jack Kevorkian, Andrew Kimbrell, and William May. *Harper's* October 1990: 47–55.

Sammon, Paul M., ed. *Splatterpunks: Extreme Horror.* New York: St. Martin's, 1990.

———, ed. *Splatterpunks II: Over the Edge.* New York: Tor, 1995.

Sartre, Jean-Paul. "'Aminadab': Or the Fantastic Considered as a Language." 1947. Rpt. in *Literary Essays.* By Jean-Paul Sartre. New York: Citadel, 1955. 56–72.

———. *Nausea.* Trans. Loyd Alexander. New York: New Directions, 1964.

———. *No Exit. No Exit* and *Three Other Plays.* By Jean-Paul Sartre. New York: Vintage-Random House, 1955.

Scarry, Elaine. *The Body in Pain: The Making and Unmaking of the World.* New York: Oxford UP, 1985.

Schaffer, Mat. ["Interview with Stephen King."] *Boston Sunday Review.* WBCN, Boston. 31 Oct. 1983. Rpt. Underwood and Miller, *Bare Bones* 111–16.

Schlobin, Roger C. "Children of a Darker God: A Taxonomy of Deep Horror Fiction and Their Mass Popularity." *Journal of the Fantastic in the Arts* 1.1 (1988): 25–50.

Schow, David J., ed. *Silver Scream.* New York: Tor, 1988.

Seem, Mark. Introduction. Deleuze and Guattari xv–xxiv.

Seltzer, Richard. *Raising the Dead.* New York: Whittle-Viking, 1994.

Sexton, Anne. "Consorting With Angels." *The Complete Poems.* Boston: Houghton-Mifflin, 1981. 111–12.

Shone, Tom. "Disgusted, Soho." *The Times Literary Supplement* [London] 2 Sept. 1994: 4–5.

Showalter, Elaine. "Bloodsell." *The Times Literary Supplement* 8 January 1993: 14.

———. *The Female Malady: Women, Madness, and English Culture, 1830–1980.* 1985. London: Penguin-Viking, 1989.

———. *Sexual Anarchy: Gender and Culture at the Fin de Siècle.* New York and London: Viking Penguin, 1990.

———. *Sister's Choice: Tradition and Change in American Women's Writing.* Oxford: Oxford UP, 1991.

Simmons, Dan. *Children of the Night.* New York: Time Warner, 1992.

Simon, John. "The Net Gross." Review of *Stand By Me*, dir. Rob Reiner. *National Review* 10 Oct. 1986: 59–60.

"Sinister Sentinel: 'Interview' Author." *Imagi-Movies* Summer 1995: 5.

Skal, David J. *The Monster Show: A Cultural History of Horror.* New York: London, 1993.

Skipp, John, and Craig Spector, eds. *The Book of the Dead.* New York: Bantam, 1989.

———. *The Light at the End.* New York: Bantam, 1986.

———. *Still Dead: Book of the Dead 2.* New York: Bantam, 1992.

Skow, John. ". . . And One With Vanity." Rev. of *The Tale of the Body Thief*, by Anne Rice. *Time* 23 Nov. 1992: 71–72.

Slung, Michele, ed. *I Shudder at Your Touch: 22 Tales of Sex and Horror.* New York: Penguin-Roc, 1991.

———. *Shudder Again: 22 Tales of Sex and Horror.* New York: Penguin-Roc, 1993.

Slusser, George, and Tom Shippey, eds. *Fiction 2000: Cyberpunk and the Future of Narrative.* Athens: U of Georgia P, 1992.

Sobchack, Vivian. *Screening Space: The American Science Fiction Film.* 2nd ed. New York: Ungar, 1987.

Sontag, Susan. *Illness as Metaphor.* 1977. New York: Vintage, 1979.

Spignesi, Stephen. *The Second Stephen King Quiz Book.* New York: New American Library-Signet, 1992.

———, ed. *The Shape Under the Sheet: The Complete Stephen King Encyclopedia.* Ann Arbor, MI: Popular Culture, Ink., 1991.

———. *The Stephen King Quiz Book.* New York: Signet, 1990.

Spitz, Bob. "*Penthouse* Interview: Stephen King." *Penthouse* April 1982. Rpt. in Miller and Underwood, *Bare Bones* 181–91.

Stade, George. "His Alter Ego Is a Killer." Rev. of *The Dark Half*, by Stephen King. *New York Times Book Review* 29 Oct. 1989: 12.

Stephen King Library, The. Advertisement. *The Book of the Month Club News* Summer 1995: [insert].

Stewart, Bhob. "Flix." *Heavy Metal* Jan.–Mar. 1980. Rpt. in Underwood and Miller, *Bare Bones* 125–37.

Stoker, Bram. *Dracula.* New York: New American Library-Signet, 1965.

Straub, Peter. "Meeting Stevie." Underwood and Miller, *Fear Itself* 7–13.

Strauss, Bob. "Flickering Frights." Van Hise 129–46.

———. "The New King." Van Hise 91–94.

Strieber, Whitley. *The Hunger.* New York: Morrow, 1981.

Süskind, Patrick. *Perfume.* New York: Knopf, 1987.

Thomases, Martha, and John Robert Tebbel. "Interview with Stephen King." *High Times* Jan. 1981. Rpt. in Underwood and Miller, *Bare Bones* 197–210.

Thompson, David. "Really a PART of Me." *Film Comment* Jan.–Feb. 1995: 17–18, 23–24, 26–29.

Thompson, William Irwin. *At the Edge of History.* New York: Harper & Row, 1971.

Todorov, Tzvetan. *The Fantastic: A Structural Approach to a Literary Genre.* Trans. Richard Howard. Cleveland: P of Case Western Reserve U, 1973.

Tompkins, Jane. *Sensational Designs: The Cultural Work of American Fiction, 1790–1860.* New York: Oxford UP, 1985.

Tucker, Ken. "The Splatterpunk Trend, And Welcome to It." *The New York Times Book Review* 14 March 1991: 13–14.

Tuttle, Lisa. "Every Fear Is a Desire." Jones 215–25.

Twitchell, James B. *Dreadful Pleasures: An Anatomy of Modern Horror.* New York: Oxford UP, 1985.

———— . *The Living Dead: A Study of the Vampire in Romantic Fiction.* Durham, NC: Duke UP, 1981.

———— . *Preposterous Violence: Fables of Aggression in Modern Culture.* New York & Oxford: Oxford UP, 1989.

Underwood, Tim, and Chuck Miller, eds. *Bare Bones: Conversations on Terror with Stephen King.* New York: McGraw-Hill, 1988.

———— , eds. *Fear Itself: The Horror Fiction of Stephen King.* New York: New American Library, 1982.

———— , eds. *Kingdom of Fear: The World of Stephen King.* New York: New American Library, 1986.

Van Hise, James. *Stephen King and Clive Barker: The Illustrated Masters of the Macabre.* Las Vegas: Pioneer Books, 1990.

VerMeulen, Michael. "What People Earn." *Parade Magazine* 20 June 1993: 4–7.

Walpole, Horace. *The Castle of Otranto: A Gothic Story.* 1764. London and New York: Oxford UP, 1964.

Waxman, Barbara Frey. "Postexistentialism in the Neo-Gothic Mode: Anne Rice's *Interview with the Vampire.*" *Mosaic* 25.3 (Summer 1992): 79–96.

Weeks, Brigitte. "Needful Things." *Book-of-the-Month-Club Book News* Fall 1991: 10–11.

Weinberg, Susan. Letter. The Stephen King Library. Advertisement. *Book of the Month Club,* 1992.

West, Paul. "Witchcraft Is Their Science." Rev. of *Lasher,* by Anne Rice. *New York Times Book Review* 24 Oct. 1993: 38.

Wiater, Stanley. "Anne Rice." Interview. *Writer's Digest* Nov. 1988: 40–44.

———— . "Catching Up with Clive Barker, Part Two." *Fangoria* July 1986: 46–49.

———— . "Clive Barker." *Dark Dreamers: Conversations with the Masters of Horror.* New York: Avon, 1990. 9–17.

———— . "Horror in Print: Clive Barker." *Fangoria* July 1986. Jones 191–97.

———— , and Roger Anker. "Horror in Print: Anne Rice." *Fangoria* Jan. 1988: 14–16, 66.

Williams, Linda. *Hard Core: Power, Pleasure, and the "Frenzy of the Visible."* Berkeley: U of California P, 1989.

———— . "When the Woman Looks." *Re-Vision: Essays in Feminist Film.* Ed. Mary Ann Doane, Patricia Mellencamp, and Linda Williams. Los Angeles: U Publications of America, 1984. 83–99.

Winter, Douglas. Introd. *Prime Evil: New Stories by the Masters of Modern Horror.* New York: New American Library, 1988. 1–9.

———— . "Less Than Zombie." Sammon 84–98.

———— . "Raising Hell with Clive Barker." *Rod Serling's The Twilight Zone Magazine* Dec. 1987. Rpt. Jones 195–97.

———— . *Stephen King: The Art of Darkness.* Rev. Ed. New York: New American Library, 1986.

————. "Talking Terror With Clive Barker." *Rod Serling's The Twilight Zone Magazine* June 1987. Rpt. Jones 209–14.

Wittig, Monique. *The Lesbian Body.* Trans. David Le Vay. Introd. Margaret Crosland. Boston: Beacon, 1975.

Wolf, Leonard. Introd. *The Essential Frankenstein: The Definitive Annotated Edition of Mary Shelley's Classic Novel.* Ed. Leonard Wolf. New York: Plume, 1993. 1–20.

"World of Anne Rice, The." *Day One.* Narr. John Hockenberry. ABC. WKRN, Nashville. 27 Sept. 1993.

Yarbro, Chelsea Quinn. *Blood Games.* New York: St. Martin's, 1979.

————. *Hotel Transylvania.* New York: St. Martin's, 1978.

————. *The Palace.* New York: St. Martin's, 1978.

Yeats, William Butler. *Collected Poems.* Ed. Peter Allt and Russell K. Alspach. 1957. Rev. Ed. London: McMillan, 1966.

Zagorski, Edward J. *Teacher's Manual: The Novels of Stephen King.* New York: New American Library, 1982.

Filmography

Addiction, The. Dir. Abel Ferrar. 1995.

American Werewolf in London, An. Dir. John Landis. 1981.

Anchoress. Dir. Chris Newby. 1994.

Back to the Future. Dir. Robert Zemeckis. 1985.

Birth of the Vampire: A Biography of Anne Rice. Dir. Anand Tucker. 1994.

Blade Runner. Dir. Ridley Scott. 1982. Based on the novel *Do Androids Dream of Electric Sheep*, by Philip K. Dick.

Bloodstone: Subspecies 2. Dir. Ted Nicolaou. 1983.

Blue Velvet. Dir. David Lynch. 1986.

Bram Stoker's Dracula. Dir. Francis Ford Coppola. 1992.

Candyman. Dir. Bernard Rose. 1992. Based on the short story "The Forbidden," by Clive Barker.

Candyman 2: Farewell to the Flesh. Dir. Bill Condon. 1995. Based on the short story "The Forbidden," by Clive Barker.

Carrie. Dir. Brian De Palma. 1976. Based on the novel by Stephen King.

Cat's Eye. Dir. Lewis Teague. 1985. Based on stories by Stephen King.

Christine. Dir. John Carpenter. 1982. Based on the novel by Stephen King.

Creepshow. Dir. George A. Romero. Screenplay by Stephen King. 1982.

Creepshow 2. Dir. Michael Gornick. Screenplay by George A. Romero. 1987. Based on short stories by Stephen King.

Cujo. Dir. Lewis Teague. 1983. Based on the novel by Stephen King.

Dark Half, The. Dir. George A. Romero. 1993. Based on the novel by Stephen King.

Daughters of Darkness. Dir. Harry Kumel. 1971.

Dawn of the Dead. Dir. George A. Romero. 1979.

Day of the Dead. Dir. George A. Romero. 1985.

Dead Ringers. Dir. David Cronenberg. 1988.

Dead Zone, The. Dir. David Cronenberg. 1983. Based on the novel by Stephen King.

Death Becomes Her. Dir. Robert Zemeckis. 1992.

Dolores Claiborne. Dir. Taylor Hackford. 1995.

Dracula. Dir. John Badham. 1979.

Dracula. Dir. Tod Browning. 1931.

Dracula's Daughter. Dir. Lambert Hillyer. 1936.

Eraserhead. Dir. David Lynch. 1978.

Evil Dead. Dir. Sam Raimi. 1982.

Evil Dead 2: Dead by Dawn. Dir. Sam Raimi. 1987.

Exorcist, The. Dir. William Friedkin. 1973. Based on the novel by William Peter Blatty.

Faces of Death, The. Prod. Rosilyn Scott. 1974.

Faces of Death 2, The. Prod. Rosilyn Scott. 1984.

Firestarter. Dir. Mark Lester. 1984.

Fright Night. Dir. Norman Holland. 1985.

Fright Night 2. Dir. Tommy Lee Wallace. 1988.

Hellbound: Hellraiser 2. Dir. Tony Randel. 1989.

Hellraiser. Dir. Clive Barker. 1988. Based on the novella *The Hellbound Heart*, by Clive Barker.

Hellraiser 3: Hell on Earth. Dir. Anthony Hickox. 1992.

Howling, The. Dir. Joe Dante. 1980.

Hunger, The. Dir. Tony Scott. Based on the novel by Whitley Strieber.

Innocent Blood. Dir. John Landis. 1992.

Interview with the Vampire. Dir. Neil Jordan. 1994. Based on the novel by Anne Rice.

In the Mouth of Madness. Dir. John Carpenter. 1995.

I Spit on Your Grave (a.k.a. *The Day of the Woman*). Dir. Mier Zarchi. 1977.

It's Alive. Dir. Larry Cohen. 1974.

Jurassic Park. Dir. Steven Spielberg. 1993. Based on the novel by Michael Crichton.

Lawnmower Man, The. Dir. Brett Leonard. 1992.

Lost Boys, The. Dir. Joel Schumacher. 1987.

M. Butterfly. Dir. David Cronenberg. 1993. Based on the play by David Henry Hwang.

Martin. Dir. George A. Romero. 1977.

Mary Shelley's Frankenstein. Dir. Kenneth Branagh. 1994. Based on the novel by Mary Wollstonecraft Shelley.

Maximum Overdrive. Dir. Stephen King. 1986. Based on the short story "Trucks," by Stephen King.

Misery. Dir. Rob Reiner. 1990. Based on the novel by Stephen King.

My Best Friend Is a Vampire. Dir. Jimmy Huston. 1988.

Nadja. Dir. Michael Almereyda. 1995.

Naked Lunch. Dir. David Cronenberg. 1991. Based on the novel by William Burroughs.

Natural Born Killers. Dir. Oliver Stone. 1994.

Near Dark. Dir. Kathryn Bigelow. 1987.

Needful Things. Dir. Fraser C. Heston. 1983. Based on the novel by Stephen King.

Night of the Living Dead. Dir. George A. Romero. 1968.

Night of the Living Dead. Dir. Tom Savini. 1990.

Nightbreed. Dir. Clive Barker. 1989. Based on the novella *Cabal*, by Clive Barker.

Nightmare on Elm Street, A. Dir. Wes Craven. 1984.

Nightmare on Elm Street, A. Part 2, Freddy's Revenge. Dir. Jack Sholder. 1985.

Nightmare on Elm Street 3, A. The Dream Warriors. Dir. Chuck Russell. 1987.

Nightmare on Elm Street 4, A. The Dream Master. Dir. Renny Harlan. 1988.

Nosferatu. Dir. Werner Herzog. 1979.

Peggy Sue Got Married. Dir. Francis Ford Coppola. 1986.

Pet Sematary. Dir. Mary Lambert. 1989. Based on the novel by Stephen King.

Pet Sematary 2. Dir. Mary Lambert. 1992. Based on the novel by Stephen King.

Psycho. Dir. Alfred Hitchcock. 1960. Based on the novel by Robert Bloch.

Rocky Horror Picture Show, The. Dir. Jim Sharmon. 1975.

Rosemary's Baby. Dir. Roman Polanski. 1968.

'Salem's Lot. Dir. Tobe Hooper. 1979. Based on the novel by Stephen King.

Shawshank Redemption, The. Dir. Frank Darabont. 1994. Based on the novella "Rita Hayworth and the Shawshank Redemption," by Stephen King.

Shining, The. Dir. Stanley Kubrick. 1980. Based on the novel by Stephen King.

Sleepwalkers. Dir. Mick Garris. 1992. Screenplay by Stephen King.

Stand By Me. Dir. Rob Reiner. 1986. Based on the novella "The Body," by Stephen King.

Stephen King's Golden Years. CBS television miniseries. Prod. Laurel Entertainment. Screenplay by Stephen King. 1991.

Stephen King's It. ABC television miniseries. Dir. Tommy Lee Wallace. 1990.

Stephen King's The Langoliers. ABC television miniseries. Dir. Tom Holland. Screenplay by Stephen King. 1992.

Stephen King's The Stand. ABC television miniseries. Prod. Richard Rubenstein. Dir. Mick Garris. Screenplay by Stephen King. 1994.

Stephen King's World of Horror. Prod., dir. John Simmons. USA television series. 1989.

Texas Chain Saw Massacre, The. Dir. Tobe Hooper. 1973.

2001: A Space Odyssey. Dir. Stanley Kubrick. 1968.

Variety. Dir. Bette Gordon. 1984.

Videodrome. Dir. David Cronenberg. 1983.

Wes Craven's New Nightmare. Dir. Wes Craven. 1994.

Wild at Heart. Dir. David Lynch. 1990.

Witches of Eastwick, The. Dir. George Miller. 1987. Based on the novel by John Updike. 1987.

Wolf. Dir. Mike Nichols. 1994.

Women of Horror. Stephen King's World of Horror. USA Network. October 1989.

Index

About the Author

LINDA BADLEY is Professor of English at Middle Tennessee State University. She has published articles on fiction, film, poetry, and gender. She is author of *Film, Horror, and the Body Fantastic* (Greenwood, 1995).

ISBN 0-313-29716-9